*The nouveau roman
and the
poetics of fiction*

The nouveau roman and the poetics of fiction

ANN JEFFERSON

CAMBRIDGE UNIVERSITY PRESS

CAMBRIDGE
LONDON NEW YORK NEW ROCHELLE
MELBOURNE SYDNEY

Published by the Press Syndicate of the University of Cambridge
The Pitt Building, Trumpington Street, Cambridge CB2 1 RP
32 East 57th Street, New York, NY 10022, U.S.A.
296 Beaconsfield Parade, Middle Park, Melbourne 3206, Australia

First published 1980

Photoset and printed in Malta by Interprint Limited

British Library Cataloguing in Publication Data
Jefferson, Ann
The nouveau roman and the poetics of fiction.
1. Fiction
2. Criticism – France
I. Title
808.3′00944 PN3331 79–41507
ISBN 0 521 22239 7

for Anthony, Amy and Laurie

Contents

vii

Acknowledgements

This book has benefited from advice and encouragement given by many people. I would particularly like to thank the following here: first and foremost, Jonathan Culler who supervised my D. Phil. thesis on Nathalie Sarraute, and whose example, teaching and support helped me find my feet in the relatively new and sometimes mistrusted field of poetics; secondly, the late Will Moore whose teaching, talk and interest were always encouraging and invigorating; thirdly, Terence Cave who read the manuscript and whose comments, criticisms and suggestions helped to make a more consistent and more readable book; fourthly, the President and Fellows of St John's College, Oxford, whose offer of a research fellowship gave me time to complete this study; and lastly, Judy Egan of Wolfson College day-nursery who looked after my children: without her help none of what follows could have been written.

Parts of this book originally appeared in the form of articles in *PTL*, the *Modern Language Review, Comparative Criticism* and *Mensen van papier* (ed. Mieke Bal). I gratefully acknowledge permission from the respective editors to use versions of those articles.

All translations are my own except where otherwise indicated.

Fatalité de l'essai, face au roman: condamné à l'authenticité − à la forclusion des guillemets.

(Barthes, 1975, 93)

Introduction

The novel is notorious for its lack of theoretical definition, and indeed its primary characteristic as a genre has often been regarded as its very freedom from fixed generic features. E. M. Forster called it 'distinctly one of the moister areas of literature' (1949, 9), and went on to describe it as a kind of swamp lying between the sharply defined peaks of philosophy on the one hand and poetry on the other. Nevertheless, the emergence of the nouveau roman in the 1950s and the debates and polemic that accompanied it do suggest that some more or less precise definition of fiction as a genre was at stake, even if it had never been very explicitly formulated. The nouveau roman was seen as posing a serious challenge to what it vaguely called the Balzacian novel, and in so far as the label nouveau roman had any meaning at all, it was clear that this new literature also had rights of entry to the house of fiction. Certainly, of all the terms coined for this new movement (*anti-roman, école du regard, chosisme, école de Minuit*), it was only the one which characterised it as fiction (nouveau roman) which stuck.[1] All the texts discussed in this study bear the rubric *roman*.

If we accept that the nouveau roman is fiction, what theory of the novel are we implicitly proposing? Is the existence of the nouveau roman a sign that the current of fictional development is now flowing along another of the hundred unconnected rills in the marshy no-man's land of the novel, leaving the frequently invoked Balzacian and Stendhalian channels to dry up? Or is there some deeper connection between the

---

[1] For a historical account of the development of the nouveau roman see Astier, 1969.

1

so-called traditional novel and the new fiction which would constitute a coherent and all-embracing definition of the genre? It is the contention of this book that the nouveau roman itself implicitly proposes a revised definition of fiction which is necessitated by the irrelevance and inadequacy of traditional models of interpretation, but which also encompasses the novels for which these models were once appropriate. It is not a case of a new literature requiring a new theory, designed to account just for its own particularities. The nouveau roman invites us to elaborate a new poetics of fiction which instead of subverting generic classifications, alters their parameters so that we see all the pre-existing fiction in a new light. But before going any further, the view that a reading of the nouveau roman will yield a kind of retroactive poetics should be set in perspective against different assumptions concerning the novelty and nature of the nouveau roman.

The first shock on reading the nouveau roman is caused by a drastic reduction in the scope of what is represented by the fiction. Balzac confidently set out to portray the whole of French society, and even Proust and Gide in his *Faux-monnayeurs*, who are often invoked as twentieth-century precursors of the nouveau roman, have a sizeable panorama in their novels. By contrast the nouveau roman seems positively emaciated, as the title of J.–B. Barrère's hostile *La cure d'amaigrissement du nouveau roman* confirms. Furthermore, representation in these novels often seems inaccurate or unrealistic, as the complaints made to Robbe-Grillet by some of his readers testify: '"Things don't happen like that in real life", "There aren't any hotels like the one in your *Marienbad*", "A jealous husband doesn't behave like the one in your *Jalousie*", "The adventures that your Frenchman has in *L'immortelle* aren't realistic", "Your lost soldier in *Dans le labyrinthe* isn't wearing his badges in the right place"' (Robbe-Grillet, 1963, 69). Apart from Robbe-Grillet's defence of his supposedly non-anthropomorphic descriptions in his essay 'Nature, humanisme, tragédie' (1963, 45–67), hardly any attempt was made to justify the nouveau roman in terms of what it directly portrayed. Seen in a hostile light, the insubstantiality of what one might call the content of the nouveau roman is an unwelcome novelty which automatically prevents it from being regarded as fiction at all, since it appears to lack a serious realist purpose.

A less hostile view of this novelty, however, sees it as a part of a developing tradition in twentieth-century fiction whereby the burden of realism is gradually shifted from content to form (and thus renders the form–content distinction redundant). The apparent novelty of the nouveau roman then constitutes no more than a sign that this shift is more or less complete. There are two different kinds of interpretation concerning the nature and relevance of this formal realism; one which holds that the formal organisation of the novel mirrors the organisation of the society in which it is produced; and another which assumes that it mirrors the structure and patterns of human consciousness.

The first view is exemplified by Lucien Goldmann who takes as his starting point the assumption that there is a *'rigorous homology* between the literary form of the novel [. . .] and the everyday relations that men have with goods in general, and by extension, with other men, in a society devoted to market production' (1964, 24). Thus, in the novels of Robbe-Grillet, the reduction of the role of character and the increased dimensions of the descriptions can be seen as formal equivalents of a society organised in terms of a market economy, whose chief concern is with the exchange-value of the objects it produces, and whose operation ignores the non-economic and private values that men place on objects and each other.[2]

To the extent that this view of fiction implies a more or less committed Marxist position and cannot account for the nouveau roman's particular novelty it does not have a very wide critical currency, and it is the phenomenological interpretation of the formal features of fiction which is most widely accepted. The supposed rejection of plot and character is necessitated by changes in the way that people structure their experiences. There has been a change in our notion of the experience of time, for example, so that the linearity of plot now seems a false

---

[2] For fuller examples of the possibilities of this kind of approach in relation to the nouveau roman see Leenhardt, 1973.

representation of time. Instead, we can read the confused chronological structure of many of the nouveaux romans as a more
appropriate representation of the experience of time, a formal
equivalent of what Sturrock calls the 'play of the mind', free
to 'rearrange the images or memories of the past without
reference to perceived reality' (1969, 22). This view is very
closely related to that of Sartre for whom a 'novelistic technique always reflects the novelist's metaphysics' (1947, 71),
and who saw Mauriac's use of an omniscient author in his
novels as a betrayal of authentic human experience (1947,
36–57). This view continues a development which the new
novelists are happy to trace back to Proust, Joyce, Kafka
and Faulkner. Formal realism implies that what is new in
fiction is determined by what is new in reality – 'Nouveau
roman, homme nouveau' as Robbe-Grillet has it in the title
of one of his essays (1963, 113–21). This theory, in both its
sociological and its phenomenological form, is undeniably
attractive, not least because of its ability to account for change
in the novel in historical terms. But it has the serious disadvantage that it still implicitly defines the novel as a swamp,
an amorphous hotchpotch of techniques determined not by the
genre itself, but only by external factors, such as the economic
structure of society or cultural agreements about the nature of
human experience.

There is a third and more distinctly literary view of the nouveau roman which fully endorses its novelty and defines it in
terms of its opposition to traditional fiction. Ricardou, for
example, sees the nouveau roman as an attempt to subvert
the conventions which imply that the novel is a copy of reality,
in order to demonstrate that the nouveau roman is constituted
instead primarily by writing itself, which produces rather than
copies reality (1971, 9). The interest of a given nouveau roman
for Ricardou will consist first in the way in which realist conventions are subverted or contested, and secondly, in the structural development of the strictly formal features of the writing.
For example, Robbe-Grillet's novel *Le voyeur* is not (says Ricardou) to be read as a depiction of a man who is a voyeur in any
psychological sense of the word. Instead the novel is created by

a kind of pun; it was originally entitled *Le voyageur* and it became *Le voyeur*, just as Mathias is transformed from a commercial traveller (*voyageur de commerce*) into a guilty *voyeur*, simply by the omission of the central syllable of the word *voy(ag)eur*, an omission which generates the plot itself, with its crucial silence in the middle concerning Mathias's whereabouts at the time of the murder (1967, 38–41). The nouveau roman is therefore defined as an example of the 'practice of writing' (Heath, 1972), an antithesis to the mainstream of realist fiction. It has forebears in aspects of the writing of Flaubert and Proust, more especially in the previously underestimated works of Edgar Allan Poe and Raymond Roussel, and in most exemplary form in Joyce, Artaud, Bataille and Borges. Originally a radical movement on the margins of realist fiction, it has now reached sufficient proportions to supplant it. Like formal realism, this view has the advantage of enabling one to make historically-based distinctions between different kinds of literature (although the distinction between literal and realist is the only criterion it has for doing so). But it categorically rules out any possibility of arriving at a generic definition of fiction, since the concept of writing does away with all distinctions between genres.

All of these theories, realist and anti-representational alike, stress the novelty of the nouveau roman at the expense of the novelistic. In this study I hope to give weight to both elements of the term, by recognising from the outset that the very need for a redefinition of the poetics of fiction springs from a crisis in the reading of fiction which can be quite precisely dated in historical terms, and by working towards a theory of fiction which will at the same time extend beyond the works of the particular writers in question. And indeed, these projects are very far from being antithetical, for the crisis in the concept of the novel that began in the 1950s led to an extremely intense and fertile exploration within fiction itself of the nature and limits of its own being as fiction. A high degree of reflexivity can be seen as a major consequence of the crisis in the theory of fiction.

This reflexivity has often been regarded as the special feature of the nouveau roman that marks it off from pre-existing fiction, and, for some, makes it a sterile and limited kind of literature. But reflexivity is not necessarily a sign of imaginative impoverishment. On the contrary. The nouveau roman's overt preoccupation with things novelistic may well constitute its novelty, but it also has an extremely enriching and enhancing effect on the genre as a whole. The elements of fiction that are re-evaluated by the nouveau roman affect our reading of those novels that the nouveau roman supposedly subverts. The entire genre is reassessed in a perspective that alters the way in which we see even the most familiar examples of it. Plot, character, representation now appear as complex operations that are interesting in their own right in any text. And, furthermore, having been alerted by the nouveau roman to the workings of self-representation, we discover reflexive operations in even the most representationally orientated texts. So, an analysis of the specific novelty of the nouveau roman will also contribute towards a fuller and richer definition of what we understand by the novelistic.

The question of the practical interpretation of the term nouveau roman is a somewhat different one. There must be many novels that can be read as a reflexive response to a critical moment in the history of the genre, but not all of them belong to the group which critics and literary historians have dubbed the nouveau roman. It is not my intention here to see how far the label extends and I have chosen as examples writers who have always been happy to accept it.[3] Restricting myself to three writers was the result partly of wanting to keep the corpus to manageable proportions and partly of a wish to build up some sense of the specificity of each writer within the general theoretical context, which might have been lost if I had also included works by other equally interesting writers. The reason for choosing Butor, Robbe-Grillet and Sarraute was, to a certain degree, a matter of personal preference, but another important factor determining my choice was the existence of differences between them which would, I hoped, create a broad enough

[3] For a discussion of the practical definition of the nouveau roman see Ricardou, 1973, 5–25.

base to validate the theory. Although the term nouveau roman derives from the state of the art in the 1950s, I have concentrated as much on the later novels of Robbe-Grillet and Sarraute as on the earlier ones, again in order to promote as wide-ranging an exploration of the issues as possible. As *Degrés* is the last of Butor's writings to be defined as a novel, I have not included any discussion of his work published after 1960.

In organising the book I have begun with the topics which were most vigorously and repeatedly contested on the emergence of the nouveau roman, namely character and plot. The first two chapters will demonstrate how the novels explore and redefine these concepts which were once regarded as the linchpins of fiction, and so justify a definition of the nouveau roman as new in its apparent rejection of these concepts and novelistic in its reflexive meditation on them. The third chapter will investigate the ways in which the apparently realistic use of certain narrative techniques encourages reflexivity and self-preoccupation in the novel. And the final chapter will attempt to determine the generic features of fiction which make possible both the subversion and the reflexivity which are so often presented as being the defining characteristics of the nouveau roman.

At every stage the theory will be read through the fiction, assuming that fiction articulates theory more interestingly and exhaustively than any explicitly theoretical writing; and the fact that Butor, Robbe-Grillet and Sarraute have all written essays on the novel therefore bears only incidentally on this enterprise. It is the novels which produce the theory and not the theory which produces the novels. For, as Robbe-Grillet himself has written, 'A novel which was only an example to illustrate a grammatical rule – even if it is accompanied by its exception – would of course be useless: it would be enough to state the rule' (1963, 12). This strategy should also have the advantage of showing the practical relevance of theory. Theories of literature have often been accused, particularly in recent years, of operating at too great a distance from actual literary works. I hope to make it clear that interaction between literary theory and text is not only possible but crucial to our reading of literature, for literature both feeds on theory and propagates it. In my use of the texts in question, I have contrived to discuss as many of them as is compatible with the discussion of the relevant aspects of the theory. Because some texts seemed to lend themselves more readily than others to being read around a given theoretical issue, a few have not been dealt with at any length, and others have been discussed more than once, each time in a different context. But although some questions seem more pertinent to some texts than to others, I do not wish to imply that each one invokes only one aspect of theory, or, worse, that if a particular novel has not been discussed at all it has no theoretical significance. In the to-and-fro between text and theory we cannot expect anything to be more than provisional, for it is in this shifting mutual scrutiny that the greatest illumination lies.

1

Unnatural narratives

Last things first

In any discussion of the poetics of the novel it is almost inescapable that one should start with the topic of plot. We class the novel under the generic heading of *narrative* fiction, and it seems likely that what we understand by fiction here will depend on what is meant by narrative. One is perhaps best advised to broach this topic with the caution, if not reluctance, shown by E. M. Forster who describes himself as 'drooping and regretful' as he concedes, 'Yes – oh dear yes – the novel tells a story' (1949, 27). Forster was not sure that the story was the heart of any novel, and indeed story is not the sole defining feature of the genre. Fairy tales, myths, epics and plays tell stories, as do films, cartoon strips and newspaper reports; we frequently speak of ourselves, of others and of our society in narrative form. But this very pervasiveness of the narrative mode serves to show how powerful a structuring device it is. Stories are the means whereby we combat the contingent and give sense to time, a task which is assigned most particularly to the novel.

Narrative constructs have varying degrees of rigour and they reveal more or less single-mindedness in answering the questions which call narrative of any kind into being, namely, 'and then?' and 'why?'. 'The king died' proposes Forster in his discussion of plot as the first term of a narrative sequence which is completed as narrative when it tells what happened next ('the queen died'), and why ('of grief'), to give the sequence: 'The king died and the queen died of grief' (Forster, 1949, 82–4). Or one may take a more complex version which Forster offers

9

as an alternative: 'The queen died, no one knew why, until it was discovered that it was through grief at the death of the king.' This second version, which inverts the time-sequence and is organised to make more of the question 'why?', shows that causes tend to be more powerful structuring devices than sequences, and that sequences are most interesting when they imply a cause (*post hoc ergo propter hoc* attests to this preference). In the first example it is the tiny phrase 'of grief' which plays the most effective role in narrativising the elements, since it provides a causal link between two events and so enables us to make sense of them in thematic terms. It is not the events in themselves which make a story, but the meanings that are proposed to link them. Forster's second example illustrates more amply what one might term the semantic delay which narratives create and depend on for the production of meaning. 'No one knew why' is the condition of the narrative's existence before it reaches its goal where the revelation of 'grief' as an organising principle is all the more forceful for its final position. As a structuring element, meaning is far more important than time: in the second example the inversion of the order of events, which tends to diminish the significance of the temporal elements, actually strengthens the causal or thematic aspect of the story.

These examples suggest that there is nothing inherently narrative about an event or a series of events. Events only become narrativised with the addition of a meaning, which may have the appearance of a goal towards which everything tends, but which is nevertheless an imposition from without. One only has to substitute 'of poverty' or 'of boredom' for 'of grief' to change the meaning of the narrative. The report of the two deaths remains unaltered ('The king died and the queen died') but the causal explanation radically alters their significance.

Viewed in this light it seems that it is sense that makes narratives, although as readers our normal procedure is to turn to narrative to make sense. When we give a summary of a novel (perhaps of anything), we tell its story because we assume that by doing so we also convey its meaning. Gérard Genette summarises Proust's *A la recherche du temps perdu* in the phrase:

'Marcel becomes a writer' (1972, 75), and so conveys some of
the sense of the novel. However, it is only possible to sum-
marise in retrospect, and Genette's summary of *A la recherche
du temps perdu* can only be made after reading the very last pages
of the novel. Meaning is never given *in toto* before the end is
reached, and reading consists in the recognition that the meaning always lies ahead and in the expectation that the close will
bring thematic illumination. In his introduction to *Glissements
progressifs du plaisir* Robbe-Grillet draws attention to this alteration in the availability of meaning depending on whether one is
placed in the middle or at the end. Having summarised the
film, he goes on to say: 'Let us note straight away that the synopsis provides us first and foremost with "meaning"; this is its
avowed aim; but it is the synopsis which is least able to account
for the structural organisation of the film' (12). The contrast
between narrative organisation and structural organisation
may be particular to Robbe-Grillet in this case (especially in
its subversive aspect) but the combination of uncertainty and
anticipation which guides us through a story is common to
all narrative forms. The end determines all that precedes it, and
it is only this finality that enables the sense of the whole to be
constructed. Norman Friedman's categorisation of basic plot
types (1955a) shows very clearly that it is a comparison of beginning and end that enables us to distinguish between, say, a
'tragic' and a 'sentimental' plot, and to make this typological
distinction is already to begin to organise meaning. In a 'tragic'
plot the hero is partly responsible for the misfortune to which
he finally succumbs, whereas in the 'sentimental' plot, the sympathetic and responsible hero undergoes a number of perils
from which he emerges finally as a victor. We identify one plot
as 'tragic' because the hero is vanquished *at the end*, the other
as 'sentimental' because the hero prevails *at the end*. It is always
the end which determines the significance of the whole.

In his essay 'Vraisemblance et motivation' (1969, 71–99)
Gérard Genette has demonstrated very clearly how the dynamic
of plot operates retrogressively, working backwards against
the unfolding of the text. If a story beings with the words 'The
marchioness went out at five o'clock', whatever follows will

be determined not by the possible sequels to this act (going for a drive, visiting a friend), but by the conclusion. So that if that conclusion is suicide, for example, then everything that intervenes will derive from that suicide and not from the marchioness's exit. If we read the phrase 'the marchioness, in despair . . .' it is a consequence not of what precedes it, but of what succeeds it: 'took a pistol and blew her brains out'. The teleological structure of plot makes the final suicide determine the despair, and not the despair the suicide. In plot, the determinations are always what Genette calls 'retrograde', means always follow from ends, causes are produced by their effects. This knowledge, that it is the goal or *telos* that governs all that precedes it, is an important part of reading. Indeed, it may be what makes any reading possible, since there is no direction-less reading. Reading consists of asking questions (like 'and then?' or 'why?') and these questions, precisely because they are questions, are highly directive. They orientate our reading and, more importantly, they imply an answer. We read on on the assumption that mysteries will finally be explained, problems solved, truths revealed. 'Mystery is essential to a plot', says Forster (1949, 84), essential because by forming a question it directs reading towards the end and an explanation. 'The queen died, and no one knew why' poses a mystery, and by virtue of that act directs us towards the answer: 'through grief at the death of the king'.

The choice of *telos* is partly a question of literary convention. In Friedman's enumeration of the forms of plot one can see, if only from the examples that he provides for each category, that certain forms are more frequently associated with one genre, period or author than another. For example, the 'intrigue of action' (where the only question raised is 'and then?') is particularly frequent in popular literature (Friedman cites R. L. Stevenson's *Treasure Island*). The 'tragic plot' is of course most frequently associated with tragic drama (*King Lear, Oedipus the King*). The 'maturing plot' where the hero begins by being inexperienced and naïve and finally matures as the result of his experiences, is particularly frequently associated with the novel (Friedman cites Dickens's *Great Expectations*). The 'pathetic plot' where a sympathetic but weak hero suffers misfortunes which he in no way deserves and to which he finally succumbs, is exemplified by Hardy's *Tess of the d'Urbervilles*, and is typical not only of all Hardy's fiction but of that period in the nineteenth-century novel which we call naturalist. The 'degeneration plot' where all the hero's initiatives fail, so that he finally abandons his ideals, is the form of *Uncle Vanya* and *The Seagull*, and is indeed the form that we conventionally associate with Chekhov. Our cultural experience will often orientate our reading, so that confronted with a new Chekhov play or a new Zola novel, we anticipate (although on the understanding that it is nevertheless provisional) the degeneration plot and the pathetic plot, respectively.

In addition to this general orientation, texts themselves, as Roland Barthes has shown, provide us with material which provokes questions and so points us to the possibility of solution. In his discussion of what he calls the codes of the literary text, he distinguishes between the 'proairetic code' (or the code of actions) and the 'hermeneutic code' whose function is to pose, sustain and finally solve an enigma (1970a, 25–8). This indication of an enigma and the delaying of its solution profoundly structure our reading of the text and the sense which we ultimately make of it:

Truth is skimmed over, deflected, lost. This accident is structural. The hermeneutic code does, in fact, have a function, the same as the one attributed [. . .] to the poetic code: just as rhyme (notably) structures the poem according to the expectation of and the desire for its return, so the hermeneutic terms structure the enigma according to the expectation of and desire for its resolution. The dynamic of the text (from the moment that it implies a truth to be deciphered) is thus paradoxical: it is a static dynamic: the problem is to *maintain* the enigma in the initial absence of its reply; whereas the sentences hasten the 'unfolding' of the story and cannot help leading the story on and advancing it, the hermeneutic code exercises a reverse action: it has to set *delays* in the flow of discourse (obstacles, halts, diversions); its structure is essentially reactive, for it counters the ineluctable advance of language with a play punctuated with halts.[. . .] In this way expectation becomes the condition on which truth can be founded: the truth, these narratives tell us, is what lies *at the end* of expectation. (1970a, 81–2)

Narrative is thus a delayed truth, and its truth is that which is delayed, a pattern which was already evident in Forster's miniature narrative: 'The queen died, and no one knew why [a phrase which simultaneously creates an enigma and delays its solution] until it was discovered that it was through grief at the death of the king', where grief is the truth that awaits us at the end of the sequence and solves the mystery.

When Todorov asserts that no narrative is ever natural he seems to have every reason for doing so: narratives work backwards against the 'natural' flow of time and the almost as 'natural' flow of language; the essential element of narrative, the magnetic current which links its elements into a chain is both constructed and arbitrary (since meanings are never found, and always have to be made). 'No narrative is natural, choice and construction will always direct its appearance; it is a discourse and not a series of events. There is no "proper" narrative in contrast to "figurative" narratives (just as there is no proper meaning); all narratives are figurative. There is only the myth of proper narrative.' (Todorov, 1971, 68). The myth of proper narrative is indeed extremely powerful, and it is one which the polemical writings of the new novelists delight in exploding. But their essays should be read with caution, as they are coloured with a marked tone of indignation that so-called realist fiction could have beguiled us so successfully with this most unnatural (but perhaps finally most irresistible) of artifices.

Robbe-Grillet firmly consigns plot to his pile of 'outdated notions' (1963, 29–32). It is with scorn that he records the primary definition of the novel as narrative: 'For most readers – and critics – a novel is primarily a "story". A real novelist is someone who can "tell a story". His vocation as a writer is synonymous with his gift for telling stories, which carries him through from the beginning to the end of his work. Inventing thrilling, moving and dramatic incidents constitutes both his joy and his justification.' (29) In contrast to this supposedly naïve and old-fashioned view, the modern novelist recognises that 'story-telling has become strictly impossible' (31). The reason for this impossibility is that a story lends an utterly arti-

ficial air of naturalness to a novel. The presence of narrative
in a novel is doubly deceitful: first, narratives pretend to give
a real view of the world ('A tacit agreement is set up between
reader and author: the author will pretend to believe the story
he is telling, the reader will forget that everything is invented
and will pretend to be dealing with a document, a biography,
some real-life story', 29–30); and secondly, the very order and
coherence of the plot give a false view of the world as ordered
and intelligible.

All the technical elements of narrative – the systematic use of the
preterite and the third person, the unconditional adoption of chronological development, linear plots, a regular graph of the emotions,
the structuring of each episode towards an end, etc.; everything was
designed to impose an image of a stable, coherent, continuous, unambiguous, entirely decipherable universe. Since there was no doubt
about the intelligibility of the world, telling stories posed no problems. The novel's writing could be innocent. (31)

The natural air of narrative is false because it does not give us
the world as it is, or as we experience it, and so must be condemned for its lack of realism. Equally, at the other end of the
representational scale, plot deceives us by masking the fact
that the novel is constituted by writing, and so mistakenly suggests that writing is innocent, something copied from or dic-
tated by the world to which it supposedly refers: 'Even if we
admitted that there was still something "natural" in the relationship between man and the world, writing, like all art forms,
proves, in contrast, to be an invention. The very strength of
the novelist is due to the fact that he is totally free to invent.'
(30) Whichever of these two points of view one chooses (that
of realism or that of the freedom of writing) Robbe-Grillet
seems to be claiming that the narrative form of fiction no longer
has any value or currency.

    The same scornful tone is evident in Nathalie Sarraute's
discussion of plot. It is a prejudice on the part of critics, she
says, to insist that a novel 'is and will always remain, above all,
"a story where one sees the lives and actions of characters"'
(1956, 55). Plot for her is an artificial form of representation
which 'by wrapping itself around the character like a bandage,

creates an impression of coherence and life, but also gives him the rigidity of a mummy' (64). For Sarraute, plot is a literary convention which gives a false illusion of the real, is merely *vraisemblable*, and it is in the name of a greater realism that her condemnation of plot must be read. There was a time, she implies, when people experienced their lives in the form of a narrative and for this reason the use of narrative in fiction was justifiable. But this era is over and the way in which we experience the world in the middle of the twentieth century can no longer be faithfully represented in narrative form. The reader 'has seen time cease to be the rapid current which carried the plot forward to become instead a stagnant pool at the bottom of which things slowly and subtly decompose; he has seen our actions lose their usual motives and their accepted meanings, he has seen unknown feelings appear and even the best-known ones change in appearance and name' (1956, 65). To convey this new concept of time and motivation, we must, she says, dispense with narrative.

For all their evidently polemical rhetoric, these attacks which date from the early days of the nouveau roman (Nathalie Sarraute's from 1950 and Robbe-Grillet's from 1957), seem nevertheless to be aimed at the foundations of the way in which our reading of novels is structured and to threaten the ways in which we go about making sense of them. Are we then to take these writers at their word? Should we look for alternative structuring principles in our attempts to make sense of the nouveaux romans? Was the incomprehension and suspicion which greeted the appearance of these works in the 1950s proof that the expectation of a narrative form is indeed a handicap to our appreciation of them? But if we can no longer read novels as stories, how are critical and interpretative activities to proceed? What kinds of things should we be looking for?

One answer is not to dispose of narrative at all, but instead to alter the way in which we look at it. Michel Butor in his essay 'Le roman comme recherche' (1960, 7–11) suggests that the novel is best regarded as the 'laboratory of narrative' (8). His starting-point is that we hear of the world and speak of ourselves to a great extent in narrative form. Narrative is: 'one of the essential constituents of our apprehension of reality. Until we die, and from the moment that we understand words, we are perpetually surrounded by narratives, first in our family, then at school, then through the people we meet and the books we read.' (1960, 7) In this bath of narrative the novel appears simply as one 'particular form of narrative' (7). Its particularity lies in its fictionality: the events which it narrates cannot be verified, and fictional stories stand or fall by something other than the fidelity of its representation. The novel is thus free to explore various *forms* of narrative and, perhaps, being itself narrative, can make us aware of the narrative forms in which we habitually but unconsciously perceive, hear and talk of the real.

Instead of employing narrative as a form of mystification and trying to pass plots off as natural, the novel as laboratory will revel, on the contrary, in the consciousness of plot as un-natural: 'Exploration of different novelistic forms reveals what is contingent in the form that we are used to, unmasks it, frees us from it, and allows us to discover beyond this fixed narrative everything which it camouflages or passes over in silence, all the fundamental narrative in which our whole life is steeped' (1960, 9). In another essay Butor writes: 'Narrative gives us the world, but it is doomed to give us a false world' (1964, 88), and it is the incorporation of this recognition into our reading of novels which makes of them a laboratory, and enables us to be rid of the otiose and rather invidious distinction implied by Robbe-Grillet's writings between naïve or deceitful fiction on the one hand, and modernist fiction on the other. *All* novels can be read as a laboratory of narrative. Butor makes of this a general principle: 'The novel tends naturally and it must tend towards its own elucidation' (1960, 11). This self-elucida-tion is not a key to crack the code, or what Proust called the price-tag on the goods (*A la recherche du temps perdu* III, 882), but implies that what is brought into play in fiction is not only the object of representation but also the means of representa-tion. The poetics of fiction become engaged in the reading of fiction and are incorporated into its 'subject matter'.

The exploration of narrative form is a feature not just of

the nouveau roman (although the nouveau roman may oblige us to acknowledge that exploration more cogently than other novels), but is a striking feature of most fiction of this century. Even as long ago as the eighteenth century we find that such novels as Diderot's *Jacques le fataliste* and Sterne's *Tristram Shandy* very explicitly and playfully incorporate questions of poetics into their subject matter. And Todorov, in his analysis of the thirteenth-century work, *La quête du saint-graal*, discovers that 'narrative appears as the fundamental theme of *La quête du graal*', and adds, importantly, 'as indeed it is of all narrative, but always in a different way' (1971, 149). It remains now to see how far this theme (or, at least, different aspects of it) is present in the nouveau roman.

The absent 'telos': 'Les gommes'

Les gommes, Robbe-Grillet's first published novel, and, indeed, one of the earliest of all the nouveaux romans (it appeared in 1953) lends itself admirably to the kind of reflexive reading that I am proposing as a general method of approach. *Les gommes* presents itself, at least superficially, as a detective story and, in addition, the text is studded with allusions to the Oedipus legend. These two genres, the detective story and Greek tragedy, both depend heavily on a delayed truth which is only revealed at the end. Both genres are highy teleological and seem to conform closely to the structural norm which emerged from the foregoing discussion of narrative organisation.

W. H. Auden, in his essay on detective stories, 'The guilty vicarage' (1962, 146–58), makes an explicit comparison between the detective story and Greek tragedy and finds many points in common between the two. The most essential of these he describes as follows: 'there is Concealment (the innocent seem guilty and the guilty seem innocent) and Manifestation (the real guilt is brought to consciousness)' (147). The very words *concealment* and *manifestation* indicate how central is the notion of a delayed truth to both forms, although in the detective story it is primarily the reader who is kept waiting for the truth, whereas in tragedy it is the hero who awaits a final recognition. *Oedipus*, for example, ends when Oedipus himself discovers that he has unwittingly fulfilled the oracle's prophecy. The detective story closes with the discovery of the murderer, and, very often with an account by the detective of how he pieced together the clues to arrive at the truth (a piecing together which the reader is by definition incapable of and which can only be grasped in retrospect).

Sophocles's *Oedipus the King* is punctuated with frequent invocations of the 'truth'. Already at the beginning Oedipus makes it clear that the discovery of truth is his prime purpose: 'I'll find the truth', he asserts (line 132), and as the events move to a climax and the horror increases, he stubbornly insists, 'I *will* know the truth' (line 1027). When he finally learns the true story of his birth, he leaves the stage, lamenting in anguish, 'Ah God! This is *the truth, at last*' (line 1137, my emphasis). The truth is out *at last* and the entire plot is structured around the anticipation of its revelation. Robbe-Grillet picks up this theme of the final truth and alludes to it in the epigraph of *Les gommes*: 'Time, which sees to everything, has given the solution, despite you', a version of two lines from Sophocles's tragedy: 'Time sees all, and Time, in your despite,/Disclosed and punished your unnatural marriage' (lines 1165–6). In both the original and the altered form, these lines emphasise the notion of (inevitable) revelation, be it in the form of *solution* (to an enigma) or *disclosure* (of a truth). The novel itself, however, fails to reveal anything or to solve any mystery. The detective, instead of uncovering a murderer, commits the crime himself at the end of his enquiry. As Jean Ricardou says, 'the enquiry *precedes* the murder and, in preceding it, *engenders* it' (1973, 35). This is the reverse of *Oedipus the King* which ends with the revelation of the origins of the sequence of events, namely the circumstances of Oedipus's birth and upbringing. Time does indeed reveal all in Sophocles's tragedy, but, contrary to the claim of the epigraph to *Les gommes*, Robbe-Grillet's novel neither reveals nor solves anything. Not only is there no murder until Wallas, the detective, pulls the trigger at the end, but the several mysteries which are raised during the course of the investigation remain unsolved. If we accept that there is a gang under the leadership of a certain Bona which is responsible for a murder committed at the same time every day, we certainly never discover whether or not the minister Roy-Dauzet is in league with them. The so-called victim, Dupont, and a certain Marchat are said to belong to an organisation whose nature and function remain obscure. Dr Juard who hides Dupont after the first murder-attempt and falsely certifies his death, might in fact belong to Bona's gang – the question is never settled. It is normally the function of a detective novel to elucidate all the aspects of a mystery (often in the detective's final explanation), so that, for example, the strange behaviour of an innocent suspect is accounted for and placed in the overall pattern of events. But in *Les gommes* mysteries are multiplied rather than solved. The novel constantly invites us to ask 'why?' but then declines to answer.

If the detective aspect of the novel proves unfruitful, one might look for narrative coherence in another strand. And here it would seem reasonable to turn to the title as a guide to the theme of the narrative. Wallas's search for the ideal eraser coincides with his search for the (non-existent) murderer on a few occasions, but the two pursuits seem never to be meaningfully integrated. Although the proprietress of one of the stationer's shops visited by Wallas is Dupont's ex-wife, although she has a large picture of Dupont's house in the shop window, and although the agent Garinati buys a postcard of the house in the shop, these facts are never woven in with Wallas's criminal investigation. The erasers seem more likely to lend themselves to being integrated with the Oedipal theme, which then might make possible a rereading of the criminal themes of the novel: Wallas-Oedipus kills Dupont-Laius, and the role of Jocasta is then filled by the seductive Madame Dupont pictured in Wallas's mind's eye as 'the attractive young woman waiting for him [Dupont] in front of the open door of her bedroom ... with her cooing little laugh, which seems to rise from her whole body ... provocative and inviting' (187). The specific place of the erasers in this formulation is implied by Wallas's description of the one he is searching for: 'The brand name was printed on one side, but was too worn to be legible any more: only the two middle letters "di" could be deciphered; there must have been at least two letters before and two more after' (132). This name is easily completed as 'Oe-di-pe' (a completion, which, however, the young woman is unable to make). But once this association with the legend has been made, what are we to make of it? For here too there is a profusion of loose threads, allusions to significances which are never revealed. There are many references to the Oedipus legend in the novel: the riddle, the Sphinx (in the form of the 'fabulous animal' in the canal), the shepherds rescuing an abandoned child (depicted on the curtains in the houses in the town), the chariot with its symbolic figures signed by 'V. Daulis', the picture of the ruins of Thebes in the stationer's shop, Madame Jean's recurrent nightmare with its 'sybilline writing', the unintelligible oracular loudspeaker at the station, the Rue de Corinthe, the Apollonian sculpture of an athlete killing a dragon, the blind old man being led by a child, Wallas's swollen feet.[1] But none of these references seems to contribute towards the revelation of a truth: the riddle is never properly formulated and Wallas never answers it, there is no deciphering either of the sybilline writing or of the oracular loudspeaker, and if Wallas's feet swell, he suffers neither the anguish nor the self-inflicted blindness of his potential counterpart in the legend.

Much has been made of the fact that Wallas gradually remembers that he once visited this nameless town as a child to visit his father – whom he never saw. But the text does not give us enough information to allow us to integrate this memory into a significant relation either with Dupont's death or with Wallas's hand in it. The Oedipal associations are all in peripheral details:

[1] Morrissette's study of this novel includes useful explanations of these allusions. For example, the name Daulis can be read as an 'allusion nette, mais qui échappe naturellement à Wallas, à la "route de Daulia" dans *Oedipe-Roi*, sous une forme (Daulis) qui renferme en plus, comme par pure coïncidence, une anagramme de Laïus'. The sculpture of the athlete killing the dragon is apparently a reference to the classical pose in which Apollo, the god of oracles and prophecy, is frequently represented. The old man being led by the child is an allusion to 'Tirésias guidé par un jeune garçon dans *Oedipe-Roi*' (Morrissette, 1963, 57).

The scene takes place in a city built in the Pompeian style –and, more
particularly, in a square one end of which is occupied by a temple
(or a theatre, or something of the sort) and the other sides by various
buildings of a smaller size, separated from each other by wide paved
streets. Wallas cannot remember where this picture comes from. He
is talking – sometimes in the middle of the square – sometimes on
some steps, some very long steps – to some characters whom he can
no longer tell apart, although they began by being quite clearly
characterised and distinct from one another. He himself has a well-
defined role, probably a major one, perhaps an official one. Suddenly
the memory becomes very sharp: for a fraction of a second, the entire
scene takes on an extraordinary density. But which scene? He just
has time to hear himself say: 'And did it happen a long time ago?'
    Immediately, everything has vanished, the gathering, the steps,
the temple, the square and its buildings. He never saw anything of
the kind before. (238)

The 'Greek' setting and Wallas's central role all point to the
legend, but the novel seems to refuse to support these indications in thematic terms. Instead of developing the thematic
potential of the paralleling of Wallas and Oedipus, the text
instead seems to emphasise the theatrical elements of the Oedipal situation in which Wallas finds himself in his memory. He
remembers a *scene*, where he played a central *role*, speaking to
characters outside a building which might itself be a *theatre*. The
Oedipal allusions have the function not of pointing to a meaning, but of drawing attention to the drama as a *means* of representation.

    On closer inspection, it seems that the erasers too share in
this emphasis. Contrary to Morrissette's assertion that the
erasers are a sign of the self-destruction or self-cancellation
of Wallas–Oedipus (1963, 65), they draw attention instead
to the novel as a *construction*. Wallas himself acknowledges
that the eraser he asks for at the stationer's is a '*fictional* object, attributed to a *mythical* brand' (133, my emphasis). Wallas's
quest is not for an object that will bring illumination and
significance to the world. Fiction and myth lie at the heart
of this novel, which therefore has no *telos*, no centre full of
truth. The Greek legend does not serve as a model to guide our
interpretation and enable us to discover a meaning or a truth,

but is represented as a representation – a drama, a fiction, a myth. The highly teleological construction of the Greek tragedy is used by Robbe-Grillet's novel to draw attention to the fact that what lies at the centre is always an artifice, an invention. The truth-centred *Oedipus the King* is played off against Robbe-Grillet's *Les gommes* where nothing is ever revealed, where there is indeed nothing to reveal, no oracular truths, no 'real' meaning to sybilline utterances. Instead of truth, there is a void at the centre of this narrative.

Several critics have commented on the void in Robbe-Grillet's works,[2] but it is perhaps Maurice Blanchot's remarks about *Le voyeur* that are most valuable in this context. He speaks of the central void in this novel as 'the absence which allows everything to be said' (1959, 200), and specifically associates it with a 'new effort to make narrative speak within the narrative itself' (199). It does indeed appear that the acknowledgement of a lack in *Les gommes* is always accompanied by a marked degree of self-consciousness on the part of the narrative. The void associated with the erasers, for example, allows the text to speak of itself as *fiction*, and this pattern is repeated throughout the novel in many details. The town itself appears to have no centre. Having decided to breakfast 'in a large modern establishment, on one of those squares or avenues which must, like everywhere else, make up the *heart* of the town' (51, my emphasis), Wallas is unable to get proper instructions for reaching that centre. When he asks a woman he meets in the street, she seems perplexed by his question, as if the centre were in some way problematic: 'The centre? The woman tries to place it in her head; she looks at her brush, then at the bucket full of water.' (56) Although she gives him directions of a sort, Wallas never reaches that centre, and, every time he aims for it, emerges instead on the ubiquitous Boulevard Circulaire, where, disorientated, he resorts to a henceforward useless logic: 'He cannot have gone round in a circle, because he had been walking in a straight line all the time' (54).

[2] Bernal, 1964 is the most comprehensive and systematic account of the novels in the light of this notion.

The very existence of a detective is, conventionally, a guarantee of (narrative) purpose, and in *Les gommes*, this teleological function is alluded to from time to time. Wallas's purposeful
walk through the town (albeit a short-lived purpose) has explicitly teleological associations:

He is walking along and he is gradually winding up the uninterrupted
line of his own advance, not a succession of senseless, unconnected
images, but a continuous ribbon where every element immediately
takes its place in the weft, even the most accidental ones, even those
which might at first appear absurd, or threatening, or anachronistic,
or deceptive; they all fall neatly into place next to each other, and
the material grows longer, without any holes or any lumps, at the
regular speed of his own step.[. . .] He is walking deliberately towards
an inevitable and perfect future. He used too often to succumb to the
circles of doubt and impotence, now he is walking; he has regained
his continuity. (52)

It is impossible to take this seriously as a true description of
Wallas's position, since his presence is quite patently not sufficient to transform a series of random and meaningless
elements into a unified, linear coherence. Instead, Wallas's
professional inadequacies allow us to perceive that inevitability
and linearity are not given naturally, and that without some
teleological force or construction things remain senseless and
incoherent. The strategic function of a detective in the narrative
is also undermined by the doubts of the supreme detective,
Fabius, Wallas's boss. His detecting (or narrativising) powers
are beginning to fail:

Even his most faithful followers sometimes charge him with a kind
of indecisiveness, an unhealthy caution, which make him question
the most solid facts over and over again. His intuitive ability to pick
out a weak spot in a suspicious situation, the passionate impulse
which would take him to the *heart of an enigma*, and his indefatigable
patience in recomposing the exposed threads, all seem at times to
turn into a sterile and fanatical scepticism. It used to be said that
he mistrusted simple solutions, now it is whispered that he no longer
believes in the existence of any *solution* whatever. (60–1, my emphases)

And in the present case he wavers between seeing the plot as a
series of coincidences or as a Machiavellian invention on the
part of the government. The legendary detective appears above

all to be losing his powers of narrative. If one no longer believes in solutions, events are bound to become a series of coincidences, and to lose their narrative appearance.

The notion of solution is finally turned to derision by the text in the last few pages in connection with the 'missing' centimetre from Wallas's forehead. Fabius is calculating the size of Wallas's forehead. The regulations require that a detective's brow measure fifty square centimetres and Wallas is one centimetre short:

Forty-three multiplied by one hundred and fourteen. Four times three, twelve. Four times four, sixteen. Sixteen and one, seventeen. Forty-three. Forty-three. Two. Seven and three, ten. Four and three, seven. Seven and one, eight. Eight and one, nine. Four. Four thousand nine hundred and two. There is no other possible *solution*. 'Four thousand nine hundred and two ... It won't do, my lad. Forty-nine square centimetres: you need at least fifty, you know.'
One single centimetre – he only needed one measly centimetre. (259–60, my emphasis)

A solution is no longer a truth which retrospectively constructs a narrative; it is simply the outcome of a mathematical calculation. The missing factor in Wallas's detection is not the vital clue that will allow all the other items to fall into place so that a story may emerge; it is a square centimetre of forehead.

The missing clue, so important in the conventional detective story, loses its importance in Robbe-Grillet's novel and joins the many other irrelevant lacks. Things that one might expect to complete, instead of revealing a whole picture, as in a jigsaw for example, prove to be incidental and arbitrary in terms of the narrative. This is as true for Wallas's missing centimetre as it is for the uncompleted sentence that Dupont leaves on his desk. At the beginning of the novel, Garinati, the agent sent to kill Dupont, notices 'four words at the top of a blank page: "they can not prevent" ... It was at this point that he [Dupont] went downstairs for dinner; he cannot have been able to find the next word' (26). Later on, on seeing the same piece of paper, Wallas apparently has no trouble in completing the sentence: '"Death", of course. That was the word he was looking for when he went down for dinner.' (95) There is, however, nothing obvious about this completion: Dupont is not dead and in any case the word is unlikely to appear in a book on economics (Dupont is an economist). The sentence, as completed here, is an arbitrary construction imposed by a misguided Wallas who believes that Dupont is dead.

Sitting in the bus some time later, Wallas hears two women exchanging fragments of a story which appears to have no *telos*:

Neither of them seems to have any particular interest in the outcome of this affair. The characters in question are not relatives or friends of theirs. The lives of the two women even seem to be sheltered from this kind of drama, but ordinary people love to discuss the glorious events in the lives of great criminals and kings. Unless they are simply talking about a serial published in one of the daily papers. (130)

The Oedipal theme surfaces here again briefly as if to compare the women to the chorus in the play, and serves again to draw attention to the theme of conclusion and make all the more exemplary the ability of ordinary people to do without solutions.

One of the most striking examples of a gap in the mystery which the novel never solves and yet which allows it to speak most freely about itself, is provided by the letter which Wallas is handed at the post-office. Mistaken for a certain 'André VS' (one of the presumed gang) Wallas is given this letter which might contain vital information if only he and Laurent, the local police chief, could decipher it. Part of the letter is, literally, illegible, as Laurent says to Wallas:

I can only see one little sentence, which neither you nor I can make out, but which we can probably leave on one side as secondary – you agree. Anyway, to be complete, let us note that there is an illegible word in one of the sentences which you think are significant – a word with seven or eight strokes in it, which looks like 'ellipsis', or 'eclipse' and which could also be 'aligns', 'graver', 'idem' or a number of other things. (170)

This unreadable word in a significant sentence is never deciphered and Laurent's speculations veer off at a tangent until he concludes (?) that the letter might just as easily refer to a business deal by a timber merchant as to the next move in the gang's conspiracy. The potential clue is never picked up and interpreted, and it serves only to thicken the mystery without sowing the seed of future illumination. However, the missing word could, as Morrissette has suggested (1963, 63), be the name *Oedipe*, which is the right length and can be conflated out of the various readings that Laurent proposes for it. As I have already indicated, the Oedipal theme in *Les gommes*, instead of taking us to the heart of the mystery, invariably provides a pretext for the text's self-elucidation, and the present instance is no exception. Indeed, all the items here can be read as self-elucidation without passing through the mythological references: 'aligns' and 'graver' both refer to the construction of a text in the purely material sense – lining up the letters, engraving the words; 'ellipsis' and 'eclipse' can both be seen to take their place in the theme of the absent *telos* – the text eclipses or obscures the mystery to which it seems to refer, the revelation is lost in an ellipsis. There is further irony here, since this pointing up of the void is done by Laurent 'to be complete', as if to suggest (once more) that the novel is most present to itself as fiction when the void is most evident in the narrative.

Time and again the novel alludes to these various forms of absence and specifically associates them with its status as fiction. Just as the eraser is no more than a fictional object, so too does detection prove to be a form of fiction. Instead of unfolding the truth behind a series of events, the detective aspect of Robbe-Grillet's novel proves to be a machine for producing an indefinite number of more or less obviously fictional stories. Many of the hypotheses put forward by Laurent and Wallas to explain Dupont's death are narrated by the text as if they really happened, without at first making it clear that they might be merely speculation. The various explanations (that it was suicide, that Madame Dupont was the murderer, that an illegitimate son shot Dupont) are presented in just the same way as the original account of Garinati's botched murder attempt. The search for truth simply leads the text to multiply its fictions.

Similarly, Wallas's search for the truth obliges him frequently to invent fictions concerning himself. When he wants to get to the central police station, he asks for directions to the central post-office in order not to create suspicion about himself. But this pretext leads him into a proliferating fiction. He finds himself having to justify his need for a post-office, and says that he needs to send a telegram:

> This remark seems unfortunately to attract the lady's sympathy:
> 'Oh, it's for a telegram!'
> She glances down at her brush while Wallas thinks he can extricate himself with a vague 'yes'.
> 'Nothing serious, I hope?' says the lady.
> The question was not put in an explicitly interrogative way, more like a somewhat dubitative polite wish; but then she says nothing else and Wallas finds himself having to reply:
> 'No, no,' he says; 'thank you.'
> That is a lie too because a man died last night. Ought he to explain that it is not anyone in his family?
> 'Well,' says the woman, 'if it's not urgent, there is a post-office over there which opens at eight.'
> That's what you get for making up stories. Whom should he send a telegram to, and what should it say? How on earth could he get back to where he started? (55)

Wallas's mission to discover the truth is severely threatened by the fictions the pursuit of that truth forces him to invent.

Later on, Wallas's search for the truth is again threatened by fiction, but this time in a different way. He feels that he is on the right track, but in telling the incredulous Laurent of his hunch, he becomes aware that his 'discovery' is simply a story:

> As he spoke, he became increasingly aware of the unbelievable nature of his story. Perhaps, in any case, it was not just the words he was using: other, more carefully chosen ones would have had the same fate; no sooner were they uttered than people stopped taking them seriously. Wallas got to the point of no longer reacting against the ready-made formulae which sprang naturally to mind; on the whole, they were the best.
> To crown it all, there was the commissioner opposite him with his amused expression, and his all too evident incredulity finally destroyed the *vraisemblance* of his construction. (174–5)

The truth becomes a fiction because Wallas does not have the narrative skill to give it the necessary air of naturalness, and we see that the greatest naturalness is a consequence of the greatest artifice.

Robbe-Grillet's own concern here is not with *vraisemblance*, and instead artifice is advertised everywhere, and in such a way as to enable the text to speak of itself. Already at the beginning, as Garinati walks up the stairs of Dupont's house, the idea of inevitability (on which conventional narrative depends) is made artificial as the text turns it into a product of a well-performed play. It is not what the gods, or in this instance, Bona, decree, but what literature writes: 'The immutable course continues', begins the episode, but the immutable is produced by writing, and not copied by it: 'You only have to *follow the text*, speaking line after line, and the word will be accomplished' (23, my emphasis). Doom, or even simply plots are created by words on paper.

Perhaps the most striking advertisement of artifice is provided by what, in the story, is in fact an advertisement: the stationer's window has a life-size model of an artist at work:

an 'artist' [is] drawing 'from life'. A dummy, wearing a smock smeared with paint and an enormous 'bohemian' beard which hides his face, is hard at work in front of his easel; standing back to be able to see his painting and his model in one glance, he is putting the final touches to a very delicately executed landscape drawing – which must in fact be the copy of some master. It is a hill with the ruins of a classical temple rising out of some cypress trees; in the foreground there are some bits of broken column lying here and there; in the distance, in the valley, one can see an entire city with its triumphal arches and its palaces – which, in spite of the distance and the number of constructions in it, has been treated with a rare concern for detail. But in front of the man, instead of the Greek countryside, by way of scenery there is a huge photographic print of a crossroads in a town in the twentieth century. The quality of the picture and its skilful positioning give the panorama a reality which is all the more striking for its being the negation of the drawing which is supposed to reproduce it. (131)

The artist (himself a representation of a standard image) is not reproducing what he sees before him (in fact a photograph of Dupont's house) but has produced a reproduction. Instead of copying reality (or at least a photograph) he has copied art. The artifice of art is indeed advertised and, again, in connection with the most apparently teleological elements of the narrative: the Oedipal and the detective.

Artifice is everywhere and we see that everything is construction. There is clearly no pre-existing story which the novel unfolds to its conclusion, fiction no longer relays truth through narrative. The novel as the laboratory of narrative becomes a powerful producer of explicitly fictional narratives and simultaneously makes quite audible the narrative's own discourse on itself.

The gamma point: 'L'emploi du temps'

One consequence of the teleological nature of plot is that all stories are explicitly or implicitly told in the past tense. There is neither mystery nor meaning in a narrative unless there is retrospect, for, since the sense of a plot is constructed in reverse, the ultimate term and all that precedes it must already be known to the story-teller, and therefore be given in the past tense. As if in recognition of this fact, the French language has a past tense reserved exclusively for narrative, the past historic (also known as the preterite).

Roland Barthes describes this tense as the 'cornerstone of narration' and explains its function in the following terms:

Through the preterite, the verb implicitly belongs with a causal chain, it partakes of a set of related and orientated actions, *it functions as the algebraic sign of an intention*. Allowing as it does an ambiguity between temporality and causality, *it calls for a sequence of events*, that is, for an intelligible Narrative. This is why it is the ideal instrument for every construction of a world; it is the unreal time of cosmogonies, myths, History and Novels. It presupposes a world which is constructed, elaborated, self-sufficient, reduced to significant lines, and not one which has been sent sprawling before us, for us to take or leave. Behind the preterite there always lurks a demiurge, a God or a reciter. *The world is not unexplained since it is told like a story*; each one of its accidents is but a circumstance, and the preterite is precisely this operative sign whereby the narrator reduces the exploded reality to a slim and pure logos, without density, without volume, without spread, and whose sole function is to *unite as rapidly as possible a cause and an end*. (1972, 26)[3]

The preterite is thus the tense which guarantees causality, the

[3] This English version is taken from the excellent translation of *Le degré zéro* by Annette Lavers and Colin Smith (Barthes, 1967, 36–7).

linking of the chain of events leading to a solution, and the promise of the revelation of truth.

In the nouveau roman this tense has almost entirely disappeared,[4] a disappearance which is bound to have consequences for the role and function of narrative in the various novels. The particular nature of these consequences is explored and elaborated in different ways by each novel but Butor's *L'emploi du temps* dramatises the absence of the preterite in a particularly striking way. Jacques Revel, the narrator of the novel, decides during the course of his stay in an English town to write an account of his time there, with the result that what he writes is part record of the past and part diary of the present as he seeks to recall the first weeks and months in the town and to keep abreast of the events that occur in the present at the time of writing. At first, however, the present does not intervene except in the dating of the writing (Revel's account of his arrival in October is dated 1 May, 2 May, 5 May, etc.). He describes his venture as a search. ('It is now that the real search is starting', 37) a classical narrative form, and he sees that this search consists of placing events in order: 'I must retake possession of all the events which I can feel swarming within me and falling into place despite the fog which is trying to obscure them, I must evoke them one by one in their order, so as to save them' (38). This ordering of events in search for significance seems a conventional and, at first, apparently a simple task. On a number of occasions in the book it is suggested that it is a quite natural activity, that one way in which we seek to understand and give sense to an event is to establish the sequence of the events that preceded it. Indeed, this is the way that all narrative functions: we begin with the marchioness's suicide and

---

[4] So much so that Jean Bloch-Michel's (hostile) book on the nouveau roman is entitled *Le présent de l'indicatif*. The only novels to use the preterite are Nathalie Sarraute's *Portrait d'un inconnu* and Robbe-Grillet's *Le voyeur*. In *Portrait d'un inconnu*, the past historic alternates with the present tense, with the effect that teleology is repeatedly interrupted, and so, finally, disrupted. In *Le voyeur* the past historic is misused rather than refused. As Genette has pointed out, the same past historic is used for four different temporal levels, the distant past, the recent past, the 'real' present, and the imagined future, thus creating a considerable amount of confusion and destroying the intentionality and the order that the past historic generally guarantees. See 'Vertige fixé' (1966, 69–90).

work backwards through the revolver and the despair. But although all teleology operates in reverse, most stories reconstitute a sequence of events so that they follow a forward direction, with the result that the despair comes first, then the revolver, and finally the suicide. However, the detective story, that most teleological of narratives, bears marked traces of the construction in reverse, and is, as George Burton, the crime writer in Butor's novel, says, the natural way in which the narrativisation of our experiences begins:

in detective stories, the narrative is constructed in reverse, since it begins with the crime, the outcome of all the dramas which the detective has gradually to uncover, which is in many ways more natural than telling stories without ever going back, [. . .] in the detective novel the narrative gradually explores the events which took place before the one with which it opens, which could be disconcerting, but which is quite natural, because, in real life, it is clearly only once we have met somebody that we become interested in what he has done in the past, because in real life, too often, it is only when some misfortune arises and upsets our life that we are alerted and seek out its origins. (171)

Revel's own narrative is of course motivated by this retrospective enquiry which is intended to illuminate his present self. At times, the narrative is even written in reverse, although it is in no sense a detective novel, and Revel makes a number of references to the reverse direction of his narrative. But in the end, neither forward nor reverse presentation can be sustained, and in the final chapter, written in September, it is clear that there is no linear organisation for the narrative at all which deals instead with an apparently random time-sequence:

> August
> August, July
> July, March
> March, September
> September
> September, February
> February
> August
> August, July
> July
> March
> September

September, February
August
August, July
July
July, March
March, September
September
September, February
August, July, March, September
September, February.

The use of the months of the year as chapter- and page-head-
ings draws attention to the chronological organisation of the
novel, and by the final chapter it is quite evident that the
narrative has lost all linear chronology. On one level the temporal organisation of the novel corresponds to a purely formal
patterning, as Jean Ricardou has shown (1967, 63). But on
another level the confused chronology is also a result of the
novel's exploration of narrative constructions, a topic with
which the book is deeply concerned.

One important reason why the narrative is unable to move in
a straight line is because the point of view from which it is told
is always shifting. The advancing present of the narrative
utterance is indicated by the dates, and in Chapter 1 which tells
of Revel's arrival and first acquaintance with the town, the
present is otherwise barely alluded to. But it erupts in the
second chapter which opens with an account (dated 2 June)
of the events that took place the previous day, Sunday 1 June.
This immediately introduces a new narrative orientation. The
question which guides the narrative in Chapter 1 and which
reappears intermittently during the course of the novel, is 'what
changes have taken place in Revel during the months between
his arrival and the present? and what is the significance of the
events that have occurred?'. But suddenly, at the beginning of
Chapter 2 we are faced with a quite different question which,
instead of trying to fill the gap between October and May, projects the narrative forward into June and beyond, into time
which has not, as yet, been lived, and about which Revel therefore knows nothing. He cannot possibly know the answer to the
question evoked by the events he narrates – namely, has he,

by telling the Bailey sisters the real name of the author of *Le meurtre de Bleston*, put the life of his friend George Burton in danger? Subsequent events prove to make this question even more pertinent, although it never in fact receives a definitive answer. As the months go on through July, August and September, other things happen which raise other questions and so serve to disperse the narrative even more widely.

The temporal levels become more and more intertwined, so that there is not simply one question to guide the narrative of the past (what has become of Revel since his arrival in Bleston?) and one to guide the present (has he put the life of his friend at risk?). Events in the present constantly alter the questions that Revel asks of the past. This is the case, for example, with his love first for Rose Bailey and then for her sister Ann. His present love structures the way in which he sees his past. Unlike a detective novel, there is no single event in the novel (like a murder) which provokes a coherent search for its origins. The different events of the present, constantly altering, provoke a search for their different origins (his love for Rose, his love for Ann). As Burton says of what he calls the best examples of his genre (detective novels), 'narrative is not simply a flat projection of a series of events, but the reconstruction of their architecture, their space, since they appear differently depending on the position from which they are viewed by the detective or the narrator' (161). In Butor's novel, the narrator's position is always changing, so that the architecture of events never offers a stable perspective.

Revel's narrative becomes a shifting, plural construction because he is never placed at what Sartre calls the 'gamma point' which, in the stable world of the pre-war French novel 'represented absolute rest' (1948, 252). In refusing to opt for the gamma point, he simultaneously refuses timelessness, or what Sartre calls the 'leap into the eternal' (257). He, like Sartre's writer in 1947, is 'involved in a system in full evolution' and so can 'only know relative movements' (252). The abdication of the gamma point is thus a serious threat to narrative order, since a strict linear causality becomes impossible with an ultimate term that is always shifting, and chronology, on which causality depends, ceases to be operative. Events, instead of arriving as an answer to the question 'and then?' become mere allusion in a narrative that is always constructed as a backward glance from an ever moving present. The allusive presentation of events increases as the chronology becomes more confused. Revel's first accidental meeting with George Burton in a Chinese restaurant is alluded to many times before it is narrated in full (288) some pages before the end of the novel. But this complete narrative itself contains allusions to people, items and events in other, chronologically unconnected narrative sequences (the detective in Burton's book, the Old Cathedral with its stained-glass window depicting the story of Cain, Rose Bailey, Ann Bailey, James Jenkins, Lucien, Revel's purchase of the second-hand copy of Burton's book), so that in explaining previous allusions, the narrative diffuses its *telos* in the inclusion of numerous other allusions.[5]

With the narrative discourse so firmly located in time, the use of the past historic would be unthinkable. The preterite is the tense used when the narrative is uttered from the atemporal gamma point. It both guarantees causal, consecutive logic and makes narrating an instantaneous, timeless act. Indeed, a logical ordering of past events seems actually to depend on maintaining silence concerning the conditions of the narrative discourse which conveys that order. The alternative past tense in the French language, composed as it is of past and present elements (the *present* auxiliary, the *past* participle: 'il a fait') is bound, therefore, to link the present utterance to past events, and so breaks the chain which links past events to each other. This linking of what is conventionally regarded as two quite separate temporal levels is repeatedly evinced in *L'emploi du temps*, and there are times when distinctions between present and past can no longer be made. The novel draws attention to the possibilities of such confusion through remarks made by

---

[5] This dispersal of events through allusion becomes the systematic narrative mode in *Degrés*, where every element demands a narrative of its origins, and every narrative contains references to items in another chronological sequence whose origins also demand to be heard.

Burton about detective fiction, which, he says, exploits and emphasises the two different temporal levels:

in the detective novel, the narrative [. . .] superimposes two temporal sequences: the days of the enquiry which begin with the crime, and the days of the drama which lead up to it, which is quite natural since, in real life, thinking about the past takes place during time when other events are piling up. (171)

And he goes on to show how these two levels can become confused:

very often things are made more complicated, with the detective frequently being called in by the victim to protect him because he is afraid of being murdered, so that the days of the enquiry begin even before the crime has happened, starting with the darkness and fear which it casts before it, precipitating the final event, so that the days of the drama can continue after it until other crimes take place as a kind of spin-off, echo or emphasis of it, and so every event belonging to the enquiry sequence could, seen from the retrospective standpoint of a later time, be placed in the other sequence. (172)

And just as the detective's presence can precipitate the very events into which he has come to enquire (as in *Les gommes*), so Revel's record of the events of his life can in turn affect the course of those events. This is the case when he loses Rose to his friend Lucien: 'Rose whom I allowed to escape [. . .] because I shut myself up in this room, never dreaming that it could go so far' (188). Rose is lost to him because he spent his time writing, and so neglected her. Writing does not take place in a timeless vacuum but occupies a quite tangible place in the calendar and the narrator's life.

To record events is not a neutral, transparent activity but can have dire consequences, and itself become part of the events it narrates. The reciprocity of narration and events is mutual. In this instance, it is not just the writing which becomes an event, but the events themselves change the nature and function of that writing. Revel writes that on hearing that Lucien and Rose are to be married, 'At that moment all these pages seemed to have turned to dust' and he asks himself, 'What use is it now to go on with this vast, absurd attempt to understand, which has only served to make me lose my way even more? What use is it to go on with this futile, dangerous business of excavation and staking out, to try and retie the thread which has been broken?' (189) The nature of writing itself is thus altered by the events that it would record; whereas, before, writing was seen as the means whereby order and significance could be brought to events, it is now reduced to a state of chaos and absurdity by them.

As the novel progresses it becomes increasingly clear that writing cannot be an invisible means of throwing light on a subject outside itself; the very gesture of casting light can obscure or deform the object under inspection. A passage in Chapter 3 states very clearly the consequences of this deforming search for the past:

It is already quite dark; it is Thursday now; I only have tomorrow, Friday, left in this week, to bring the events of January up to the surface from where they lie at a depth of seven months, like the events of my arrival in October when I retrieved them, fished them out and narrated them in May at the same distance of seven months which I hoped to reduce, but which I have managed only to sustain (and even then with what difficulty!), so many shadows, so many consequences, so many accidents, so many ghosts have intervened in waters seven months deep and increasingly less transparent because the disturbance has stirred up the mud. (218)

The metaphor here is doubly apposite: first, it suggests that events do not simply present themselves for inscription, but have to be fished out and brought to the surface with all the patience and effort that this implies; and secondly, it suggests that the very business of retrieving the objects actually obscures our vision of what those objects are.

The material nature of the narrative discourse itself becomes an ever greater preoccupation of the narrative as the novel draws towards a close, almost to the detriment of the events which it records. It is as if the text preferred to take stock of itself as discourse rather than passively record events as they progress towards resolution (which they do not). Revel's narrative is by turns 'this pathetic heap of futile sentences' (252), 'this long path of writing' (246), an act of defiance against the spell that he thinks the city is trying to cast on him, a 'necessary and laborious writing to enable me to understand [...], to understand myself, before it is too late, before things are decided without me' (218). In a sense Revel's life comes to depend on his narrative, and the chain of sentences becomes a lifeline:

The cord of sentences curled up in this pile and which links me directly to the moment on 1 May when I began to plait it, this cord of sentences is an Ariadne's thread because I am in a labyrinth, because I am writing in order to discover where I am, all these lines being the signs with which I mark out the paths which I have already retraced, the labyrinth of my time at Bleston, infinitely more confusing than the palace of Crete, since it grows larger as I move about it, since it alters as I explore it. (187)

In a world where exploration changes the form of what is explored it does indeed seem safer to privilege the discourse over its object.

This growing importance of the narrative discourse itself succeeds finally in changing the notion of narrative form. The recognition of the present tense of narration made a linear cause-and-effect model of narrative impossible to adhere to (and, incidentally, proves its artificial, constructed nature), and gives rise to an image of a different narrative order. This image is evoked in the stained-glass window in the Cathedral and in the tapestries of Theseus which the novel describes. The stained-glass window depicts all the major events of the story of Cain and Abel *simultaneously,* although there is, significantly, a problem of perspective in trying to embrace the whole in one glance. In the same way, the eighteen tapestries depicting scenes from the life of Theseus are a simultaneous presentation of successive events, and in some cases a single tapestry represents in one image a number of events that are strictly speaking separate in time. Successivity, linearity and causality are replaced by an attempt at simultaneity.

The final narrative image is a musical one, where the principle of construction is likened to harmonics. A backward glance towards the past evokes not a linked chain of events, but

a 'whole series of bands of varying degrees of brightness separated by wide zones of shadow, like the stripes of an incandescent
light when it is broken down on the black screen of a spectro-
scope, a whole series of resonances of varying degrees of intensity, separated by wide intervals of near silence, like the
harmonics which the tone of a note can be broken down into'
(292). Every day, every event has its 'historical harmonics' (295)
and it is in this context of *associations*, and not in a context of
causes, that each takes on its significance. This means of producing significance is so powerful that it overrides the properly
narrative orientation with which the novel opens, so that by the
end questions that are posed about events in February remain
unanswered, as do all the other enigmas and mysteries (for
example, was George Burton's accident caused deliberately?
and if so, by whom?). This construction by harmonics is one
that is effected by the narrative discourse and would be entirely
lost if one were to try and reconstruct a chronological sequence
of events. It is a construction that the reader must continue
from his own reading of that discourse ('this exploratory description, the basis for a future deciphering', 264), and to which
every narrative is ultimately subject. Greimas, in his study of
narrative, says that every narrative has to submit to what he
calls a 'paradigmatic interpretation', and claims that 'this
paradigmatic interpretation [is] the necessary condition for
the understanding of the narrative as a whole' (1966, 204).
Although narratives give us sense, that sense cannot be fully
grasped until, once the end of the story is reached, the syntag-
matic organisation of the narrative is collapsed into paradigmatic (or harmonic) structures. In Butor's novel, it is as if the
narrative were anticipating its own fate at the hands of
future readers.

L'emploi du temps demonstrates that the language of narrative
is the ultimate determinant of the form of the story to which it
refers and on which it appears so often to depend. It operates
a dramatic shift from the attempt to order events into a narrative sequence, to the discovery that the language in which that
ordering is carried out, refuses to comply with cause and effect
in this way – perhaps because its own existence is imperilled

by the silence which a teleological, purely retrospective narrative imposes on the discourse which proffers it.[6]

The real in question: 'Vous les entendez?'

It is a major part of the business of narrative (as either story or history) to answer the question 'what happened?', and this appears a simple enough task. But, in fact, to answer this question one needs to make a number of qualitative distinctions that the nouveau roman shows us should not be taken for granted. In order to be able to say what happened one needs to be able to distinguish between what actually happened and what was remembered, anticipated, dreamed or entirely invented. If we take Forster's example of a plot, we can see that it clearly answers the question 'what happened?': the king died and the queen died of grief. But we could make a longer version which might read: 'The king died and when the queen then died it was supposed that she had caught the disease which had killed the king. It was only later that it was discovered that it was through grief at the death of the king.' In this version we can see that the narrative record of the real is strongly opposed to what one might call hypothesis (it was supposed that she had caught the disease which had killed the king), and indeed that its status as a record of the real is greatly reinforced by the contrast with the hypothetical. This distinction is as true for fiction as it is for history or newspaper reportage, since when we read a novel, we read *as if* the narrative were a record of the real.

In many of the nouveaux romans these distinctions are frequently ignored. The confusion at the beginning of *Le voyeur*,

[6] Gérard Genette's essay 'Frontières du récit' (1969, 49–69) argues that the limits of narrative are marked by the opposition between narrative and discourse, and concludes that in twentieth-century fiction 'Tout se passe [...] comme si la littérature avait épuisé ou débordé les ressources de son mode représentatif, et voulait se replier sur le murmure indéfini de son propre discours' (68). Literature's need to become audible to itself is quite evident in Butor's *L'emploi du temps*. But it is less certain that it has necessarily abandoned the representational mode (Butor's novel never questions the reality of the world to which it refers but only makes clear that the way in which that reality is perceived and understood is entirely dependent on the constructions which we make and employ). Equally, it seems doubtful that literature has ever been able to dispense with 'the indeterminate murmur of its own discourse'.

for example, is due to the mixing of past, present and imagined events through the indiscriminate use of the past historic (the tense which conventionally designates the real). In *La jalousie* decisions about what is real, remembered, imagined or simply invented have constantly to be altered and finally suspended, in part because we are never sure whether the text has a narrator, and in part as a result of the ubiquitous use of the present tense. In *La maison de rendez-vous* and Robbe-Grillet's subsequent novels the confusion between different levels becomes systematic and any attempt to distinguish between them is bound to be frustrated and to make the novel less, rather than more interesting. The novels appear to have little concern with the question 'what happened?'

It is Robbe-Grillet's novels which have drawn most attention in the context of this aspect of narrative, and, apart from the four versions of a single scene in *Martereau* (207–37), Nathalie Sarraute's novels have not come under scrutiny. This is surprising in view of her claim that *most* novels ignore distinctions between different levels of reality. Writing about *Entre la vie et la mort* she says: 'Here, as in most novels, the real, the potential, the merely possible, the entirely imagined blend and merge together to the extent that even the author would have difficulty in distinguishing them' (*Prière d'insérer*). If this is true, then it seems that the definition of the novel as a member of the class of *narrative* fiction is entirely inappropriate, since narrative depends on distinctions of this kind being made. In *Vous les entendez?* the narrative consequences of the text's reluctance to distinguish between 'the real, the potential, the merely possible and the entirely imagined' can be reasonably easily documented.

The novel opens with two old men sitting over coffee and brandy admiring a sculpture which belongs to the host. The peaceful atmosphere is disturbed by the sound of laughter coming from upstairs as the host's children prepare to go to bed. For the first few pages there is a fairly clear narrative syntax that enables one to reconstruct a sequence of events. The evocation of the children's leave-taking for the night is introduced in the past tense ('they were tired', 9) and so enables

one to place it before the moment with which the book opens,
even though the leave-taking subsequently shifts to the present
tense (which we therefore accord the status of historic present):
'they stand up'. The way in which the friend carries the sculpture from the mantelpiece to the table (10) is also given in the
past tense, and, as the children appear still to be in the room,
it seems logical to place this event before their leave-taking.[7]
A page or two later, the father goes upstairs to tell the children
to be quiet, an event which is narrated in the present tense, and
which appears as a logical sequel to the opening scene where
the men sit peacefully with the sculpture. However, as the discussion between the two men is resumed and pursued, the
father appeals to his children to confirm his assertion that he
has never been a collector (an assertion which they go on to
mock, 22–5). At this point, there seems to be an infringement
of the narrative syntax which normally makes possible a reconstruction of the real: if this scene is to be read as real, the
children must have come downstairs again for a reason which
the text fails to give. And if the scene itself is not real, in order
to preserve some notion of the real, the only alternative is to
assume that the scene is imagined by the father who mentally
pictures what his children's response *might* be *if* they were
there. But the text itself bears none of the conventional marks
for signalling imagination or hypothesis and the scene is given
as if it were real. This realism has the effect of profoundly
threatening any notion of the real in the novel's overall narrative.

It is challenged too in the following sections by a profusion
of repetitions: on page 28 the children are upstairs – again?
still? A page later the friend (again?) takes the sculpture from
the mantelpiece. The threat posed by these repetitions is due to
the fact that there is a certain ambiguity about whether they are
in the text or the reality to which the text supposedly refers:

---

[7] Genette, in his discussion of the temporal zigzags which characterise the beginning
of Proust's *A la recherche du temps perdu*, points out that this structure is typical of
most narratives: 'Ces ouvertures à structure complexe, et comme mimant pour mieux
l'exorciser l'inévitable *difficulté du commencement*, sont apparemment dans la tradition
narrative la plus ancienne et la plus constante' (1972, 88). It is in this ancient tradition
that we may place the opening of Nathalie Sarraute's novel.

is the text repeating its account of a single event? or is it recording several similar events? Is the repetition in the writing or the reality, in the narration or the story? There is no unambiguous answer, and as the novel develops, an answer becomes increasingly impossible. Everything is given in the present tense which contributes to the obscuring of any narrative syntax or hierarchy, so that ultimately it seems preferable to regard the text not as a narrative of the real, but as a juggling of the original *données* of the opening pages (the leave-taking, the discussion about the sculpture, the laughter upstairs, and so on), a juggling which appears to use narrative events for what are probably quite *un*-narrative purposes. On page 46 the friend (once again) fetches the sculpture; on page 49 the children (again) go up to bed; on page 58 the father (again) goes upstairs to reprimand his children and on page 64 this is repeated (again). The cumulative effect of these repetitions is to break down or make irrelevant the original sequence which the opening pages allowed us to postulate and which originally allowed answers to the narrative questions 'and then?' and 'why?':

(1) the friend fetches the sculpture;
then (2) the children go up to bed;
then (3) the men smoke their pipes, drink brandy and discuss the sculpture in peace (because the children have left them alone?);
then (4) the children laugh upstairs (because they find the two men comic?);
then (5) the father goes upstairs (because he is disturbed by the children's laughter).

The juggling of these items breaks any sequence or causality that this (original? constructed?) version implies.

In addition to the juggling of these *données*, the novel contains a number of scenes which do not appear to be in any way integrated into this narrative order and which are equally hard to categorise as reality, memory, or imagination. For example, in one scene the father visits a headmaster to discuss the progress of his children in school and discovers that they are bad pupils. It is impossible to decide whether this is a memory

of a real event or an imagined scene which the father (?) invents
in order to corroborate his view of the children at that moment.
In another such scene the father visits what appears to be a
kind of reference library in search of a definition of his feelings
towards his wife. Again, this could be either memory or imagination. There are a number of such apparently implausible
scenes in the novel, as for example, the visit of the social worker
who is called in by the neighbours because of the father's
suspected cruelty, or the trial of the friend on a charge of having
called the children mediocre. The *invraisemblance* of these scenes
makes it possible to regard them as imaginary, but when the
father roars with pain at the thought that his children dismiss
his love of art as simple madness, is this fact or imagination?
On the one hand the roars of pain seem *invraisemblable* in the
context of a discussion about aesthetic values, and yet, on the
other, the scene's dialogue is not out of tune with the dialogue
that surrounds it, and unlike the headmaster, the social worker
or the judge, the characters are those in the rest of the novel (the
father, the children, the friend). A decision seems impossible.
In this novel there is no certainty about *what happens*. Even
if one rules out 'a social worker calls' or 'some children make
their father roar with pain', we must share in the sustained
uncertainty about the children's laughter: does it signify their
scorn for traditional values (especially on aesthetic matters)?
Or is it simply a token of innocent fun? It is not clear whether
there is anything to the laughter, and therefore whether there
is any justification for many of the narratives or scenes that
comprise the novel.[8]

Uncertainty here is so pervasive that one can never be sure
what is real and what is not. We cannot speak of a coherent
narrative since the disruption of narrative syntax obstructs any
ordering of events into a temporal sequence (we cannot reconstruct a chain of events from the text) and, as a corollary,

[8] This negation of the narrative enterprise is quite common at the end of Sarraute's
works and is almost systematic in the plays (which, in many ways, the novels come
more and more to resemble). At the end of *Isma*, for example, one of the characters
denies that the way another character pronounces the syllable *-isme* has any significance and so cancels the whole action of the play. In the same way, *Le silence* ends with a
denial that there was anything special about a certain Jean-Pierre's silence. This
silence is the starting point for the whole action of the play, which is therefore entirely
cancelled by the final remark: 'Je n'ai rien remarqué.'

into what one might call an ontological hierarchy (real, remembered, imaginary, possible). Instead we do better to use a term,
such as the one coined by Mary McCarthy to describe *Entre
la vie et la mort* – 'an auditory pantomime' (1970, 172). Voices
speak and the novel meditates on the implications of what they
have to say. Viewed in this light the scene with the headmaster,
for example, can be read as an exploration of the implications
of calling the children 'dunces', without any regard as to
whether the scene is real or not: the scene makes us realise that
the word 'dunce' reflects more on the people who use it than it
does on those whom it is supposed to describe. The irritated
schoolmaster who sits tapping a pile of exercise books with his
pen and talks of the children's lack of curiosity, their atrophy
and their rigidity, instead of reinforcing the father's values
over those of the children, finally makes the father want to
escape through the dusty, damp corridors where 'mediocre
minds obediently swallow insipid mush' so that he can rejoin
his children, and through them 'that part of himself which he
had spent his life helping to eradicate, which he had thought
was buried and which has been resurrected in them' (54). It
becomes clear that to use the word 'dunce' places one in the
drab, regimented world of the schoolroom, and the qualities
which the father finally opts for are the very ones which con-
demn them as 'dunces' in school.

Similarly, the social-worker-scene constitutes an exploration
of a suggestion by one of the children that the sculpture has
certain Cretan features and of her father's furious response.
The report given by the children to the social worker initiates
the exploration of this exchange of words. 'It looks like a
Cretan sculpture' the daughter had said, and she goes on to
explain to the social worker: 'sometimes I lose my head, I say
anything, just to be able to say something . . . Then he went for
me, he barked . . . "What sort of sculpture?" in a horrible
voice . . . his mouth was all twisted with hatred . . . "What sort
of sculpture?" . . . he bit me . . . Then we left, we thought it was
wiser.' (105) It seems somewhat *invraisemblable* in this context
that a father should bark at and bite his children, just as it seems
implausible that the social worker should be there in the first
place. But these incongruities do not need to be explained away

into some kind of realistic order if we regard *all* the scenes in the novel (whether apparently real or not) as constituting an exploration of different kinds of language. For these purposes it does not matter whether the visit to the school is remembered or imagined, since its primary purpose is to render perceptible the significance of calling one's children 'dunces'. And the social worker's visit serves to demonstrate that remarks that appear to be purely aesthetic judgments (a sculpture looks Cretan) can in fact be a last resort in a desperate bid for contact with one's interlocutor.

Instead of structuring the overall architecture of the novel, narrative is used here as a means of elaborating the significance of apparently chance remarks. Brief narrative sequences are engendered by utterances like 'They are cheerful, aren't they?' (7), 'I have never been a collector' (22), 'It's good enough to be in a museum' (38). Narrative is used to produce meaning, but only, so to speak, on a short-term basis, and without any regard for overall coherence and *vraisemblance*. Here, instead of fulfilling its documentary function, narrative has separated itself from its traditional siamese twin, history, freed itself from the obligation to answer, or rather, to provoke, the question 'what happened?', and to prove that it has other, independent potentialities, such as the production of meaning without particular regard for the factual world.

Nathalie Sarraute's claim that distinctions between real and imaginary are irrelevant to fiction can therefore be said to have considerable justification. *Vous les entendez?* exemplifies the independence of narrative from any pre-existing reality which it is conventionally supposed to copy. The force of narrative lies in its *productive* or *generative* capacity, which operates without any concern for ontological hierarchies, hierarchies which it is quite capable of producing or constructing, but to which it is never bound.

Narrative euphoria: 'La maison de rendez-vous'

La maison de rendez-vous attests most forcefully to the almost irresistible power of narrative as a form of discourse and demonstrates that far from having been eliminated from the nouveau roman, narrative has actually extended its range and dominance. Already within the first few pages of the novel narrative emerges triumphant from a tussle with other forms of writing.

The novel opens with a sentence which seems to have little narrative potential, describing as it does the narrator's habitual state of mind: 'The flesh of women has, without doubt, always taken up a large place in my dreams', and goes on to say: 'Even when I am awake, I am constantly assailed by images of it.' There is nothing narrative about this use of the present tense which here is being used to express a habitual action or state one of the three major functions which grammarians attribute to this tense (Wartburg and Zumthor, 1973, 208–9). After a list of some of these images, we go on to read:

I often linger to watch some young woman dancing in a dance-hall. I prefer it when her shoulders are naked, and also, when she turns round, her cleavage too. Her polished flesh shines with a soft glow, in the light from the chandeliers. With grace and concentration she performs one of those complicated steps where the woman stays at a distance from her partner, a tall, dark figure, standing back from her, as it were, who restricts himself to indicating the movements in front of her, while she concentrates, keeping her eyes lowered as if watching for the least sign from the man's hand, in order to obey immediately while still observing the detailed rules of the ceremony, then, on an almost invisible command, turning round again in a supple about-turn, once again offering her shoulders and the nape of her neck.

She has moved off now, a little to the side, to do up the buckle of her delicate strap shoes, made out of narrow gold thongs which criss-cross over her bare feet. Sitting on the edge of a sofa, she is bending forwards, and her hair slipping sideways reveals more of her delicate skin and the blond down on it. But two characters walk in and the scene is hidden by them, a tall figure in a dark dinner jacket, and a large red-faced man who is telling him about his travels. (12–13)

Between the beginning and the end of this passage a marked shift takes place from the habitual present ('I often linger') to the 'narrative' present ('She performs ...'). One may call this use of the present tense narrative since its function is, according to Wartburg and Zumthor to mark the 'concomitance of the

action expressed and the words which express it', a function
which has narrative potential since it particularises events and
thus makes possible the institution of a sequence, as indeed
becomes the case later on in the sentence: '*then*, on an almost
invisible command, turning round again ... '[9] The second
paragraph is entirely narrative and a quite explicit sequence:
'She has moved off now ...', where the past tense and the temporal indication given by the word 'now' serve to consolidate
a narrative.

The order of events which emerges from this passage can be
presented as follows:

(1) a woman dances some complicated steps;
(2) she twirls round;
(3) she sits down to do up her shoe;
(4) two men appear and the woman is hidden behind them.

This account both evokes and answers the question 'and then?',
and also provides strong enough causal links between items to
answer the question 'why?': the woman twirls around *because*
her partner signals to her to do so; she sits down *because* her
shoe has come undone (*because* the dancing was so strenuous?);
she is hidden from sight *because* the two men appear. The
narrative ends, or rather is interrupted at this point. But
although it appears not to have reached its goal, it has established itself forcefully enough to replace the narrator's opening
general discourse about his habitual fantasies.

The following paragraph contains a similar shift, in this
instance from a descriptive to a narrative present. Wartburg
and Zumthor characterise this third major function of the present tense as the expression of an 'action or state independent
of any temporal limitation', and give as examples 'the earth is
round' and 'the sum of the angles of a triangle is equal to two
right angles'. This is clearly the function of the present tense at
the beginning of the following passage, and it is equally clearly
not the function of the present tense with which it ends:

[9] The English language is able to distinguish this particular use of the present tense
from other uses by means of the continuous present. The French language has no
equivalent tense, and it is the French system which is under discussion here.

Everybody knows Hong-Kong, its harbour, its junks, its sampans, the office-blocks of Kowloon, and the close-fitting dresses with the slit up the side to the thigh, which the Eurasian girls wear, their tall supple figures outlined in their sleeveless sheath of black silk with its narrow upright collar, cut off straight at the armpits and the neck. The thin shiny material is worn next to the skin, following the contours of the belly, breasts, hips, and wrinkling at the waist in a bunch of tiny furrows, when the girl, who stopped in front of a shop window, turned her head and body towards the glass. (13–14)

Time, and with it, narrative, erupt into the atemporal description with the word 'when' and the sequence implied by the use of the past tense ('who stopped', *qui s'est arrêtée*).

It is, of course, possible to pass from a temporal description to narrative without anomaly by using a conventional narrative syntax. It is quite feasible to say 'I often linger to watch some young woman dancing' and to go on to introduce a narrative with a link phrase such as: 'One day I was in a dance-hall when I saw a particular young woman . . . ' Equally, a general description of the clothes worn by Eurasian girls in Hong-Kong might serve as a background to a narrative if it were followed by a statement like: 'One day, a girl in just such a dress could be seen walking down the street with her dog on a lead . . . ' By choosing the present tense for his novel, Robbe-Grillet is able to confuse general statements, descriptions and narrative which, if transposed into the past are normally quite easily distinguishable by their different tenses (in the French tense-system), the present being reserved for general, atemporal statements, the imperfect for descriptions and habitual actions, and the past historic for narrative proper. As it is used in *La maison de rendez-vous* the present tense not only creates confusion but also positively encourages conflict. There is no syntax to subordinate narrative to description, or vice versa, and instead, narrative proves itself markedly insubordinate and ultimately the most powerful form of discourse available to the novel.

This power is linked with a kind of narrative euphoria in the text which exuberantly produces narratives with minimal regard for *vraisemblance*. Causality is joyfully pursued to the point where it begins to bite its own tail (tale). Franklin Matthews's summary of one of the narrative threads in the novel makes this circularity quite evident:

a certain Edouard Manneret is murdered in strange circumstances; the chief suspect – who goes by the name of Johnson – finds himself having to leave Hong-Kong for Macao as soon as possible in order to avoid the enquiries being carried out by British police; but Johnson wants to take the pretty prostitute Laureen [sic] with him, and he has to buy her back from the luxury brothel run by Lady Ava; in order to get the necessary money, he embarks on a crazy chase which takes him round and round in circles until he ends up at Manneret's house, as Manneret is in the end the only person in a position to lend such a large sum of money; but Manneret pretends not to understand and Johnson, in a fit of exasperation, kills him! (1972, 33)

The generative power of narrative is quite evident from this summary, since the *invraisemblance* of this circular structure obliges us to recognise that the story is not copied from a pre-existing reality, but is instead constructed. In this, the text is fulfilling what Roland Barthes regards as the primary function of literature, which is to place language at the centre of the stage and free it from the mediating function which is normally ascribed to it: 'Language is literature's Being, its very world; the whole of literature is contained in the act of writing, and no longer in those of "thinking", "portraying", "telling" or "feeling"' (1970b, 411). This liberation from its mediating function makes possible what Barthes calls the 'Eros of language' (415) and this happy phrase may serve to illuminate the blatantly sexual themes of *La maison de rendez-vous*.

The erotic and the narrative seem to go hand in hand in the fiction of Robbe-Grillet, so that as the world is eroticised it is also narrativised. This is clearly the case in the opening paragraphs of the novel quoted above, where the objects of the narrator's sexual obsessions (the bare shoulders of a woman dancing, the close-fitting dresses of the girls in Hong-Kong with the slit up the side) become transformed into narrative as they are developed. The coupling of the narrative and the erotic is to a certain extent explicable in terms of their shared dependence on the same patterns of expectation and delay. But it is in the Eros of language that the sexual and the narrative combine to take on their greatest force. The euphoria promoted by this Eros is perhaps at its most intense when the text becomes not just a narrative of the erotic, but a narrative of narrative (although the two are often synonymous).

Story-telling seems to be a major form of communication between the characters: the large man with the red face is always telling some story; Lady Ava always begins her conversations with the news that Manneret is dead and an account of the events that led up to his death; Manneret is writing a story in his note-book; and the narrator himself (despite the fact that the novel opens with a description of the erotic images that fill his mind) characterises his purpose as primarily a narrative one: 'So I shall now try to tell what happened [*raconter*] that evening at Lady Ava's, and in any case to indicate which were, to my knowledge, the main events which marked it' (23), a task which, partly because of his frequent disappearances, he proves unable to complete.

In addition, Hong-Kong and the Villa Bleue are both full of objects which tell stories: magazine covers, sculptures, theatrical performances, an engraving on a ring. Descriptions of pictures almost invariably become narratives in an exuberant proliferation. An example of this occurs in the case of a magazine cover which first appears amongst the rubbish in a street where one of Lady Ava's servants is walking along with her dog. A road sweeper's brush turns up the image for a moment and the text pounces on it in order to describe what is represented on it:

Under a large heading in square-shaped ideograms, which takes up the whole of the top of the page, the drawing – crudely executed – represents a huge drawing-room in the European style, whose wooden panelling, which is very heavily decorated with mirrors and stucco-work, is probably supposed to give an impression of luxury; a few men in dark suits or in cream or ivory jackets are standing around in small groups talking; beyond them, towards the lefthand side, behind a sideboard covered down to the ground with a tablecloth on which there are several platters full of sandwiches and petits fours, a waiter in a white jacket is offering a glass of champagne on a silver tray to a fat, important-looking character who, with his arm already stretched out to pick up his glass, is talking to another guest much taller than himself, so that he has to look up. (35–6)

This scene is entirely descriptive and we recognise Lady Ava's villa, and some of the characters and objects (the two men, the waiter, the petits fours on the buffet, the champagne and so on) from the opening pages of the novel. The text inches closer to narrative as it continues:

right at the back, but in an empty space, so that one sees them straight away – especially as it is the centre of the picture – a large double door has just opened to let in three soldiers in combat uniform (parachutists' suits with green and grey camouflage markings) each of whom is holding a machine-gun at hip level, standing quite still, ready to shoot, with their weapons trained in three different directions so that they have the whole room covered. But only a few people have noticed their entry in the hubbub of the social gathering, a woman in a long dress directly threatened by one of the barrels, and three or four men in the immediate vicinity; their heads and bodies are caught in a movement of recoil, while their arms are frozen in instinctive gestures of self-defence, or surprise, or fear. (36)

A sequence of events is implied by the words 'a large double door has *just* opened' but is for a moment restrained by the text's insistent description of the poses in which the characters have been caught. But in the next paragraph which begins with a description of two women placed in the foreground of the picture, a narrative emerges and the scene is finally released from immobility:

After a few minutes, the young woman turns *again* towards the lady who is sitting down; seen from the front, her face appears grave, exalted, *suddenly* decisive; she takes a step towards the red sofa and, *very slowly*, lifting the hem of her dress a little with a supple and graceful movement of her left arm, she places one knee on the floor in front of Lady Ava, who in a completely unaffected, unruffled way, and without ceasing to smile stretches out a majestic, or condescending hand towards the kneeling girl; and, gently grasping the fingertips with their laquered nails, the girl bends over to place her lips on them. Her bent neck, beneath the blond hair . . .

But the young woman *immediately* gets up again in one swift movement, and, once on her feet again, turns aside to walk bravely towards Johnson. *Then suddenly* things happen *very fast*. (37–8, my emphases)

The many temporal indications in the passage turn the verbs into actions and sequences so that poses become gestures and movements. The final hasty narrative that follows concludes by sliding back to the spot where it had been operating before the description of the magazine cover began – in the streets of Hong-Kong where Kim is out on her mission to collect the drugs:

the crystal glass which falls onto the marble floor and breaks into tiny sparkling pieces, the young woman with the blond hair who stands and looks at them with an empty gaze, the Eurasian servant girl advancing like a sleepwalker through the debris, still preceded by the black dog pulling on its leash, the delicate gold shoes moving away past the shops with their dubious trade, the rice brush, which, in completing its arc, sweeps the illustrated magazine cover into the gutter, whose muddy water carries away the coloured picture as it eddies in the sunlight. (38)

The narrative's struggle for existence against other forms of discourse (here description) is similar to those with which the novel opens, but with one important difference: the triumphant narrative here is contained within another narrative, which thus becomes, as it were, a narrative of narrative.

This embedding (*enchâssement*) of narratives one within the other makes explicit what, according to Todorov, is the most fundamental aspect of narrative: a meditation on its own being. In the course of his discussion of *The Thousand and One Nights* where embedding is the chief principle of construction ('She-herezade tells that, Dja'far tells that, the tailor tells that, the barber tells that, his brother (and he has six) tells that ...' 1971, 83) Todorov makes the following observation:

embedding is a manifestation of the most essential property of all narrative. For the embedding narrative is the *narrative of a narrative*. In telling the story of another narrative, the first one arrives at its fundamental theme and at the same time is reflected in this image of itself; the embedded narrative is both the image of that great abstract narrative which all the others are only a tiny part of, and also of the embedding narrative which directly precedes it. It is the fate of every narrative to be the narrative of narrative, and this is achieved through embedding. (85)

In *La maison de rendez-vous*, then, it is not simply narratives that proliferate, but something more fundamental – *images* of narrative. It is this imaging of narrative that should be stressed in preference to any apparent destruction that conventional forms of narrative might appear to undergo. If the conventional syntax of embedding is perverted (as when the narrative of the magazine cover and its containing narrative of Kim's mission are merged rather than articulated) its effect is rather to intensify the imaging of narrative which, as Todorov says, is a part of all narrative, *vraisemblable* or not, embedded or not.

Another form that this imaging takes can be seen when, in contrast to the magazine cover, apparently real events are transformed into representations. This is the case with the narrative of Kim's mission a few pages after the interlude of the magazine cover. Kim arrives at her destination:

The large black dog stops of its own accord at the usual entrance: a narrow, dark, very steep staircase, which starts right at the edge of the building, without a door or a passage of any sort, and which leads to depths where the eye cannot follow. (39)

Then we read:

The *scene* which takes place then is not very clear
(my emphasis)

before the narrative moves on again. The use of the word *scene* is ambiguous here, since it makes it possible to regard the events as represented in a theatre. At the same time, we frequently speak of real events constituting a 'scene', or we say that the 'stage is set' for such and such an action. In fact, this ambiguity only emphasises the fact that it is we who construct life into plots and that it is not life itself which dictates them to us – a point that the text itself makes again when the narrative definitively becomes theatre a little later on. After a review of the various possibilities concerning what the dog is doing while Kim is upstairs (does he wait for her without being tied up? or does the girl attach his lead to something? and, if so, what? or is there someone else there to hold him?) Kim re-emerges, not with the envelope full of heroin but with a young Japanese girl. The text speaks briefly of the 'episode', of this '*fragment de scène*' until the narrative is finally transferred completely to the theatre:

I believe I have already said that Lady Ava put on performances [...] on the stage of the small private theatre in the Villa Bleue. This stage here must be Lady Ava's. The audience is in darkness. Only the footlights are on when the heavy curtain parts in the middle, to open slowly on a new set. (41)

And here the action continues with Kim, the Japanese girl and the dog in a kind of strip-tease executed by the dog who tears the clothes off the terrified girl on orders from Kim. With this shift from the street to the stage, from the real to the represented (which is accompanied, significantly and almost comically by the erotic), the text again operates a kind of embedding, so that the narrative narrates itself, in further proof that events in fiction never simply happen but are always a product of a narrative.

The framing of narratives can be repeated indefinitely (as *The Thousand and One Nights* already attests). There is nothing to prevent an embedded narrative from becoming in turn the container for a further embedded narrative (Sheherezade tells that, Dja'far tells that, the tailor tells, and so on) and there is a clear example of this in *La maison de rendez-vous* during one of the theatrical performances:

Then comes the scene with the dress shop window, outside an elegant shop in the European town, in Kowloon. However, it cannot belong exactly at this point, where it would not really make sense, despite the presence of the same Kim who is also on stage now in the little theatre where the performance, which continues, has reached the few minutes before the murder. The actor playing the part of Manneret is sitting in his chair at his desk. He is writing. *He is writing that* the Eurasian servant girl is crossing the circle without being able to see a thing, cracking the splinters of sparkling glass beneath her delicate shoes, in the silence, all eyes having at once turned towards her and following her as if fascinated, as she moves with her sleepwalker's gait towards Lauren, and stops in front of the terrified young woman, stands and stares at her relentlessly for a very long time, too long and unbearable a time, and says finally in a clear, impersonal voice, which leaves no hope of escape: 'Come. They are waiting for you.' (66, my emphasis)

This is full of *invraisemblances*, since what is written on a stage cannot be read by the audience. And, furthermore, the strict hierarchy which normally goes with the framing principle of construction is very often ignored in *La maison de rendez-vous* (as it is here) so that it is always the same events (albeit with variants) or fragments of events which are evoked at whatever level of representation – 'real', or as represented on the stage or the magazine cover, or as told by Manneret or the big man with the red face. But whatever the infractions of the code, the narrative's most intense euphoria is always associated with its self-imaging in these embedded narratives.

This multiple framing of what is basically the same narrative material suggests that the narrative is more interested in discoursing on its own mode of production than on relaying (in a realistic manner) a series of events in the form of a story. As Todorov says:

Every narrative is bound to make explicit the process whereby it is narrated; but in order for this to be done a new narrative has to appear where this narrating process is merely a part of what is narrated. So the narrating story always becomes a narrated story as well, where the new story is reflected and finds its own image. (1971, 90)

This is the activity to which *La maison de rendez-vous* is primarily and joyfully committed.

If our view of the nouveau roman were conditioned solely by the essays on the novel written by Nathalie Sarraute and Robbe-Grillet, we might, on turning to the texts themselves, expect to be confronted by a new brand of fiction altogether, a fiction which had entirely disposed of constricting conventions (amongst which plot would be extremely prominent) in order to achieve the freedom either to represent the world more accurately or to manifest the powers of writing without any referential obligations. But a reading of the novels themselves gives us a quite different picture. They have not disposed of narrative at all, and they demonstrate that it is impossible either to represent the world or simply to write without making these enterprises engage with a speculation on the nature of narrative itself. Narrative can come under every form of attack. It can be degenerated, damaged, transmuted or just bogged down (Ricardou, 1973), but in these attacks it merely makes its discourse on its own nature (albeit an unnatural nature) all the more audible.

The novels do, it is true, oblige us to shift the focus of our attention, so that, instead of (or as well as) giving us the world *through* narrative, they give us the world *of* narrative. But in obliging us to refocus in this way, they alert us to the fact that narrative is always loquacious about itself, and that in every fiction narrative's own noisy voice is to be heard testing, probing and imaging the ways in which we construct and organise the world for ourselves. The nouveau roman may have rejected particular forms of narrative, but by bringing narrative so ostentatiously into play as the object as well as the means of representation, it reminds us that whether the novel explores the nature of fiction or the nature of the world, narrative remains an integral element of the genre.

2

Character and the age of suspicion

Unforgettable figures: 'Portrait d'un inconnu' and 'Le voyeur'

The most furious debates occasioned by the emergence of the nouveau roman in the 1950s were centred around the question of character. It was felt that the attacks on character made by Robbe-Grillet in *Pour un nouveau roman* and Nathalie Sarraute in *L'ère du soupçon* struck at the very heart of a genre which was commonly defined primarily as 'a story where one sees the lives and actions of characters' (1956, 55). The conservative critics hostile to the nouveau roman condemned the new fiction as inhuman and 'formalist,' and the responses of the new novelists themselves had little or no effect in altering this point of view. Furthermore, much of the critical support for the nouveau roman came from quarters where the notion of character was in any case regarded as an 'ideological prejudice' (Culler, 1975, 230). For example, Jean Ricardou's essay 'Nouveau roman, Tel quel' is designed to prove that novels like *La maison de rendez-vous* or Robert Pinget's *Le libéra* repeatedly emphasise the death of fictional character, and that Jean-Louis Baudry's *Personnes* and Philippe Sollers's *Nombres* institute the era of the 'grammatical person' which eliminates any representational aspect of character and so fosters the 'formalisation of fiction' (1971, 245–51).

Despite the heat of these debates, there was, however, a good deal of confusion about what is to be understood by the concept of character. Does the so-called abolition of character necessarily imply the elimination of all human elements from the novel? To read the debates, one might easily think so. But even in his most vigorous attacks on character, Robbe-Grillet argues that the redundancy of fictional character is determined by social changes in the world in which we live, and that it is not simply the result of a 'formalist–nihilist' literary fashion:

The character novel belongs well and truly to the past, it typifies a certain era: when the individual was at his height.

Perhaps it is not a sign of progress, but we are now in the age of the regimental number. For us, the fate of the world is no longer related to the rise and fall of a few men or a few families. [. . .] To have a name was doubtless very important in the days of the Balzacian bourgeoisie. A character was all the more important as it was also a weapon in any confrontation, it represented the hope of success, it was a means of wielding power. It meant something to have a face in a universe where personality was both the means and the end of all endeavour. (1963, 28)

And in a later essay, he asserts that the disappearance of conventional character does not entail the disappearance of humanity:

As there were no 'characters' in our books, in the traditional sense of the word, people somewhat hastily concluded that there were no people in them at all. This was a serious misreading of them. Man is present on every page, in every line, in every word. (1963, 116)

In the first essay Robbe-Grillet defines the status of human beings in modern fiction (and in modern society) as one of anonymity. And in the second essay, he draws attention to the role of character as subjective consciousness:

Even if there are lots of objects [in our books], which are described in great detail, there is always first and foremost the eye that sees them, the mind which visualises them, the emotions which distort them. *Objects in our novels have no existence outside human perception, real or imaginary.* (1963, 116, my emphasis)

In other words, Robbe-Grillet is claiming that the existence of human beings in his fiction takes the form not of individuality and objective representation, but of anonymity and point of view. And he points out that anonymity and point of view have constituted an increasingly important part of fiction in the course of its development since the beginning of the twentieth century, citing Kafka, Faulkner and Beckett as examples.

Nathalie Sarraute's discussion of character in fiction describes the role of character in similar terms. The continued existence of 'Balzacian' characters in contemporary novels has led, she says, to a mutual distrust between author and reader (and it is this distrust which is the cause of the 'age of suspicion'):

appearances suggest that, not only does the novelist no longer believe in his characters, but that the reader, for his part, is no longer able to believe in them. So that we see character in the novel toppling and disintegrating, stripped of the double support, the novelist's and the reader's faith in him, which used to keep him upright, firmly on his feet, bearing the entire weight of the story on his broad shoulders. (1956, 56–7)

The individuated, externally portrayed character has no place in modern fiction which, according to Sarraute, since Proust's *A la recherche du temps perdu*, Gide's *Paludes* and Rilke's *Malte Laurids Brigge*, has seen an increasing development of the anonymous, subjective role of characters:

Nowadays, we are being inundated by an ever-increasing flood of literary works which still claim to be novels and where an indefinable, elusive and invisible creature with no sharp outline, an anonymous *I*, who is everything and nothing, and who is usually just a reflection of the author, has usurped the role of the main hero and taken the place of honour. The characters around him, with no existence of their own, are no more than the perceptions, dreams, nightmares, illusions, reflections, modalities or dependencies of this all-powerful *I*. (1956, 57–8)

The mark of a hero now is his invisibility and his anonymity, and the world and society take the form of his particular point of view.

Whereas Robbe-Grillet's justification for the change of status or mode of existence of character in fiction was based on the change of status of individuals in modern society, Sarraute's justification is chiefly psychological. She argues that the level of our interest in human beings has changed since the first half of the nineteenth century, and that we have, so to speak, gone beyond a preoccupation with personality to a deeper level of psychological reality, which after Joyce, Proust and Freud, we recognise to be common to all people: '[The reader] has seen the water-tight compartments, which used to separate characters from each other, collapse and the hero of a novel become an arbitrary limitation, a conventional outline cut in the common woof which each of us contains in its entirety and which captures and holds the whole universe in its innumerable meshes.' (1956, 65) Whether the realist justifications for these changes in the mode of existence of character in fiction are social or psychological, the effects, at least to judge from the theoretical standpoint, are similar. But although we have been familiar with the limited point of view of characters since Fabrice del Dongo's experience at the Battle of Waterloo, and with their anonymity at least since Musil's man without qualities, we should not minimise the fictional consequences that the almost exclusive use of these modes has in the case of the nouveau roman.

In the European novel of the nineteenth century the *telos* of fiction was largely provided by character, which took precedence over plot as the basis of artistic coherence, and this is what Sarraute is suggesting when she speaks of character bearing the entire weight of the plot on his broad shoulders. The novel was a biography of one or more individual characters whose personalities provided the main focus of interest in the text. This view is still evident in assertions such as 'characters are the primary vehicles for meaning in narrative' which Scholes and Kellogg give as an explanation for the fact that their typology of narrative is based on the character-type of the protagonists of plot (1966, 104). This may be true for a certain era in literary history (say, the late eighteenth to the early twentieth century) and in that era, character was an extremely powerful 'totalizing force' (Culler, 1975, 230). As Barthes says, character ceased to be the agent of an action and subordinate to that action, and became instead a 'person', a 'being' (1966, 16). The existence of character as 'person' is frequently indicated by the titles of novels (*La Cousine Bette, Anna Karenina, Tess of the d'Urbervilles, Portrait of a Lady*) which act as a sign that the novel in question will be primarily concerned with the life and personality of an individual character. The characters of these fictions are not merely protagonists or agents of plot, they are separate psychological essences ('avarice *was* Père Grandet' as Nathalie Sarraute says, 1956, 62) which organise the thematic material whether or not they participate in any action.

When a character 'bequeaths his name to a human type', as Robbe-Grillet puts it in speaking of nineteenth-century conventions (1963, 27), it is a mark of the degree to which the novel in which he appears has succeeded in arranging its thematic material around its characters. The definition of a character as a psychological essence is achieved by the construction of themes through ceaseless differentiation. For example, in Balzac's *La Cousine Bette*, the spinsterhood of Bette is contrasted to the prostitution of Madame Marneffe, Bette's selfish scheming to the self-sacrificing family loyalty of Madame Hulot, her single-mindedness to the dissipation of the young Wenceslas Steinbock, her peasant-like stinginess to the reckless squandering of Hulot, and so on, until a composite identity is built up for the character whose name provides the title of the novel. Along with the construction of this composite identity of a character goes the elaboration of the novel into some overall thematic significance, so that theme can be seen to be articulated through character. The convention of this kind of character-based interpretation has become so deeply ingrained in our reading habits, that it often continues to operate whether or not it is appropriate to the text in question. But a novel whose characters are relatively anonymous cannot articulate its semantic material through character, since the differences which are so essential to this procedure do not exist, or are not great enough to support a thematic reading at this level of the text. Where characters are anonymous, we must change the whole hierarchy of our expectations concerning the operations of texts.

The disruption caused by the change of status of character in the nouveau roman is doubly disconcerting. Not only does character seem no longer to serve as a 'primary vehicle for meaning', so ruling out a reading based on character as 'person' or 'being', but also the lack of narrative coherence would make a reading of character as agent of plot decidedly problematic. In these circumstances, and in the light of the results brought

from a reading of narrative in the previous chapter, the best procedure for discovering the nature and function of character in
the nouveau roman is to embark on a reading of character in
these novels in the full expectation that they will be less likely
to yield thematic coherence than to occupy the space of character
in order to initiate some reflexive discourse on the text as
text.

On the whole, the titles of the novels in question do not imply
a character-based fiction: *L'emploi du temps, Le planétarium,
Dans le labyrinthe*. There are three notable exceptions: *Portrait
d'un inconnu, Martereau,* and *Le voyeur*, each of which draws
attention to a different aspect of the conventional character
novel. The notion of portrait is strongly implied in any character-
based fiction, especially as this type of novel does not require
a strong narrative element (Henry James's *Portrait of a Lady*
is the revelation of the life and personality of Isabel Archer).
The use of proper name in a title frequently acts as a sign that
the character referred to will serve as the *telos* of the novel in
question (*Anna Karenina* does just this), and, furthermore,
names themselves support the individualism which character-
based conventions require for semantic organisation. Finally,
Le voyeur points to a psychological theme which we would
expect a conventional novel to explore through the medium
of a given individual (Dostoievsky's *The Idiot* explores and
transforms the notion of idiocy through its treatment of Prince
Myshkin). Portrait, individual and theme are the three major
aspects of conventional character evoked by these titles. By
exploring these conventional elements, it may be possible to
discover a new poetics of character in a self-confessedly anonymous fiction.

The title of Nathalie Sarraute's *Portrait d'un inconnu* appears to
support a conventional poetic not only in its notion of portraiture but also in its reference to an unknown man. All characters in fiction are unknown in the sense that we do not know
of them independently of the novels in which they appear, and
the fact that this is not so in Balzac's *Comédie humaine*, with its
recurring characters, or of historical novels which narrate the

lives of real people is precisely what makes them a case apart in fiction. But once we turn from the title of Sarraute's novel to the text itself, it is impossible to say who the unknown man is whom the title seemed to promise to portray. Could it be the narrator? or the old man? But if it is the old man, why does the title not also refer to his daughter whose role seems equally important? Or, perhaps, by an ironic twist, the unknown man is Dumontet, the only named character in the novel, who appears in the last few pages and brings the novel to a close? There seems no way of resolving these uncertainties.

Furthermore, the notion of portraiture itself is made problematic by the novel. Whether or not the title refers to the old man, the greater part of the narrator's activity consists in deciding if descriptions like 'selfish old man' or 'tight-fisted' are appropriate to him, or if he too is as prone to the 'tropisms'[1] which constitute the substratum of psychological life which the narrator suspects is the basis of most human behaviour. In other words, the narrator is undecided whether to paint the portrait of a 'miser' or to see all the characters as subject to what Sarraute calls 'this terrible desire to establish contact' (1956, 33). Is he to focus on the 'miser' and the 'crank' in the father and daughter respectively, and if not, how can he be sure that the tropisms which govern his own sensibility are equally powerful for others?

The psychiatrist's cure for this dilemma and uncertainty is conventional portraiture. Portraiture will cure the narrator of

---

[1] 'Tropism' in the sense in which Sarraute uses the term is a neologism coined by her. One might be tempted to offer an explanation of this key term in her work if she had not always insisted that although her writings are almost exclusively concerned with the tropism, the concept itself resists definition. And since in any case the novels always represent the attempt to classify and categorise as both inauthentic and futile, the only gloss one would hazard is that of Sarraute herself. Speaking of her tropisms, then, she writes: 'These movements, of which we are hardly cognizant, slip through us on the frontiers of consciousness in the form of undefinable, extremely rapid sensations. They hide behind our gestures, beneath the words we speak and the feelings we manifest, all of which we are aware of experiencing, and are able to define. They seemed, and still seem to me to constitute the secret source of our existence in what might be called its nascent state. [...] Thus my first book is made up of a series of moments, in which, like some precise dramatic action shown in slow motion, these movements, which I called *Tropisms* came into play. I gave them this name because of their spontaneous, irresistible, instinctive nature, similar to that of the movements made by certain living organisms under the influence of outside stimuli, such as light.' (Sarraute, 1963, 8–9)

his 'sterile brooding', his 'tendency towards introversion, and empty day-dreaming which is simply a way of avoiding having to make any effort' (77). Conventional characterisation is the psychiatrist's prescription for a return to good health: 'So show us somebody really life-like and, if you want, put all the masks on him that you please. But make him live first, make him concrete, tangible.' However, for the narrator, this tonic induces a kind of mental paralysis. The psychiatrist's thumbnail sketch of the old man and his daughter, far from making them life-like, turns them into painted dolls. 'These people of yours are highly nervous individuals', says the psychiatrist (75), and adds, 'don't take offence, many immortal literary types are also neurotics from our point of view' (76). And as the narrator listens to this picture of his characters, 'their appearance alters, they move closer, become hard, them too, finished, with clear colours, sharp outlines, but rather like the dolls made of painted cardboard that are used as targets in a fairground. One pull of the trigger and they will topple over.' For the narrator, the psychiatrist's portraiture has the effect of taking all the life out of its subjects; the psychiatrist's characters are merely effigies. There is an additional negative overtone to the psychiatrist's characterisation in that he uses the exercise to bring the session to a close, to forestall further discussion between doctor and patient, and it is thereby implied that this kind of characterisation is a means of preventing contact and communication.

The negative elements of the psychiatrist's enterprise are even more apparent in the light of the narrator's experience when he visits an art gallery to see a picture entitled 'Portrait d'un inconnu'. It is this painting (and not a character) to which the title most probably refers. And from what is said about the picture in the text, its importance for the narrator lies not in the character of the unknown man, but precisely in the picture's lack of interest in character. Anonymity and not individuality is the keynote: the painting is not signed, neither painter nor subject has a name, and the art of the painting consists in avoiding delineation of the represented figure:

The lines of his face, his lace jabot, his doublet, his hands, seemed to be the kind of fragmentary and uncertain outlines that the hesitant fingers of a blind man might haltingly discover. It was as though all effort, all doubt, all anxiety had been overtaken by a sudden catastrophe, and had remained fixed in full action, like corpses which have petrified in the position they were in when death struck. Only the eyes seemed to have escaped the disaster and to have achieved fulfilment: it was as though they had attracted and concentrated in themselves all the intensity, all the life that was lacking in the still formless, dislocated features. They seemed not quite to belong to this face and they made one think of the eyes of those enchanted beings in fairy tales, in whose bodies princes and princesses are held captive by a magic spell. Their distressing, insistent entreaty made one strangely aware of his silence and the tragedy of it. (86)

The unknown man is captive in a form which does not define him or signify anything to the spectator. Unlike the psychiatrist's characters with their sharp outlines and bright colours, his outline is vague and carries no significance. The narrator's response is not to individuate his subject, not to say 'modest' or 'sorrowful', words which another text (such as the psychiatrist's) might explore. Where the psychiatrist's portrait is finished and polished, this one is fragmentary, and, except for the eyes, explicitly incomplete. The painting's dislocated, unformed features are the very opposite of the hard, painted dolls of the other portrait, and, where they are dead and ready to topple, this unknown man's eyes are full of intensity and life. Where the psychiatrist's portrait closed communication, this one initiates a dialogue. The man's importance lies not in what he represents, but in his appeal, and the narrator's function is not to name him but to respond to that appeal. 'There was no doubt about it – his entreaty was addressed to me, and to me alone' (86). The painting itself responds to the narrator's own response, until they become merged in a dialogue based on mutual communication. The effect of this communication instigated by the painting is liberation: 'I suddenly felt free. Liberated. The Unknown Man – I said to myself as I ran up the stairs in the hotel – the "Man with the doublet", as I called him, had freed me.' (87) This unknown man is no unforgettable figure, no immortal type, and the liberation which he achieves for the narrator is from the deadly values of conventional portraiture. Indeed the mutually enhancing communication seems to gain in force in inverse proportion to the degree of conventional portraiture – the more fragmentary the delineation, the greater the communication. The title of Sarraute's novel seems, then, to be pointing us to a *mise en abyme*[2] in the text which is concerned specifically with characterisation. The old values are deconstructed and other values foregrounded. Character is no longer important as a kind of representation, and instead, its value consists now in its existence as a form of communication.

I shall be dealing below with the question of proper names, which is the aspect of character evoked by Sarraute's second novel, *Martereau*. But in the context of this discussion of titles, it can be pointed out that the individuality of which we conventionally assume the proper name to be a guarantee is deconstructed by the novel. Martereau's character is not revealed, and instead, as Stephen Heath says,

The firm outline of his character begins to blur until he too flows into the same sea of anonymity as the others. [. . .] The dissolution of Martereau is the essence of the novel: the arabesque of individuality is discarded before the very eyes of the reader to make way for, on Nathalie Sarraute's terms, the more profoundly realistic study of the impersonal life (1972, 52).

The title of Robbe-Grillet's second published novel, *Le voyeur*, seems to promise a conventional thematic representation of a given character. However, once we turn to the text itself, we find that the main protagonist, Mathias, is a decidedly weak vessel for this theme. Even Bruce Morrissette, whose readings of Robbe-Grillet's novels are aimed at demonstrating the totalising function of his characters, is more than ready to concede that 'voyeur' is not a very apt description of Mathias: 'Mathias is not the *voyeur* of the title'. The word does not refer to the hero: 'Mathias, instead of being a passive voyeur, commits a murder involving sadistic acts and possibly even rape.' (1963, 103) The only act of voyeurism that the text attributes

[2]This term which has come to have such wide currency was originally coined by Gide. It can be roughly defined as a representation within a representation which mirrors the representation which contains it. For further discussion of the concept and Gide's use of it see Dällenbach, 1977. See also below, Chapter 4.

to Mathias occurs in a brief remembered incident that takes place before Mathias leaves for the island.

Morrissette defines Mathias in terms of a psychology, as a 'classic case of cyclical schizophrenia, accompanied by sado-eroticism' (103), and he concludes that every major aspect of the novel illustrates this psychology. Morrissette's conclusions about the coherence of Mathias's character are questionable; but in any case, it is strange that the title should function in such a misleading way in relation to the text. Morrissette argues that the real voyeur of the novel is Julien Marek, the boy from the farm who appears to have witnessed Mathias's supposed crime. But his brief and inconsequential appearance in the novel does not endow him, as a character, with enough power to serve as the *telos* of the novel. Having demonstrated the relative thematic irrelevance of the title, Morrissette suggests that we regard it as 'if not a coincidence, at least [as] the result of "objective chance"' (105). But to regard this title as an accident while asserting that psychological themes provide the underlying unity of Robbe-Grillet's novels is a flagrant contradiction.

Instead of presuming, like Morrissette, that some theme other than voyeurism will provide the coherence of the novel, we should perhaps start with the title itself, and see if we can hear more distinctly what the novel is saying about the kind of thematic coherence which it seems to promise and which it fails to achieve. In the first place, and at a very basic level, Mathias is someone who *sees*, and as a voyeur is thus an agent of the verb *voir*. As such, he simply provides a conventional realist pretext for descriptions. As Philippe Hamon points out, it is a frequent feature of realist descriptions to have a spectator on the scene described, to provide a superficial motivation for descriptive writing (1972, 467). Mathias serves in this way as a pretext for the frequent and abundant descriptions in this novel. What Mathias sees is what is visible: 'he saw' is interchangeable with 'one could see'. The description of the town on the island is typical of the many descriptions motivated by this trope:

He looked up towards the windows over the café in the hope of attracting someone's attention. The house, which was simple to the point of destitution, had only one upper storey, like the ones next to it, whereas most of the ones along the quay had two. Now *he could see* in the alley opposite him, the backs of the houses whose fronts he had passed on the way here – built in the same rudimentary style despite being somewhat taller. (46, my emphases)

Each of the descriptive sentences is introduced by a reference to Mathias seeing. What he sees is what anyone might see, so that through this suggestion of an objective situation there emerges a sense of what Culler calls 'narrative contract' which serves to guarantee the mimetic status of the text (1975, 192–202). To this extent, then, the novel's frequent references to what Mathias has before his eyes are a notable element in the rhetoric of realism. Mathias as the agent of the verb *to see* has no thematic significance and instead is little more than a figure of speech in the kind of description which gave rise to the notion of an *école du regard* in the early days of the nouveau roman.

Another, if somewhat different, feature of the rhetoric of realism is provided by the limitation of Mathias's viewpoint which is indicated on several occasions. The conventions of the novel over the last hundred years have taught us to regard the restriction of a character's viewpoint on the world as a step forward in the direction of realism, since life itself never affords any of us a complete overview of any situation or event. This limited point of view is evident in the most trivial descriptions in *Le voyeur:*

Mathias could no longer see the landing slip, because of its steep slope, so that the causeway seemed to have been cut off at this point without any reason. (43)

If the mimetic contract is further strengthened by these allusions to what Mathias sees, the interpretative consequences of his seeing are almost nil. In *Le voyeur*, accounts of what Mathias sees tend to emphasise the lack of thematic coherence or meaning, as in the instance just quoted, where the angle from which Mathias surveys the port makes the road seem to come abruptly to a halt 'without reason'.

Mathias's inability to interpret or understand what he sees is frequently alluded to. The people and objects whom he comes across are liable not to make sense to him. The cinema poster, for example, is a visual jumble:

He stepped back three feet, to get a better overall picture; but the more he looked, the more it seemed blurred, changeable, incomprehensible. (168)

All the characters encountered by Mathias are impenetrable and indecipherable, but perhaps none more so than Madame Leduc. She is quite visible, but quite uninterpretable:

The features of her face were frozen in the pose in which they had first appeared – as if they had unexpectedly been fixed on a photographic plate. Far from making it easy to decipher, this immobility only made each attempt at interpretation more questionable although her face obviously had a meaning – a very banal meaning which one began by thinking one could easily discover – it kept slipping out of the references which Mathias tried to trap it in. (40)

The thematic emptiness insistently asserted by these descriptions, and which normally supports a mimetic contract, becomes so widespread as to be suspicious. Is there a thematic motivation behind Mathias's view of the world? Is the apparent objectivity in fact a feature of Mathias's own particular (schizophrenic? sado-erotic?) personality?

Certainly Mathias's own act of voyeurism (in the psychological sense) is associated with a limited point of view, and this might allow one to postulate some link between the realist rhetoric and a character-based theme. Mathias the voyeur stands outside a window, and what he sees is limited and partial: 'The folds of the curtain prevented him from making out the furniture inside very clearly. All one could see was what the electric light lit up very brightly at the far end of the room: the cone-shaped lampshade on the bedside light and the less distinct outline of an unmade bed.' (28) Indeed, every time Mathias finds himself in a similar room, the sado-erotic overtones ('Standing next to the bed, leaning slightly over it, the figure of a man was raising his arm towards the ceiling') and the limited point of view simultaneously present again. But can these two factors of vision (the subjective viewpoint and the voyeurism) be meaningfully integrated? On the whole the answer appears to be no. Instead we should recognise that the text is teasing us with the juxtaposition of two incompatible conventions: limited point of view as a formal index of realism, and voyeurism as a psychological theme. Similarly, the text deliberately hesitates in its descriptions: does the text inventory items because they were objectively visible, or does it record only those elements which Mathias's psychological nature makes him notice? The text refuses to make it clear which convention is the more appropriate, and indeed, hesitation itself becomes finally more interesting than either of these mutually exclusive alternatives.

The topic of seeing extends beyond Mathias himself. As Morrissette points out, Mathias is as much the object of the gaze of others as he is a spectator. The innumerable and interchangeable seagulls are almost always mentioned in association with their fixed, inscrutable stare, and here too the text continues to balance its alternative conventions. Is the gaze of the seagulls a simple, objective fact, or is it a sign that they know of Mathias's (real or imaginary) crimes? This ambiguity is repeated in the gazes of most of the other characters in the novel, like the *patronne* in the café where Mathias stops for a drink, whose gaze is persistent but ambiguous. Does it or does it not signify? Julien Marek (Morrissette's voyeur) has the most ambiguous and therefore disconcerting gaze. Mathias is particularly disturbed by the insistence of the boy's stare which could be a sign that the boy had witnessed Mathias's crime; but the gaze is consistently expressionless and therefore finally uninterpretable. Mathias decides that 'Julien had "seen". It was useless to deny it any more. It was only the images imprinted on those eyes, for ever, which gave them that unbearable fixity which they would have from now on' (214). So Julien's gaze signifies reproach? accusation? Yet only a page later, Mathias loses his grip on its interpretation: 'He looked at Mathias straight in the eyes, with his own hard and curious eyes – which might have been unconscious, or blind even – or subnormal' (215). Perhaps Julien is mentally defective and, like Mathias himself, unable to make sense of the things that he sees? All that can be said with any certainty about Julien's eyes is 'they were very ordinary grey eyes – neither ugly nor beautiful, neither large nor small – two perfect, motionless circles, placed next to each other, each with a black hole at its centre' (214). Julien's gaze has no meaning, his eyes just have a certain geometric shape: two juxtaposed circles – like the rings on the harbour wall, the bits of string twisted into figures of eight, the wheeling of the seagulls, the patterns on the watch, the bicycle which Mathias hires, or like the shapes in the paint on the Leduc's front door – all figures which betray Mathias's obsession or which indicate the auto-representation of the text.

The description of the Leduc's front door sums up these ambiguities:

The varnished paint, which had recently been redone, was a perfect imitation of the grain and irregularities of wood. Judging from the sound of his knock, there could be no doubt that beneath this deceptive layer the door really was made of wood. At eye-level, there were two round knots painted side by side which looked like two large eyes – or more exactly, like a pair of glasses. They were represented with an attention to detail which is rare in this kind of decoration; but, although the technique was realistic in one sense, the lines were so perfect that it ceased to be *vraisemblable*, the face was altogether artificial as a result of seeming contrived, as if the very blemishes were governed by laws. It would, however, have been difficult to prove the flagrant impossibility of such a pattern in nature, by pointing to any particular detail. Even the suspect symmetry of the whole could have been explained by some common technique of carpentry. If one scratched the paint at this exact spot, one might perhaps have found two real knots in the wood, cut in just this way – or at least showing some very similar configuration. (36–7)

Robbe-Grillet's novel is like the Leduc's front door; it represents gazes (that of Mathias and those of the other characters) with a realist rhetoric that is so impeccable that it ends by casting doubt on itself. Furthermore, the description of the door, like the novel itself, hesitates between a variety of explanations without choosing between them: the paint on the door is arbitrary and artificial, or it is an exact copy of the wood underneath it. The theme of seeing is doubly present here, both in the paint's representation of a pair of eyes and in the gaze that attempts to make sense of the paint. The geometric figure of eight, which has so often been regarded as a sign of Mathias's psychological obsessions, is also related to the title in a non-psychological sense through its application to eyes, and the notion of gaze itself in turn has a double value as signifying or non-signifying.

The pursuit of the theme of seeing which started with the title brings us up finally against this front door, which sums up and deliberately maintains the ambiguities that the title gives rise to. Instead of providing a psychological theme to give coherence to the novel as a whole, it creates ambiguities on the level of representation which divert our own gaze to the text itself and its own artificial base.

Le voyeur and *Portrait d'un inconnu* which seemed through their titles to offer the possibility of a conventional character-based reading, demonstrate, each in its own way, that such a reading is inappropriate to them. There are no more real characters, no more unforgettable figures, no more psychological essences. Instead the novels' treatment of the old conventions leads us to a different level of relevance, a level which requires us not to look through the novel to a world and a population beyond it, but to take account of the laws of fiction itself.

From the eponymous to the anonymous: 'Les fruits d'or'

At first sight the notion of proper names may seem a somewhat unpromising point of departure for a discussion of the poetics of character in fiction. If we were told that someone is called John Smith, for example, we should probably not feel that we had gained much illumination from this piece of information (beyond the fact that its bearer is probably male and Anglo-saxon). To know someone's name may be useful (because it enables us to make a distinction between John Smith and Arthur Jones without having to say more), but it is finally trivial because names themselves tell us so little. Philosophers and linguists tend to concur with this view. The functions associated with proper names are those of reference and identification. To use a name is to refer to a unique person (or place), to pick him out for scrutiny, to assert the existence of the person in question, about whose identity speakers are in agreement; but to suspend, if only temporarily, all questions of definition. Or, in the words of John Searle:

the uniqueness and immense pragmatic convenience of proper names in our language lies precisely in the fact that they enable us to refer publicly to objects without being forced to raise issues and come to an agreement as to which descriptive characteristics exactly constitute the identity of the object. They function not as descriptions, but as pegs on which to hang descriptions. (1969, 172)

Defined in this way, proper names seem a most obliging and unproblematic aspect of language.

How surprising, then, to find Roland Barthes asserting that 'All subversion, or all novelistic submission [...] begins with Proper Name' and that 'The thing that can no longer be written is Proper Name' (1970a, 102). What is at issue when fiction uses or refuses the proper name? One of the most powerful effects of literature (in general) is its transformation of the normal use of names through its ability to make them speak, so that they not only refer but also signify. The name of the hero of Sophocles's tragedy, Oedipus, does just this. Or, to take a more modern example, the name Goriot not only refers to a given character, but also acquires a meaning which one might sum up, in the words of the novel itself, as something like 'the Christ of fatherhood'. The ability to make names signify is something that literature shares with history. History is notoriously able to turn the proper names of its protagonists into nouns with semantic definition, so that we can speak of 'a Napoleon' or 'a Hitler', and mean something by it. We can speak of 'a Hitler' (or more likely of 'a little Hitler') without referring specifically to the man who was chancellor of the Third Reich and responsible for the murder of six million Jews, and so on, but in order to imply that the person described by his name has all the qualities (petty tyranny, ungentlemanliness, loud-mouthedness) which history has ascribed to its original bearer. And there are some characters who have become almost lost to sight

under the semantic significance which their names have acquired. How many of us remember the Norwegian Major when
we talk of 'a Quisling'?

History and literature, through their attempts to make
names signify, tend to invert the conventional, everyday function which John Searle ascribes to proper names. They allow
names to acquire so much meaning that they can engender
nouns and adjectives with dictionary definitions. Before the
appearance of Flaubert's novel in 1856, the name Bovary
signified nothing. But now the name has entered the dictionary in the form of the noun *Bovarysme*. *Le petit Robert*
defines this as 'novelistic dissatisfaction; "the power of man to
conceive of himself as other than what he is" (J. de Gaultier)',
dates it from 1865, and gives the title of Flaubert's novel as
its etymological origin. 'Quixotic' and 'Gargantuan' are adjectives which have their place in every dictionary. In their semantic motivation of that (supposedly) purely referential item –
proper name – history and literature are both engaged in
transforming anonymity into eponymy. By this I mean that
before literature or history begin to work on a name, that
name is, to all intents and purposes, anonymous. An anonymous person is, according to the OED, 'nameless' or 'of
unknown name', but, so far as literature is concerned the
definition of an anonymous person is primarily 'featureless'
or 'undistinguished', even if he bears a name. *Le petit Robert*
defines the word as 'impersonal' or 'neutral' and gives as an
example: 'His anonymous clothes blended with all surround-
ings'. In literature, anonymity consists not in the absence of a
name, but in the absence of the meaning or characteristics of
which a name could, in some way, become a token or a sign.

Gérard Genette calls this kind of semantic motivation of
proper name 'eponymy' whose opposite would be 'anonymity'.
He defines the term as follows:

The eponymy of a person is due to the fact that he has a nickname;
the eponymy of a name, is created by its nickname value, by the coincidence of its reference and its meaning, by its indirect motivation.
By extension, we could say that eponymy as a 'science' (as one says
'toponymy'), is the search for this type of motivation. It is thus

constituted by taking a proper name when one knows *whom it refers to*, asking in addition *what it means*, and recording – or imagining – how these two functions coincide. (1976, 23)

In this way, we might say that the study of literature consisted in a kind of eponymy. Reading, especially in the case of a character-based fiction, consists in discovering what names mean (the name Bette in Balzac's novel 'means' spinsterhood, single mindedness, destructiveness, selfishness, etc.). But in his discussion of Plato's *Cratylus*, Genette explains this desire to construct meanings for names in terms which go far beyond the notion of 'fact of reading' or 'ideological prejudice'. His reading of the *Cratylus* emphasises the strength of our desire to abolish the arbitrary nature of all linguistic signs by providing some motivation for them, and he describes literature as one of the most powerful and systematic means of this abolition, which he characterises as 'a secondary cratylism':[3]

I propose to call this attitude *secondary cratylism* (or *mimologism*), because of the almost irresistible wish to *correct* somehow or other the nomothetes mistake which Mallarmé called the '*défaut des langues*' – and so by means of some device to establish or re-establish in language the natural state which 'primary' cratylism, that of Cratylus, naïvely thinks it can still see. (36)

It is perhaps not surprising, therefore, to find that proper names with their purely referential function and their lack of any semantic element, should provide a particular fascination for the mimological activity of literature. The eponymy of name becomes proof of the achievement of a secondary cratylism.

Eponymy, as a particular form of this mimologism, is most evident in the novel. Since its origins as a distinct literary genre, it has habitually used proper names for titles. It flaunts its cratylist activity in this evocation of its tirelessly eponymous heroes. Indeed, the birth of the novel is often dated from the first appearance of that most eponymous of heroes, Don Quixote. His appearance has been followed by that of a wide

---

[3] Cratylism is the term Genette uses to describe the belief (held by Cratylus) that words are determined by the things to which they refer, and that they are not arbitrary signs for those things.

variety of heroes and heroines whose names have provided the titles of the books which depict them: La Princesse de Clèves, Gil Blas, Moll Flanders, Tom Jones, Clarissa, Tristram Shandy, Emma, Waverley, Eugénie Grandet, David Copperfield, Madame Bovary, Daniel Deronda, Tess of the d'Urbervilles, Anna Karenina, Mrs Dalloway, Thérèse Desqueyroux, even Beckett's Molloy. The whole economy of the novel as a genre could be said to revolve around the transformation of a name into a sign or token.[4] Barthes describes the economic character of names in the following terms: 'in the novelistic system (elsewhere too?) it is the instrument of an exchange: it allows one to substitute a nominal unit for a collection of traits' (1970a, 101). Indeed, this system of exchange operates at such a deep level of the text, that Barthes goes so far as to say that name provides the *telos* of the narrative itself: 'One may say that the essence of narrative is not the action but character as Proper Name: the semic material [. . .] *fills* essence with being, the name with adjectives' (197). This exchange-value of names is seriously threatened by the anonymity of the characters of the nouveau roman.

Robbe-Grillet's ironic attack on character (which heads his list of outdated ideas) is primarily aimed at eponymous heroes. 'Everybody knows what the word "character" means', he begins ironically. And he goes on:

It is not some *anonymous*, translucid 'he', simple subject of the action expressed by the verb. *A character must have a proper name*, two if possible: a surname and a first name. He must have parents and a heredity. He must have a profession. If he has property, all the better. Finally, he has to have a 'character', a face which expresses it, a past which has moulded them both. His character dictates his actions, makes him react in a predetermined way on every occasion. His character allows the reader to judge him, love him, hate him. It is thanks to this character that one day he will *bequeath his name to a human type*, which was, as it were, awaiting the consecration of this baptism. (1963, 27, my emphases)

In focusing his attack on the named status and naming function

---

[4] There are varying degrees of eponymy in fiction, so that a name does not always exert its semantic effect outside the novel in which it appears. Nevertheless, names always function inside the novel as tokens of exchange.

of character in fiction, Robbe-Grillet is calling for extremely far-reaching changes in the poetics of character. Anonymity of the kind that he outlines here implies characters who are neither named nor distinguished, and so effectively rules out eponymy as a means of constructing and organising his texts. Sarraute's universal psychology of the tropism which severely reduces our ability to distinguish between characters makes proper names equally redundant. The anonymous replaces the eponymous, and fiction no longer appears to be moved by the cratylist challenge created by the semantic vacuum of the proper name. The secondary mimologism of this literature must have turned its attention elsewhere.

Anonymity is certainly the hallmark of Sarraute's fourth novel, *Les fruits d'or*, where for the first time in her fiction characters can no longer be distinguished from one another for any length of time, and where proper names appear only incidentally in the dialogue of the indistinguishable characters.[5] The narrative itself never takes on the responsibility of naming the characters. And as we read, we find that instead of themes (or semes, as Barthes has it in *S/Z*) being predicated to names, naming itself becomes a theme.

This theme begins to be elaborated in the opening pages of the novel, which consist in speculation on the part of two (anonymous) characters about the significance and motivation of the gestures and words of a third character when he pulls a postcard reproduction from his pocket and says, 'Have you seen this . . . this Courbet . . . wonderful . . . Look' (8). This seems an innocuous beginning. But something sinister seems to lie behind the continuation given on the next page:

A large face with bulging eyes sways, thick lips protrude . . . his voice drops, he is overwhelmed by respect . . . Courbet. He's the only one. The greatest. I say so. I'm not afraid to say so: he is the greatest genius. Shakespeare and him. I always say so: Shakespeare and Courbet. (9)

---

[5] *Portrait d'un inconnu* and *Martereau* have only one named character each, and although both novels can be read as a denunciation of proper names, the characters are, none the less, distinguishable. In *Le planétarium* the characters are named as well as distinguished although, as in the first two novels, individuation is counterpointed against the theme of psychological anonymity, summed up in the final words of the novel, 'Je crois que nous sommes bien tous un peu comme ça.'

Why Shakespeare and Courbet? What have an English Eliza-
bethan playwright and a nineteenth-century French painter in
common? The only thing that they appear to have in common
is a name. The speaker seems to clutch Shakespeare's name out
of the air in order to add weight to the respect which in any
case is almost more than he can bear. The crushing effect that
great names appear to have is explored again in the *sous-
conversation* of the art-lover's interlocutor who, on hearing the
mention of the name Courbet, places the art-lover in 'a civilised
country where true values are respected, where merit is re-
warded, where justice reigns, where right triumphs' (26). These
values are opposed to the 'arbitrariness' and the 'obscurantism'
which typify the second character's experience and which are
the very qualities of the general universal tropistic psychology
with which Sarraute is concerned. Order and justice thus become suspect virtues.

In subsequent episodes names are repeatedly found in conjunction with a similar kind of violent order. Many of the names
are evoked in connection with the discussions about the novel
called 'Les fruits d'or' which form the main body of the book.
The following is a typical and typically violent instance:

'Very good, Brulé's article on Les Fruits d'Or. Absolutely first rate.
Perfect.'
    The detached tone is that of someone coldly stating a fact. In the
motionless face, the staring eyes are looking straight ahead, like the
mouth of a cannon which the soldier standing motionless on his tank
points directly forward, while he parades with the victorious army
through the streets of the occupied city. (47)

The order here is achieved by an army occupation which depends on betrayal and brutality for its existence, and it is an
order which, although it is not directly caused by names, always
has names as a prominent feature. The mention of Brulé has
only a tyrannising function, since we do not know and are not
told who he is, what sort of a man he is or what his article says.
A page or two later the same speaker (probably) begins to pile
up proper names in an attempt to demonstrate his admiration
for 'Les fruits d'or': 'Since La Rochefoucauld, Madame de La
Fayette, I say, since Stendhal, Brulé is right, since Constant'

(49). Taken literally this statement is nonsense. 'Les fruits d'or' cannot be the best book since Madame de La Fayette *and* Stendhal. But read as a sign of the speaker's determination to institute order, the profusion of names testifies only too clearly to his violence, as the preceding *sous-conversation* makes evident:

In one stroke, all the forces of evil have been swept away. Order reigns at last. We are free. Now we will teach all those layabouts, those ignoramuses, those children of nature, those strong personalities, to toe the line. To respect the rules of decency and good behaviour. We will teach them – oh, it's difficult, isn't it? – that literature is consecrated, forbidden ground, which only a humble apprenticeship and patient study of the masters gives a chosen few the right to enter. Tricksters, upstarts, intruders will not be admitted. (48–9)

Naming names will coerce people into stereotyped admiration and a devastating order will reign: 'you will be forced to admire, you will be locked into admiration, you will be penned in, like bleating sheep, surrounded by dogs' (39).

This incidental naming of names in conjunction with violence is a recurrent feature of Sarraute's fiction, even where names are also used in a more conventional manner to identify separate characters. Already in *Tropismes* there is an exemplary case of violence through naming. Number XV is devoted almost entirely to an elaboration of this effect. A young girl falls victim to an old man who, it appears, has all the impeccable and reassuring virtues of ripe old age:

She liked old gentlemen like him so much, you could talk to them, they understood so many things, they knew about life, they had known interesting people (she knew that he had been a friend of Félix Faure and that he had kissed the hand of the Empress Eugénie). (93)

But any reader of Sarraute will know that when a character claims to have worldly experience it is always a form of bullying, and the mention of the names of Félix Faure and the Empress Eugénie, instead of guaranteeing the old man's credentials, serves as a warning about his latent brutality. This brutality becomes evident as the old man begins to speak in names:

'England ... Ah! yes, England ... Shakespeare? Eh? Shakespeare. Dickens. I remember, by the way, when I was young, I amused myself

by translating Dickens. Thackeray. Have you read Thackeray? Th . . .
Th . . . That's how they pronounce it, isn't it? Eh? Thackeray? Is that
it? That's how they say it, isn't it?'
    He had grabbed her and was holding her entirely in his fist. (94)

The incident ends in a sadistic frenzy of proper names:

He was going to keep on without pity, without respite: 'Dover, Dover,
Dover? Eh? Eh? Thackeray? Eh? Thackeray? England? Dickens?
Shakespeare? Eh? Eh? Dover? Shakespeare? Dover?' while she
would try to free herself gently, without daring to make any sudden
movement that might displease him [. . .].
Not until he saw her parents arrive, would he come to himself,
relax his grip, and a bit red, a bit dishevelled, her pretty dress a bit
crumpled, she would finally dare, without being afraid of displeasing
him, escape. (95–6)

    Another feature of this violence of names is their association
with the naming of characteristics. In rejecting a proposition
such as 'avarice was Père Grandet' Sarraute is drawing attention
to the impossibility not only of writing proper names (so con-
curring with Barthes's assertion that 'the thing that can no
longer be written is Proper Name'), but equally of writing
words like 'avarice' as synonyms for those names. A novel
like *Portrait d'un inconnu* demonstrates the irrelevance and super-
ficiality of using terms like 'miser' and 'crank' to describe its
main characters. In *Les fruits d'or*, the attempt to use terms of
this kind is always accompanied by incidental naming and is
almost always violent.
    One of the characters (or rather, voices) tries to name the
qualities of 'Les fruits d'or', and in doing so mentions the name
Charlie Chaplin, as if by chance, and uses the name as support
for his argument:

it's irresistible . . . really *Chaplinesque*. A *style* . . . A *strength* . . . Better
than *Chaplin*. It's true. *Great comedy*. No one has seen it. Who has
thought of saying it? Both *comic* and *tragic*. That's what defines all
great works. (127, my emphases)

The authoritative tone of this utterance is the result of the naming of names and qualities. But unlike the conventions of
eponymous literature, the naming of qualities never leads us
towards a truth, and instead founders finally in nonsense:

A humour . . . A savage humour. Macabre. Macabre and ingenious. A sort of innocence. Light. Dark. Penetrating. Confident. Agreeable. Human. Pitiless. Dry. Moist. Icy. Burning. It transports me into an unreal world. It's the realm of dreams. It's the most real world there is. Les fruits d'or is all of those things.

This series of systematically contradictory descriptions of the features of 'Les fruits d'or' becomes quite meaningless. Indeed, everyone who tries to name the qualities of the book falls into the trap of nonsense and the novel comically dramatises how pathetic and futile is any attempt to name qualities at all. The voices tell us nothing about the book itself. They tell us instead that this eponymising discourse is a form of inauthenticity and brutality. We never learn what the true character of 'Les fruits d'or' is. Instead we discover that any attempt to name this true character is bound to fail, not only because an authentic language is incapable of naming, but because by a sinister effect, what is named is dead, killed by the violent order which naming inaugurates.

The survival of the discourse of Sarraute's novels seems to depend on refusing or eliminating the two sets of terms which provide the equation on which fiction previously rested: names and qualities. The eponymy of name now has a terrorising function. It connotes the crowd and no longer defines individuals.

Character and the world of platitudes: 'Entre la vie et la mort'

Character has never ceased to be a major preoccupation in Sarraute's fiction, although the emphasis shifts slightly from novel to novel. *Portrait d'un inconnu* draws our attention to the question of character in a most forthright manner with its discussion of Prince Bolkonski and Princess Marie in Tolstoy's *War and Peace* (66–72). It is often suggested that Sarraute has moved away from the question of character in her later novels in favour of more aesthetic preoccupations. But while *Entre la vie et la mort*, for example, is concerned with the theme of writing, the possibility of writing is shown to be constantly put at risk by the construction of characters.

Sarraute is at pains to point out that the *he* of her novel is not a character:

The reader who gives in to his habit of looking for characters every-where, who wastes his time trying to force the movements and trop-isms which constitute the substance of this book into pigeonholes, will realise that his efforts to get them decently housed have led him to construct a hero made out of bits and pieces which will not stay upright. *(Prière d'insérer)*

This is indeed the case. On page 12 the writer-figure describes himself as an orphan. But later on in the novel an entire sec-tion is devoted to the father's scorn when he accuses his son of having his book published at his own expense (162–73). Apart from this kind of inconsistency, coherence is further threatened by the lack of chronology. The opening section of the novel deals with an established writer describing his method of work to an admiring audience: 'I correct. With a biro. I always do. I loathe fountain pens.' (15) But on page 84 it becomes clear that the writer has not yet written anything, since someone turns to him in exasperation and says, 'Why don't you write? You only ever talk about it.' With these anomalies, then, it seems wiser not to read this novel as the portrait of an artist, but to accept Sarraute's own definition of the book's subject: 'it is about writers and writing' *(Prière d'insérer)*.

Nevertheless, within the book itself, we see endlessly renewed attempts to characterise the writer (writers?), to provide him with a character. He himself initiates the process in the first scene by describing his night-time anxieties and doubts: 'Sometimes I wake in the night, I ask myself. What's the use of so much struggling and effort. Why, my God, for what?' (8) He tries to make this experience exclusively his own, to make it the property and definition of 'a writer'. There is a moment of terror when one of the admiring crowd is foolhardy or arrogant enough to lay claim to the same experience, and tries to take on the exclusive characteristics of the writer.[6] In the second section of the novel, he recalls his childhood sensitivity to words and language: 'My bed still had bars . . . I remember . . . Sitting up in my cot at night, I used to play at words.' (23) The woman writer to whom he is talking responds, quite logically, to this blatant piece of self-characterisation by say-

---

[6] In the interests of brevity and fluency I shall use the phrase 'the writer', although I am conscious of the fact that the term obscures the fact that there is no single hero.

ing 'you really were the predestinated child', a characterisation which, on the lips of another, the writer finds repugnant. The third section of the novel shows a child at play with words. For his mother, the game is the sign of a heavenly visitation, and the section ends with the anonymous assertion that 'a poet, it has been said and it's true, is someone who can make a poem out of words' (42). Each of these sections elaborates a different definition of the writer as a character: a writer is someone who is prone to night-time anxiety and doubts (which might even be formulated as: *because* he is prone to night-time anxiety, this man must be a writer), a writer is predestinated, a writer is someone who is sensitive to language, a writer is a child genius, a writer is someone who knows how to play with words to make a poem.

We are prevented, however, from taking these definitions too seriously, since they are all placed at a certain distance and tend to involve a certain violence. And of course, it is never the narrative itself which makes these assertions, but always the characters. The woman who lays claim to the anxieties which the writer seems to regard as his own is seen by the crowd as having unleashed tremendous forces of destruction. Whether the violence is due to the writer's fury at seeing his definition shared, or whether to the woman's anger at his claiming sole rights to it, it transforms the defining characteristic into a piece of property which can easily change hands with the help of force or wealth. If the definition can circulate in this way, then it can clearly not be an intrinsic feature of the writer.

The monetary metaphors which accompany the proud mother's definition of her child as a poet make the same point. The mother is metaphorically described as pushing her child along in front of her, making him pass round the hat, begging in return for the picture of him that she has just painted (the child genius murmuring word-games):

Nobody gives a penny to any of the others, the ones who seek, holding in their hand an autumn leaf, buds, catkins, offering images of heralds, monks, eagles' nests, umbrella pines, canopies ... but she has put something in the bowl he is handing round which will encourage them to be generous ... a nice piece of silver ...

Only words ... Fingers fumble in pockets, in handbags ... There.
Take it: 'It's one of the signs ... one of the ones which count.'
(41–2)

By stressing the fact that the character of the writer is bought to
please the vanity of his mother, the text makes it clear that there
is nothing inherent or distinctive about these qualities which
she tries to arrange in the form of a character.

The metaphors which support the writer's definition as predestinated make a similar point. In laying himself open to the
definition, the writer is said to have filled in an application form
for membership of the society of predestinated children:

You didn't know what you were saying? You dare to say that? You had
no idea what your replies meant? You weren't laying claim to anything when you filled in the forms, completed the formalities? You
weren't trying to show that you were good enough to join the predestinated children, eh? (25)

The predestinated children are outside the writer in a society
which one enters by completing the formalities, not through
an intrinsic quality which defines him as a character. Characteristics are presented as something that one applies for.
Another metaphor in this section turns a quality into a uniform. Signed up as a 'cadet' in the 'society for predestinated
children', the writer is sent to get the appropriate set of clothes:

The attendant who distributes the clothes sees at a glance what he
needs. He is not the first in this position, she sees so many of them.
He is undressed, his underclothes are handed to him, they are part
of the regulation dress. He is made to put on his uniform. (24–5)

The image of the uniform here not only suggests that the
quality in question is an acquisition that is external to the
writer, but it also has the paradoxical effect of suggesting
anonymity. A uniform makes a man indistinguishable from
his fellows and thus creates anonymity, instead of definining
individuals.

So much for the character of the writer. He has no intrinsic
nature, only false personas which he constructs in moments of
inauthenticity or which others construct for him out of violence
or a misplaced admiration. Much of the book deals with typical

moments or scenes from a writer's life which imply a character. Aside from those already mentioned, there is the schoolteacher who claims to have discerned the writer's poetic gifts in his schoolboy compositions, the first acceptance of a book by a publisher, conversations with admirers about the book, the father's disbelief in the son's success, the mother's anxious pride in her son's achievement, the visit of young admirers to the writer's house, the writer's advice on what makes for good writing. In all these typical situations the writer runs the risk of inauthentic characterisation, which in turn jeopardises his ability to write. To be seen as one of the world's 'artisses' (127) is a threat to authenticity, and it is a threat which increases as a result of the success of his writing.

The scene where the writer receives his admirers at home develops the idea of this ratio (the greater the success of the book, the more marked the character of the author) which is fixed in the minds of the young visitors and provides the reason for their presence. They have come in search of the equivalent of 'Balzac's gloves and canes, Baudelaire's trousers, so many pipes, embroidered waistcoats, lamps, monocles' (190), and finally settle for the writer's teapot. Despite his disappointing ordinariness, they use his humble brew to concoct a high priest of literature until eventually they have distilled for themselves the character that they came in quest of:

You must never give up hope . . . there it is, the most obvious thing . . . why didn't I think of it? sitting there for all to see . . . no one here seems to have noticed it . . . the tea he made in his room . . . that teapot, that kettle . . . those gestures . . . it depends how you arrange it, present it . . . I'll take care of it, they're mine, I'll have them . . . I'll be able to sell them, there'll be takers for them . . . you just have to alter them slightly . . . slow down the movements . . . slow, solemn gestures like a priest when he raises the chalice . . . yes, that's it, it's perfect . . . You should have seen him . . . he looked as if he was officiating in a ceremony when he filled the teapot with water from some sort of receptacle . . . a samovar . . . you felt you couldn't disturb him . . . it took place in a religious silence . . . it was a sacred rite . . . He told us that he drank seven or eight pints a day of that very strong tea. (193)

This larger-than-life character is entirely the product of a sleight of hand on the part of this anonymous voice, which seems determined not to be done out of its pound of the writer's flesh.

A page later this monstrous 'artisse' becomes even larger than life when he is seen grumbling on a bus:

> She has got hold of one of those hideous 'souvenirs' to take home, the product of local folklore, mass-produced for foreigners, and which sentimental tourists buy . . . he looks at her with disgust, he would like to snatch the thing off her that she has just taken, and which she will put on her mantelpiece and show off to her friends: himself naïvely, crudely, grotesquely carved out of ordinary material of the poorest quality: 'a real character', 'a strong personality', 'one helluva guy'. (195)

He realises, poor man, that the qualities which are supposed to mark him off from the rest of humanity as a writer are in fact mass-produced and made of 'ordinary material of the poorest quality'. There is nothing rare or distinctive about the hieratic gestures of the sacred artist. His character does not constitute or explain his art.

The writer in *Entre la vie et la mort* bears the brunt of an increasing onslaught of the 'ready-made ideas, prefabricated images, commonplaces, clichés, *trompe l'oeil*' which, according to Sarraute, constitute our world. 'This cocoon of clichés and ready-made ideas, which we never stop producing, covers everything' (1961, 37), and the idea of 'a writer' is no exception. The discourse which we habitually use to define and differentiate people for ourselves by presenting them as characters is shown by Sarraute to be a sizeable element in the banality, which, in modern times we have succeeded in lifting 'out of the sphere of handicraft and placed [. . .] in that of a major industry' (1961, 39). The reference here to major industry corroborates most appositely the mass-produced image of the 'real character'. Speaking in characters is not a device for discovering reality. Instead it is a rhetorical tic, a certain way of talking which has no truth value whatsoever, and which, as cocoon or uniform, actually serves to disguise the reality to which Sarraute's novels most insistently refer.

Writing itself has nothing to do with being a character or with constructing characters. Rather, it depends on surviving the onslaught of platitudes about character. A writer is the agent of the verb *to write* and not the repository of a certain number of larger-than-life characteristics. Characters no longer serve as the primary vehicle for meaning in narrative, but are put on display as an obsolete and corrupting form of discourse. There are no meaningful differences between characters which can be worked into an elaboration of themes. The conventional role of character has now been shown to be just a way of talking, a trope, a rhetorical construct in which we can no longer believe, and which we use at our peril, since we are likely to be submerged in an ocean of platitudes which will be entirely of our own making.

Nevertheless, it is precisely this definition of character that restores to character (albeit as a general concept rather than as a set of individuals) its conventional narrative and thematic function in the novel. So far as the writer is concerned, character as a problem is the primary vehicle for narrative. And the major thematic material of the fiction, organised around oppositions between authenticity and inauthenticity, violence and communion, anarchy and order, etc., is also articulated through the question of character. In demonstrating that character is merely the product of a certain kind of discourse. *Entre la vie et la mort* draws our attention to one aspect of the poetics of character, and yet, in so far as narrative and theme depend on character, it still remains firmly grounded in another aspect of that same poetics.

The hidden life at its source: 'Projet pour une révolution à New York'

One of the major attractions of fiction is its ability to give us access to the minds of other people on a level of intimacy and with a degree of certainty that are denied to us in everyday life. Even if we are sure of our own motives, we can never be certain of those of others. The motives and desires of others always have to be guessed at, deduced from behaviour, gestures and utterances; other people have constantly to be interpreted. The novel is able to reprieve us from this endless speculation, for here other minds reveal themselves through their inner thoughts, letters or diaries, or else they are revealed to us by an author who is able to say what is *really* felt and thought by his characters. As E. M. Forster wrote, 'it is the function of the novelist to reveal the hidden life at its source' (1949, 45). The revelatory power of the author is often profitably aligned with the hermeneutic code of the plot, so that the mystery is, quite simply, and in accordance with our everyday experience, the inner life of other people. The narrative unmasks the mysterious and is able to show us what is real. This unmasking often accompanies the narrative's account of the hero's own discoveries about life, so that the plot consists in the uncovering of the hero's misapprehensions about himself and the world. This pattern is so endemic to fiction that it has almost become a built-in convention of the novel, and most particularly in a certain period of its history, namely from the late eighteenth century to the early twentieth century. A typical example of this maturing through unmasking of self and others can be seen in Jane Austen's *Sense and Sensibility* (first published in 1811).

The eventual marriages of the two sisters are made possible as the result of a number of discoveries that they make about themselves and other people. Many of the characters in the novel prove to have secrets which serve finally to explain otherwise mysterious and uninterpretable behaviour. For example, Willoughby, the man with whom the younger of the two sisters, Marianne, falls in love, ends his side of the attachment with inexplicable suddenness and unwonted bad manners. It is later discovered that this apparently charming and desirable young man is *really* a cold and heartless seducer. This discovery is itself then superseded by a more comprehensive revelation of Willoughby's motives when, towards the end of the book, he tells the elder of the two sisters, Elinor, of the threats that had been made to him concerning an inheritance. He explains that although marriage with Marianne has become impossible, his love for her had always been genuine. Two layers of mask and mystery are removed so that in the end the *true* picture of his character can emerge. Edward Ferrars, the man whom Elinor eventually marries, is similarly unmasked by the unfolding of the narrative. He appears at first to be in love with her, although his reticence is thought by Marianne to be odd. It is later discovered that he had been secretly engaged to another woman (Lucy Steele) for many years. And behind this revelation there lies yet another truth, which explains his apparent interest in Elinor, namely, that the engagement with Lucy is loveless, and that the woman he *really* loves is, after all, Elinor.

As far as maturing and discovering are concerned, it is Marianne who is required to modify her beliefs and preconceptions to the greatest extent. Hers is the sensibility of the title, and it is the romantic beliefs associated with her sensibility which her experience of society and of others oblige her to alter. This alteration is summarised on page or two before the end of the novel when we read, 'Marianne Dashwood was born to an extraordinary fate. She was born to discover the falsehood of her own opinions, and to counteract, by her conduct, her most favourite maxims.' (366) Marianne's discovery (which is nevertheless not quite so simplistic as this summary of her 'fate' suggests) is made through her experience of society and is achieved as the result of a compromise between individual and society – that conflict which has provided the theme for so many novels almost since the beginnings of the genre. There are certainly very good historical reasons for the perenniality of this topic, but it is not with these that I am concerned here, for there exist more purely novelistic reasons for it. The opposition between individual and society allows the novel to explore the contrast between the hidden life and the social mask. The continued existence of any society depends on its being able to maintain a huge number of elaborate codes (of behaviour, speech, dress, etc.) which all its members share and comply with, and which, by virtue of their existence as codes, turn every element of that code into a sign. Signs, by definition, need interpreting. For this reason, the behaviour of people in society must always be partially enigmatic, and it is only the author or the educated hero who are capable of interpreting it. The author of Balzac's novels and the narrator-hero of Proust's novel are always engaged in deciphering, and in the case of Proust's hero, the ability to decipher and interpret signs is acquired only as the result of a long and patient initiation. The heroes of fiction (often those whose hidden life is revealed at its source) are almost always involved in such an apprenticeship, and their happiness almost always depends on it; a happy marriage, for example, requires that each partner forms a right judgment of the other.

The need for an apprenticeship is implicitly supported in *Sense and Sensibility* in the frequent recognition of misreadings by the characters. On one occasion when Edward Ferrars acknowledges his error in describing Marianne as 'gay' and 'lively', Elinor comments on the frequence of such misjudgments: 'I have frequently detected in myself such kind of mistakes', she says, 'in a total misapprehension of character in some point or other: fancying people so much more gay or grave, or ingenious or stupid than they really are, and I can hardly tell why or in what the deception originated' (119). Such misapprehensions constitute a significant element in the poetics of fiction, not only in providing a *telos* for the narrative, but also in the creation of realism. The revelation of the hidden life at its source makes fiction appear in some way more real than history or chronicle, because fiction reveals what is secret. E. M. Forster describes the difference as follows:

The historian deals with actions, and with characters of men only in so far as he can deduce them from their actions. He is quite as much concerned with character as the novelist, but he can only know of its existence when it shows on the surface. If Queen Victoria had not said, 'We are not amused,' her neighbours at table would not have known she was not amused, and her ennui could never have been announced to the public. She might have frowned, so that they would have deduced her state from that – looks and gestures are also historical evidence. But if she remained impassive – what would any one know? The hidden life is, by definition, hidden. The hidden life that appears in external signs is hidden no longer, has entered the realm of action. And it is the function of the novelist to reveal the hidden life at its source: to tell us more about Queen Victoria than could be known, and thus to produce a character that is not the Queen Victoria of history. (1949, 45)

But if the more fully revealed Queen Victoria of fiction is not the Queen Victoria of history, in what does the difference

consist? Perhaps the gesturing, talkative characters of history
are finally more real than the impassive characters of fiction
with their concealed ennui, for the hidden life, being by definition hidden, has always to be invented. The Queen Victoria
of fiction becomes herself a fiction, although the rhetoric of
character tends to obscure this. Just as in narrative what
comes last is regarded as the truth, so in characters, what is
secret is held to be the most *real*. Discussion of characters in
fiction carries with it an arsenal of terms like *really, actually,
in fact* which suggest that fiction's invented secrets represent
the truth: Willoughby is *really* not the charming, desirable
partner that he first *appears* to be, but he is *actually* not as un-
feeling as reports of his seductions would suggest. Appearance,
rumour and deception give way to *facts, truth* and *reality* in
direct proportion to the inventiveness of fiction. Novels invert
the truth values of history so that appearances must always
be regarded as deceptive or mysterious and secrets as truth-
ful. The visible is described in terms of masks in order to
provide a realist motivation for that most fictional domain of
fiction: the hidden life at its source.

In Robbe-Grillet's *Projet pour une révolution à New York* most
of the characters are depicted as either playing a role or wearing
a mask, and the novel therefore lends itself to a reading in
terms of the opposition between the hidden life and the mask
that I have just been discussing. In the subway of the New York
of the novel there is a shop which specialises in masks. Anyone
dissatisfied with his or her hair, face, hands or breasts can equip
themselves with most attractive and realistic alternatives. The
shop window displays, for example: 'Psychoanalyst, in his
fifties, sensitive and intelligent face; attentive expression despite
signs of fatigue, which are the mark of study and hard work;
worn preferably with spectacles', or 'Business man, forty to
forty-five years of age, tough and reliable; the shape of the
nose suggests cunning as well as honesty; an attractive mouth,
with or without moustache' (53). In buying a mask you are
buying yourself a character with a complete set of characteristics (tough and responsible, upright and scheming), but they
have the kind of mix-and-match quality that is suggested by

the optional glasses and moustache. You are also buying your-self lifelikeness, a commodity which the shop specialises in; the window has a special display of a number of Presidents of the United States which are there as a kind of sales promotion,' as an indication of the high degree of the establishment's skill (so that passers-by can see for themselves the living character of the likenesses in features they are familiar with, including those of the President now in office who is seen every day on the television screen)' (53). Lifelikeness is not a fact, but the product of a certain degree of skill. And there is irony too in that television is one of the most powerful myth-makers of our culture, and the better known a face on television, the more like a mask it becomes. Reality *is* a mask or a myth, and the people that are most real are simply those that are most skil-fully constructed (either by the mask shop or by fiction itself). As distinct from what happens in the novels of Jane Austen, however, the discovery of masks here is never accompanied by the revelation of the real or the true. Masks and artificiality of all kinds proliferate in the text, and it advertises them as such, but it refuses to complete their discovery with the conventional rhetoric of the *real* and the *actual*. And strangely enough, by refusing this conventional rhetoric, and by shifting the inventiveness of fiction to other levels of the text, the novel appears highly *un*realistic and itself most artificial.

The mask shop sells the characters of most of the characters in the book: the psychoanalyst already mentioned is the character of Dr Morgan who runs a practice in the subway; the businessman is also the character of a certain Johnson, who never actually appears but who is in charge of a number of large business corporations; Ben Saïd is there, as is the trumpeter from Le Vieux Joë, the nightclub which serves as the head-quarters for most of the scheming that takes place; and Dr Morgan's sophisticated receptionist is also there. In this way, we are alerted to the stereotyped nature of the characters in the novel, stereotypes which it plays and juggles with, but which it never replaces with anything more real. Other characters who appear may not have their masks on sale in the shop, but they are none the less stereotyped: there is Laura, the precocious and difficult niece of a big banker who lives a spoiled and lonely life in a sumptuous modern flat overlooking Central Park ('in the avant-garde millionaire style', 57) and who spends much of her time with a small gang of other teenagers mugging strangers in the subway; there is the Vampire du Métropolitain who rapes and murders large numbers of young girls in the subway; there is JR the spy-cum-prostitute; there is the young adolescent with his leather jacket and his flick-knife in the subway, and so on. These are the characters who populate the New York of contemporary popular myth, and no attempt is made to suggest that reality is any different.

If a character is unmasked for any reason, all that is revealed beneath is another mask or stereotype, not a real self. Ben Saïd, one of the supposed revolutionaries, spends much of his time disguised in the exaggerated garb of a detective and watching a block of flats. JR describes his disguise and his mission in the following terms: 'Ben Saïd arrives, in the conspicuous garb of a private detective, with a badly glued plastic mask, dark glasses to hide his eyes and all the classic apparatus: felt hat with the brim turned down, trench coat with the collar turned up at the back, etc.' (104). But is his real identity any less glaringly stereotyped? JR describes him as an Arab intermediary, who speaks twenty-three different languages and who is currently working for the American revolution. Modern myth is full of these Arab itinerant professional revolutionaries. But even this stereotype may not be true, as JR is being tortured by a *false* policeman who orders her to *invent* significant and precise facts. Whether the truth is one of fiction's invented facts or simply a current stereotype makes little difference, for we never get closer to a real identity than this, and the text's remaining efforts consist in proliferating the image of Ben Saïd as mask and stereotype. The masks become dizzyingly numerous: we discover that there is also a *false* Ben Saïd – a man in detective's clothes watching a block of flats, who is not the real Ben Saïd in disguise; and a little later the false Ben Saïd turns up in the subway carriage in the very seat occupied by the real Ben Saïd only a few pages previously. This baffling confusion becomes finally unresolvable when we learn that

Ben Saïd is the name of one of the secondary characters in a book that another character called Laura is reading, and that she uses the name of this secondary character to identify the detective outside her block of flats . . .

Instead of trying to resolve this chaos of false identities, it would seem preferable and more coherent to recognise that there might be any number of real people behind the name and various appearances of Ben Saïd, none of which is more real or more false than the other. In any case, in this novel a name is never the exclusive property of anyone (there are two Lauras, for example) and the very existence of masks and stereotypes means that the same features and characteristics are infinitely repeatable. By the end of the novel, for example, the psychoanalyst has split into two apparently separate characters: there is the psychotherapist, Dr M, and the 'criminal surgeon', Dr Morgan, who both wear the same mask: 'It is [. . .] very difficult to tell them apart because they both wear the same mask, bought from the same manufacturer for the same purpose: inspiring confidence' (190). In this world of stereotypes, we find ourselves surrounded by indecipherable signs – the signifiers do not automatically yield their signifieds and their referents – and the only apprenticeship offered by the novel consists not in the discovery of a code that will enable us to read the signs, but in the reaffirmation of the semiotic basis of reality.

This confusion between the various elements of characters as signs can be seen in the cases of the main female characters. The name Laura is used for two apparently separate girls, the rich girl from Central Park, and the nervous girl who lives alone and imprisoned in an empty block of flats. But towards the end of the novel, elements from one are gradually confused with elements of another and they are unified by the sado-erotic violence which threatens them both. We shift imperceptibly from the rich Laura in the subway doing her best to escape from the Vampire du Métropolitain to the nervous Laura in the flat who is perpetually threatened with rape and violence. Instead of unmasking a real person behind either of these two figures, the text merges the masks under the uniform stereotype of the female victim of the sado-erotic (which eventually includes JR as well). The movement of the novel seems altogether to consist in making the masks and roles more numerous and more uniform. All the women succumb to the same fate which is also infinitely repeated in the advertisements for carpet shampoo in the subway: 'on the other side of the glass Laura [. . .] sees innumerable, identical, equidistant copies of a gigantic poster, placed at short intervals, from one end to the other of the curved wall covered in broken white tiles: the enormous face of a young woman with her eyes blindfolded and her mouth open' (111). And later, when this advertisement is referred to again, it is clear that the girl is 'lying in a pool of her own blood in the middle of a white nylon carpet in a modern living room' (159). Instead of giving us a world where everything appears at first to be similar and uniform but is finally differentiated, *Projet pour une révolution à New York* succeeds in casting possibly different characters into as nearly similar roles as possible. Everything is false, and by the same token infinitely repeatable: the carpet in the advertisement is synthetic (and not wool), the real Ben Saïd wears a coat made of imitation camel hair, the false Ben Saïd keeps a record of his watch on the flats in a 'little black notebook whose *imitation leather* cover is so worn that the threads of the material underneath it are visible at the corners' (114, my emphasis). The table in Dr Morgan's waiting room is made of imitation alabaster, the steps leading up to the flats where Laura is imprisoned are made of imitation stone.

In a sense, the entire novel emerges from a contemplation of the false and the imitated. The opening scene emerges from the shapes which the narrator constructs out of the lines in the imitation wood of a door:

The surface of the surrounding wood is coated with a brown varnish on which tiny lines of a lighter colour, which are the painted image of imaginary veins belonging to another substance, considered to be more decorative, make up parallel or barely divergent networks of sinuous curves around darker nodes, in round or oval and sometimes even triangular shapes, a collection of changing signs in which I have for a long time been able to make out human figures. (8)

A contemplation of the false yields shifting signs which take the form of human figures, thus stressing the semiotic and artificial basis of character from the very beginning of the novel. The scene which follows then appears to be witnessed through a 'cast iron grille of a complicated design (a crude *imitation* of wrought iron)' (7, my emphasis). Just as Proust's Combray is said to emerge from the taste of a madeleine dipped in tea, so Robbe-Grillet's New York emerges from what is artificial, imitated and mass-produced.

On one level these themes can be read as a characterisation of New York itself and the American way of life. But at the same time we cannot ignore the repercussions that they have for the notion of character as it traditionally articulates fiction. The real no longer consists of fiction's invented secret truths, the real is instead the artificial production of myths, as Robbe-Grillet has said himself:

When I read newspaper reports of scandals or crimes, when I look at the shop windows and posters which make up the façade of any large city, when I walk down the passages of the underground, I am bombarded by innumerable signs which taken all together constitute the mythology of the world in which I live, something like the collective subconscious of society, that is to say, both the image of itself that it wants to project and the reflection of the anxieties that haunt it.[...]

Fully revealed as stereotypes, these images will no longer act as a trap from the moment that they are taken up by a living discourse, which remains the only scope that my freedom has. I used to be stifled by this city, but now I know that it is imaginary; and, in refusing to be alienated by it and to submit to its pressures, fears and fantasies, I want instead to reinvest them through the power of my own imagination. (*Prière d'insérer*)

Instead of using some invented secret life as a contrast to outline the signs, codes and myths by which we are surrounded in any society, Robbe-Grillet uses the unrealistic inventiveness of fiction to draw attention to the stereotypes that haunt us. In doing so he shares with all fiction its preoccupation with signs, their elaboration and interpretation; and in rejecting the revelation of the hidden life at its source as a means of organising that preoccupation, he paradoxically makes manifest its strictly novelistic function.

Pronominal persons: 'La modification' and 'Les fruits d'or'

In their attacks on the eponymous heroes of traditional fiction, the new novelists have frequently proposed that the characters of the new fiction should exist simply in the anonymous form of the personal pronoun – as *I* or *he*, or even as *you*. In recognition of the fact that the 'character novel belongs well and truly to the past' (1963, 28), Robbe-Grillet maintains that character should take the form of an 'anonymous, translucid *he*, simple subject of the action expressed by the verb' (27). Nathalie Sarraute sees her own fiction as part of the twentieth-century tradition of the 'anonymous *I*' (1956, 58). Butor's definition of character is even less concrete; character, for him, is neither a self-sufficient entity in fiction, nor a 'physical individual', but simply a 'function which occurs within a mental and social context, in a dimension of dialogue' (1964, 72). The elimination of proper name in favour of some pronominal cipher is advocated by all these writers as a means of achieving authentic anonymity.

However, to opt for pronominal anonymity in preference to eponymous names does not so much solve a problem as introduce a new set of problems. As Butor himself says, 'it makes a great deal of difference which of these two forms is chosen' (1964, 61). To present a character as *I* or as *he* is to introduce quite divergent perspectives. The third person, according to Barthes, belongs alongside the preterite as a basic ingredient of novelistic convention: 'The "he" is a typical novelistic convention; like the narrative tense, it signifies and carries through the action of the novel' (1972, 29). There is all the difference in the world between the first and the third person, he says, since in the novel the '"I" is usually a spectator, and it is the "he" who is the actor' (29).[7] The eponymous characters of conventional fiction are also third persons: Goriot, Rastignac, Julien Sorel are all *he*, the third-person subjects of actions expressed in the preterite. Contrary to what Robbe-Grillet

[7] The translation of these quotations is that of Annette Lavers and Colin Smith (Barthes 1967, 40–1).

proposes, *he* is not necessarily an alternative to a name, and does not necessarily entail anonymity.

The difference between *he* and *I* exists not only in novelistic convention, but, according to the linguist Emile Benveniste, corresponds to a fundamental distinction in all language. Benveniste's thesis is that there are elements in every language which have no meaning outside the utterances in which they occur. *I*, for example, always and only refers to 'I, the speaker of this utterance' and *you* is equally always and only 'you, to whom this utterance is addressed'. Unlike *he*, these pronouns cannot be defined by external reference. The reality to which *I* refers is not an objective one, but is a 'discursive reality' (*une réalité de discours*) (1966, 252). *I* has always to refer to the discourse which proffers it, whereas *he* is silent about its discursive origins and refers instead to the external world. It is for this reason that Benveniste reclassifies these so-called personal pronouns. *He* for Benveniste is the pronoun of non-person, and *I* and *you* are the only properly personal pronouns. The use of these properly personal pronouns always involves some consideration of language itself, since they do not make sense without some reference to the discourse in which they appear. *He*, however, as non-person, allows one to make utterances which do not involve reference to oneself as speaker. The third person and the preterite have in common the ability (albeit a questionable one) to speak of the world without calling into question the nature of that speech. The use of *I*, *you* and the present tense must always raise questions about the language in which they take their form.

A corollary of this distinction between personal and non-personal pronouns is the question of intersubjective communication. *I* and *you* (and the various other personal items of language which Benveniste discusses elsewhere in his book) provide us with empty, non-referential signs which speakers can appropriate in order to transform language into 'discursive instances' (263) and so enter into communication with others. The consequences that the choice of pronoun has for intersubjective communication are outlined by Barthes in a comment about pronouns when he says:

'he' is nasty: it is the nastiest word in the language: the pronoun of non-person, it nullifies and mortifies its referent; one cannot use it to refer to someone one loves without a certain sense of unease; if I say 'he' of someone, I always have in mind a sort of murder by language. (1975, 171)

To speak of someone as *he* is not to communicate with that person, but amounts almost to a form of betrayal, since that *he* is reduced to the status of non-person in a communication with another *you*. Because of the different propensities of *I* and *he* – the communicative and the referential, respectively – the choice of pronoun is bound to have far-reaching consequences for characterisation in fiction. *He* invites the predicates of conventional characterisation much more readily than *I*. *He* can be bold, deceitful, ambitious, ignorant, naïve, impulsive, etc. But if I were to say that 'I am naïve, impulsive, etc.' it would create a certain jarring effect; for, as subject, I am, almost by definition, denied the objectivity that makes the use of these predicates possible. To present myself in this apparently objective way is to present myself as a character, or as a non-person, whereas my experience of myself is as a subject, as someone who says *I*; and as subject, my place is on the axis of communication rather than of reference.

These distinctions are, of course, not absolute, because behind every utterance there is always an *I* addressing a *you* however much the utterance itself may appear to be concerned with an external *he*. This is recognised by Butor in his essay on personal pronouns in fiction: 'In the novel, the story we are told is [. . .] also someone telling his own story and telling our story. Recognition of this fact leads to a shift from the third to the first person.' (1964, 62) And he argues therefore that 'in the novel [the] distinction between the three grammatical persons is much less rigorous than it can be in everyday life; they are linked to each other'. In an attempt to foreground the communicative element of narrative, Butor chooses the second-person pronoun *you* (*vous*) for the hero of his third novel, *La modification*. This unconventional pronoun emphasises the fact that behind the narrative someone is speaking (a *you* always implies an *I*, just as an *I* always implies a *you*). In addition, being what Butor calls a didactic pronoun, it reminds us that the hero of a novel is under apprenticeship:

It is because there is someone whose story is told to him, who is told something about himself which he does not know, or at least not on a verbal level, that it is possible to have a narrative in the second person, which will consequently always be a 'didactic' narrative.[...]

So, each time one wants to describe a development of awareness, the very birth of language, or of a language, the second person will be the most effective. (1964, 66–7)

It is the hero's ignorance or misconceptions, one of the major teleological forces of the novel as a genre, which justifies for Butor this strange narrative pronoun, whose efficacy is reinforced by the fact that ignorance and apprenticeship always involve questions of language. The acquisition of knowledge or understanding of self and world in fiction is always accompanied by an apprenticeship in language, or is even, as was suggested in the previous section, the pretext for the exploration of certain aspects of language.

In the very first lines of Butor's novel, the hero's ignorance is evinced in the smallest details by the use of the second-person pronoun:

You have put your left foot on the copper groove, and with your right shoulder you try in vain to push the sliding door a little wider open.

You squeeze in through the narrow opening, then you bring in your suitcase of dark bottle-green granular leather, the rather small suitcase of a man used to long journeys, you lift it by its sticky handle with your fingers which have got hot from having carried it this far, although it is not very heavy, you feel your muscles and your tendons outlined not only in your fingers, the palm of your hand, your wrist and your arm, but in your shoulder too, in one half of your back and in your vertebrae from your neck down to the small of your back.

No, it is not just the slightly early hour which is responsible for this unusual weakness, it is age which is trying to convince you of its power over your body, and yet you are only just forty-five. (9)

This hero needs to be informed of every minor twinge, of his gestures, of the colour and appearance of his possessions, of the time of day, of his age, and his deeper fears. And as he acquires this information, so too does the reader. The use of *you* implies a gap between an action and its comprehension, between a state and its recognition, and so introduces the theme of learning and understanding from the very outset. By the same token, since this information is given in the form of an explicit communication, the communicative elements of the text come to demand at least as much attention as the informational ones. What is description is also address.

As the novel proceeds, descriptions and information lose their significance as such. Léon Delmont's apprenticeship grows in importance, while questions concerning his character dwindle into relative insignificance. Although he has most of the requisite items for being a conventional character (name, age, address, profession, a certain physical appearance, some personal characteristics, etc.) the novel's themes are not elaborated through these elements. Delmont's character is more or less irrelevant to the apprenticeship which takes place on his journey to Rome. The illumination which this apprenticeship brings concerns not only his view of his wife and his mistress, and of the cities he associates with them, but also involves language itself. Delmont is initiated into language, and communication becomes a major theme of the novel. For Butor illumination is inseparable from the discovery or acquisition of language. And speaking about his use of *you* in this novel, he has said: 'The *you* allows me to describe the character's situation and the way in which language is born to him' (Leiris, 1958, 100).

This birth of a language in Butor's hero has been admirably documented by Françoise van Rossum-Guyon who traces its development through the gradual and intermittent emergence of an *I* in the novel, which marks Delmont's achievement of some sort of linguistic competence (1970a). The revaluation of his life takes the form of a double linguistic achievement: first, he is able to speak in the first person, and announces the new order by which he intends to live in the form of a first-person address to his wife rather than receiving the communication from the authorial *I* behind the text: 'I promise you, Henriette, as soon as we can, we will come back to Rome to-

gether, as soon as things have calmed down again after this disruption, as soon as you have forgiven me; we won't be so old'
(236). The second, and perhaps more compelling proof is
Delmont's decision to exercise his new-found eloquence by
writing a book, and this too is expressed in the first person.
The lessons that Delmont has learned need to be completed
and maintained by the communication that writing will entail.
Instead of receiving communication as a *you*, he will initiate
it as an *I*, and so will be able (in Benveniste's terms) to transform language into discourse. Through its particular use of
pronouns, Butor's *La modification* demonstrates that character
does not necessarily consist just in predicating or in refusing to
predicate certain facts of individuals, but that in writing characters, language itself is brought into play.

Nathalie Sarraute's fiction demonstrates very similar concerns
through the use of pronouns, although none of her characters
is referred to, or rather spoken to, by the text as *you*. In her
novels the themes of communication and linguistic competence
are elaborated and dramatised in the interpersonal relationships between the characters. As Bernard Pingaud says in his
excellent study of character in the novels of Nathalie Sarraute:
'*I* is never a character, *he* is always one. And conversely *he* sees
me in the form of a "character" who occupies the void of his
own *I*' (1963, 21). The drama of the novels consists in the tension between characterisation and communication. To see a
character as a *he* is to see him as a 'character', and so to be
denied any communication with him. Just as one cannot say
he of someone one loves, so one cannot say *you* to a 'character'.
Sarraute's novels repeatedly enact this drama, where every
character experiences himself as an *I* and longs to deconstruct
the *he* which the other always presents to the world, and to
turn him into a *you*. This is the form which 'this terrible desire
to establish contact' takes. In the words of Bernard Pingaud:

The movement (the 'plot') of the novel consists in this alternating
shifting, which by placing the other in front of me, the *he* in front of
the *I*, as a fascinating reality, subsequently devalues the *he* by reducing
him to the anonymity of a *they* or a *you* [*vous*], and then immediately
and paradoxically revalues this collectivity as a closed society from

which the subject feels excluded, and returns to the *he* for a new scrutiny which will vainly try to reduce him to the dimensions of an *I*. (1963, 23)

The whole drama consists in the changing perspective on character which is achieved through what Stephen Heath calls the 'play of pronouns' (1972, 65).

Readers of Nathalie Sarraute soon learn that apparently referential and non-personal (in Benveniste's sense) statements are really a disguised or aborted form of communication. These inauthentic and platitudinous statements are either a form of aggression or an instance of the 'terrible desire to establish contact', but in any case the *he* is never anything but a pretext for the communication that goes from an *I* to a *you*. 'Les fruits d'or', the novel in Nathalie Sarraute's novel of that name, functions nearly always as a pretext for this kind of aggression or communication. The utterances which are supposedly aimed at defining or characterising the book almost always have their true centre of gravity in the *I* and the *you*. The desire for contact is evident in one of the earliest conversations in the book, a conversation whose motivation appears to be the novel in question, but where this objective topic proves to be an anonymous pawn in the game of communication:

The earth opens up. Enormous crevasse. And he, on the other side, walking away without turning round . . . someone should cry out, call him back . . . he should turn round . . . he should come back . . . don't abandon us . . . towards you, with you, on your side, help us, we're coming . . . take hold of what I'm throwing you, this rope that I am hurling at you to pull us with, take it, I beg you . . . just one more try, you'll see, trust in us one more time . . . Tell me . . . have you read? . . . What did you think of it? (17–18)

The interrogative form of the utterance ('what did you think of it?') which appears to invite a description or characterisation by way of a reply, actually testifies to the presence of the communicative axis of language, which is made even more explicit in the *sous-conversation*; the question about 'Les fruits d'or' is thrown like a rope or a lifeline to provide a link between a desperate *I* and a frigid *he* who firmly resists the speaker's effort to turn him into a *you*. Similarly, referential characterisation can

be used as an attempt to foil communication. This is the case
when one of the characters asserts that 'Les fruits d'or' is derivative and platitudinous. His interlocutors, a group of admirers of the novel, disagree, and their response to his assertion
is a characterisation of the novel which is primarily designed to
silence the obstreperous critic and has little descriptive interest
as far as the novel is concerned:

And then, like a shot in the back of the neck, this quick crack: 'But,
you see, it's all done on purpose.'
  The victim of this salvo staggers, falls and he lies on the ground,
losing all his blood. (138)

The image here reveals only too clearly the violent intentions
behind the apparently referential remark. Description here
takes on its full significance in the context of the theme of communication, and it functions as a means of preventing inter-
course between the characters.

  The tension between characterisation and communication
is finally resolved towards the end of the novel when one of the
characters realises that instead of trying to characterise the
elusive novel in question, he can speak *to* it. He rejects the
derisory names which the others invent for 'Les fruits d'or':
'"Man in the cosmos", "A vast fresco" ... "Better than War
and Peace" ... "Modern man at grips with the great problems
of our time"' (217). Instead, he decides to address the novel
directly, to replace description with communication:

But it must be granted that, in the long run, as time passes, your
chances of survival are increasing. The silence in which you float,
divested of all the garments and ornaments with which you have
been rigged out, naked, washed adrift, with me clinging onto you,
makes our contact a very close one. We are so close to each other
now, you are so much a part of me that it seems to me that if you
ceased to exist, it would be as if a part of me had become dead tissue.
(224–5)

Address resolves the impossible problems of definition. We
discover that it is no longer possible to say anything *about*
people (and here 'Les fruits d'or' functions as a person), there
are only greater or lesser degrees of speaking *to* them. The
anonymity of character has cleared a space in the novel where
the themes of communication can be openly explored.

Both Michel Butor and Nathalie Sarraute show very clearly how character in fiction is not simply a portrait or a description but also a form of communication. Character is indeed a 'function which occurs within a mental and social context, *in a dimension of dialogue*' (1964, 72, my emphasis). We discover that even non-persons (the third-person *he*) can acquire or challenge the linguistic subjectivity of the text. Not only is *he* the means whereby a communication between text and reader takes place, but also even the most traditional and characterful characters of fiction, non-persons in the narrative discourse of the novel, become subjects when they speak in order to address other characters; and every novel, traditional or otherwise, presents characters who speak and who are themselves users of language in some kind of communication.

A reading of the novels discussed in this chapter suggests that the poetics of character in the nouveau roman has little to do with the realist concerns outlined by Robbe-Grillet and Nathalie Sarraute in their essays on the subject. The psychological realism implied by the universality of the tropism, and the social realism implied in what Robbe-Grillet calls the 'era of the regimental number' simply constitute the cultural setting in which the nouveau roman appears, but they were certainly not invented by it. The regimented anonymity depicted in Aldous Huxley's *Brave New World* and Zamyatin's *We* is already several decades old, and we have lived with the psychological anonymity of psychoanalytic discourse for even longer. Equally, the realism of the subjective viewpoint does not constitute a new departure in the nouveau roman, and this shift of focus on character goes back to the novels of Henry James, Gide, Proust and Virginia Woolf. Indeed, anonymity and subjectivity could now be said to be the platitudes of this century. So that the cultural realism associated with these notions cannot be taken very seriously in a discussion of the theory of the nouveau roman.

Viewed in more strictly literary terms, the thematic and realist coherence traditionally provided by character has been more severely undermined in the nouveau roman than in previous fiction. Thematic coherence proves either to be void (as in the case of Robbe-Grillet's voyeur) or is unequivocally under attack (as in the case of the old man in Sarraute's *Portrait d'un inconnu*). The realist coherence traditionally involved in the representation of character is also seriously threatened, for example by the constantly changing names of the characters in *La maison de rendez-vous* or by the contradictions concerning the writer in *Entre la vie et la mort*. Name as the symbol of all coherence is extensively devalued in these novels, but this too is a continuation of a practice that began with Kafka's K, Proust's narrator (named only once in 3000 pages), or Faulkner's two Quentins in *The Sound and the Fury*. The realist effect which the concept of character has made available in the past had already lost a good deal of credence by the time the nouveau roman appeared, and the nouveau roman has only continued its effacement.

The most interesting contribution made by the nouveau roman lies in its revelation of the underlying poetics of character in the novel. It shows us that the coherence provided by character is illusory because it rests on a certain kind of discourse, the kind of character-making discourse which the nouveau roman treats as platitude or mask. Secondly, it shows us that the lifelikeness of character, always so highly valued in the past, is the effect of certain rhetorical strategies. And finally, through its treatment of characters as speakers, it opens up the possibility of seeing a whole discursive polyphony in fiction, where the issues at stake have less to do with the adequacy of the novel's representation of character as mind or social entity, than with the nature of the languages that we use for these representations. It is with the consequences and implications of these issues that the following chapters will be concerned.

3

Narrative strategies and the discovery of language

To dramatise the seeing eye

When Percy Lubbock writes that the 'art of fiction does not begin until the novelist thinks of his story as a matter to be *shown*' (1965, 62) he is, in one sense, doing little more than defining narrative itself by reminding us that a narrative consists, on the one hand, of a story or a sequence of events and, on the other, of their means of presentation. Or, as Genette puts it, 'there can be no narrative [*récit*], no narrative discourse except in so far as it tells a story, failing which it would not be narrative [. . .] and in so far as it is uttered by someone, failing which [. . .] it would not in itself be a discourse' (1972, 74). There would be little value in reminding oneself of what is almost a self-evident definition if the question of presentation had not constituted such a major issue in critical and theoretical writings in this century. In discussing aspects of narrative in Chapter 1 above, questions relating to presentation and narration proved to be an integral part of narrative (as in the case of the 'gamma point'); but a poetics of the novel ought to consider the question of narration as a separate issue because its role in the interpretation of fiction has such extensive and numerous consequences.

In his discussion of what he calls 'narrative contracts' Jonathan Culler claims that the identification of narrators is one of the most powerful strategies that readers have for naturalising and interpreting fiction (1975, 192–202). By implying that its 'narrator is only a more knowledgeable version of the reader and that they share the same world' (196), a novel is able to establish its mimetic intentions. This is the case, for instance, in the opening pages of Stendhal's *Le rouge et le noir*. They not only set the scene for the action and introduce some of the characters who will be participating in it, but do so from the point of view of the ordinary observer, and more specifically, the 'Parisian traveller'. Both these are roles which the narrator invites the reader to share with him, and the values and experience of reader and narrator are linked through them in the description of M. de Rênal, for example:

When he appears all hats are quickly doffed. His hair is turning grey, and he is dressed in grey. He is knight of several orders, he has a broad forehead, an aquiline nose, and in all his face has a certain regularity: *one* even feels at first glance, that it combines the dignity of village mayor with the kind of charm that can still be found in a man of forty-eight or fifty years. But soon *the Parisian traveller* is shocked by a certain air of self-satisfaction and self-importance mixed with something limited and uninventive. *One* feels finally that this man's gifts consist just in making sure that money owed to him is paid on time, and in delaying payment of his own debts as long as possible. (*Romans et nouvelles* I, 220, my emphases.)

By making its evaluation of M. de Rênal seem like the shared judgment of narrator and reader, the text is able to establish a trust between the two which ensures the truthfulness of all subsequent statements and judgments in the novel.

The guarantee of mimesis achieved by this narrative strategy is directed primarily towards creating agreement about the nature of the world to which the novel refers, an agreement which would not in itself be effective for the mimetic effect in fiction of the post-Jamesian era. For, since the end of the nineteenth century, the realistic effects to be derived from narrative presentation have come increasingly to be associated with the perspective and language of fictional discourse itself. We do not ask Stendhal's narrator to provide plausible explanations about how he came by his information concerning the characters and what his personal involvement with those facts is; once he has been identified and cast in his role of the ordinary observer, anything (within reason) goes. In the twentieth century, however, the tendency has been to demand realist alibis for every stretch of narrative discourse. Mimesis in the modern world has come to concern not so much the objects of narrative discourse as its origins. And it is because the burden of realism has fallen so heavily on narrative presentation that the question of narration and narrative discourse requires special attention in a discussion of the poetics of fiction.

The work of Henry James is conventionally seen as the starting point of this kind of narrational realism. His notebooks and prefaces testify to his abiding concern with finding narrators or 'reflectors' for his narratives. For James himself his narrative strategies did not constitute a set of dogmatic proposals concerning the realism of his fiction. 'When I practise [the art of reflection] the whole field is lighted up', he writes; 'I feel again the multitudinous presence of all human situations and pictures, the surge and pressure of *life*' (James, 1961, xvii), as if the practice of this art corresponded to a largely personal and private need on the part of the writer. Or else, they are a purely formal means of constructing a 'masterpiece of close and finished irony' (1961, 180). And, interestingly enough, his views are very similar to those of his younger French contemporary, André Gide. In a now famous entry in the *Journal* of 1893 Gide outlines a kind of narrative strategy whose appeal Henry James would certainly have appreciated: 'An angry man tells a story; there is the subject of a book. A man telling a story is not enough; it must be an angry man, and there must be a constant connection between his anger and the story he tells.' (41) Again, the attraction for Gide of this kind of narrative strategy is based not so much on any gain in realism that it may offer, but rather on its effectiveness as a formal solution. He sees it as a kind of *mise en abyme* which he defines here as the 'retroaction of the subject on itself' (41) or the '[transposition] onto the scale of the characters of the very subject of that work' (41). Henry James might not have chosen such terms to justify his preference for such devices, but it should be stressed that neither James nor Gide was responsible for what Wayne Booth has since called the 'general rules' of modern fiction (1961, 23ff.), for which they are both seen as providing textbook examples.

These 'general rules' are set out (as rules) in Percy Lubbock's

The craft of fiction, and he attributes to them a realist purpose which neither James nor Gide, nor any writer before them would have thought necessary. By the time Lubbock came to write his book (first published in 1921) the voice of the author had acquired an 'arbitrary quality' which was unacceptable to the modern ear and which needed to be disguised by narrative techniques whose function would be to provide a spokesman for the *'mere* author' and prevent us from seeing the story as resting *'only* upon the author's direct assertion' (1965, 251, my emphases). He continues:

Is it not possible, then, to introduce another point of view, to set up a fresh narrator to bear the brunt of the reader's scrutiny? If the story-teller is *in* the story himself, the author is dramatised; his assertions gain in weight, for they are backed by the presence of the narrator in the pictured scene. It is an advantage scored; the author has shifted his responsibility, and it now falls where the reader can see and measure it; the arbitrary quality which may at any time be detected in the author's voice is disguised in the voice of his spokesman. (251–2)

In his comments on authorial assertion Lubbock displays a horror of the kind of arbitrariness which, as the preceding chapters show, also lies at the heart of the rhetoric of plot and character in fiction. Any technique, then, which provides a spokesman for the author, or at least some kind of plausible origin for the narrative discourse should be seen as a motivation designed to disguise the arbitrary, just as the false causality of narrative and the notion of the hidden life as its source do in the case of character. 'The thing has to *look* true', says Lubbock, and 'It is not made to look true by simple statement' (1965, 62). The novelist has to 'dramatise the seeing eye' in order to 'authenticate his story' (117) and so silence the arbitrary voice of what he calls the 'mere author' but what modern French writers might prefer to term *écriture*. Roland Barthes, for example, also sees fiction as an endless struggle between the arbitrariness of writing itself and the realist motivations which make interpretation possible. But in his case, his preference is the reverse of Lubbock's, and it is delight in the triumph of writing which lies behind his remarks on realism in narrative discourse: 'the essence of writing (the sense and purpose of the activity which constitutes it) is to make it impossible to ever reply to the question: *"Who is speaking?"'* (1970a, 146)

The whole question of what is loosely subsumed under the heading 'point of view' poses some interesting questions which literary history might one day provide the answer to. A number of critics have summarised the history of the notion of point of view (e.g. Friedman 1955b and van Rossum-Guyon 1970b), but no one has yet explained why, some time at the end of the nineteenth century, the author's voice should take on this arbitrary ring and why the discourse of fiction and the literary criticism which accompanies it should need to work so hard to fulfil this new demand for realist disguises. What follows here is not an attempt to answer these interesting questions, but rather a brief compilation of the kinds of realist motivation which have been invoked to provide alibis for the arbitrary language of fiction, and which cut across specific narrative techniques (e.g. those summarised by Friedman, 1955b, as 'editorial omniscience', 'neutral omniscience', 'I as witness', 'I as protagonist', 'multiple selective omniscience', etc.).

Until relatively recently it was chiefly the English-speaking world which was preoccupied with the question of point of view, as Norman Friedman's article on the development of the concept of point of view implies (1955b). The comparative lack of sensitivity to the topic in France may go some way towards explaining the surprising degree of naïvety that the theoretical writings by the new novelists reveal on this subject. Nathalie Sarraute is the most outspoken defender of the realist motivation for narrative discourse, and, while neither Butor nor Robbe-Grillet betrays a great deal of interest in the subject, most of what they write implies agreement about the need for some narrational realism. I shall therefore use their writings to provide examples of the kinds of realist motivation that are frequently adduced for fictional discourse.

It is Nathalie Sarraute who demonstrates the most marked horror of the arbitrary in narrative discourse. The effort of every novelist should, in her view, be directed towards avoiding either a speakerless narrative or one which too crudely draws attention to the presence of Lubbock's 'mere author' behind it. She imagines a novelist sitting down to write Valéry's now famous narrative introit 'La marquise sortit à cinq heures' and finding that he cannot go on with it: 'he stops, his courage fails him, no he simply can't' (1956, 68). The reason why he cannot pursue this narrative based simply on authorial assertion is that 'he thinks he hears the reader, like the child being read a story by its mother for the first time, stop him and ask: "Who ,says that?"' The solution to the novelist's dilemma is to construct an identifiable speaker (or spokesman): 'The first-person narrative satisfies the reader's legitimate curiosity and allays the author's equally legitimate scruples. In addition, it has the appearance at least of lived experience, of authenticity, which keeps the reader's respect and soothes his mistrust.' (68–9) The arbitrary is eliminated and the narrative authenticated (that is, motivated) by the device of dramatising the 'seeing eye', or, more specifically here, the 'speaking I'.[1]

One of the most frequently employed devices for dramatising this seeing eye is to make the narrative discourse a form of indirect characterisation of its narrator or reflector (the character from whose point of view the story is narrated). This is one way in which one might read the connection between story and discourse proposed by Gide in his plan for a story told by an angry man. And Robbe-Grillet, in arguing against a 'chosiste' interpretation of his novels, has on occasion also proposed that his fiction be seen as originating from a dramatised narrator who could potentially be characterised as a liar, a schizophrenic or as a victim of hallucinations. Modern fiction, he says, has a new kind of narrator: ' he is no longer just a man describing the things he sees, but he is also the person who invents the things around him and who sees the things he invents. From the moment that these narrator-heroes begin to look the least bit like "characters", they immediately become liars, schizophrenics or victims of hallucinations.' (1963, 140) Bruce Morrissette bases his study of Robbe-Grillet's novels on the assumption that this kind of indirect characterisation is indeed the basis

---

[1] In this context the distinction between the two is not relevant, but for a discussion of the otherwise usual importance of distinguishing between 'focalisation' and 'narration' see Genette, 1972, especially chapters 4 and 5, and Bal, 1977, 21–58.

of his fiction, and he finds alibis for the narrative discourse of the novels by postulating Wallas as the Oedipally obsessed reflector of *Les gommes*, a schizophrenic as the reflector of *Le voyeur*, etc. Character as motivation for narrative discourse is frequently found in critical interpretations of literary works, but as an interpretive strategy it seems itself particularly prone to the charge of arbitrariness unless there are very specific indications in a text that it will be appropriate. Jonathan Culler has also argued against its indiscriminate use in the interpretation of fiction by showing how uninteresting narrative discourse can become if we insist on constructing narrators or points of view for it (1974, 109–22).

Since individuated character seems not particularly functional in providing a *telos* for the fiction of the nouveau roman, this kind of motivation is not extensively invoked in the theoretical writings of the new novelists. Some notion of character is, nevertheless, used as motivation for narrative discourse in so far as certain narrative techniques are regarded as fostering an exploration of the (anonymous) inner life. Of the three writers in question, it is Nathalie Sarraute who makes most use of the notion of psychology in her novels, and it is she who most vigorously justifies various narrative techniques in terms of their appropriateness for the representation of the inner life. Interior monologue and the use of a first-person narrator are seen as the means whereby the evocation of the 'endless activity of psychological life and the vast regions of the subconscious which so far have hardly been opened up' can be achieved (1956, 64). First-person narrative becomes a device for ensuring the anonymity which, in Sarraute's opinion, has, after Freud, Joyce and Proust become the basis of a new view of human nature (1956, 58–9). For her the number of twentieth-century novels written in the first person (Proust's *A la recherche du temps perdu*, Rilke's *Malte Laurids Brigge*, Céline's *Voyage au bout de la nuit*, Sartre's *La nausée*, Genet's *Miracle de la rose*, etc.) testify to what she calls 'this current development of character in the novel' (1956, 59). In other words, new concepts of character are adduced to provide a realist motivation for narrative discourse. In the twentieth century the hidden life at its source has become more or less synonymous with the indirect representation of the experiencing mind by means of certain kinds of narrative technique.

A second major kind of motivation for narrative technique concerns the representation of time. Sartre's attack on the retrospective narrative stance is based on the argument that the 'gamma point' abolishes true temporality by leaping into the eternal; it denies 'historicity and the irreversibility of time' (1948, 257). By providing narrators or reflectors who are caught up inside the events of their own narrative it becomes possible to 'restore to the event its brutal freshness, its ambiguity, its unforeseeability, [to] restore to time its actual course' (254). Similar arguments are put forward by Butor and Sarraute. The use of point of view in one form or another is again motivated by the notion of the experiencing mind, and a realist reading of narrative techniques which exploit point of view will see in them the representation of the lived experience of time.

The third major type of motivation is connected with what is often rather vaguely termed 'relativity', a concept much used by Sartre and which occurs in all the theoretical writings of the new novelists. The emergence of sensitivity towards the mimetic implications of narrative stance roughly coincides in historical terms with the development of Einstein's theory of relativity, and it is a popularised version of this theory which is frequently invoked as the motivation for narrative techniques based on point of view. Sartre's famous attack on Mauriac is founded on the notion of relativity, and he concludes by accusing Mauriac of failing to acknowledge the realist implications of his narrative technique:

Like most of our authors, he tried to forget that the theory of relativity applies in full to the universe of the novel, that, in a real novel, no more than in the world of Einstein, there is no place for a privileged observer. [. . .] M. Mauriac has chosen divine omniscience and omnipotence. But a novel is written by a man for men. (1947, 56–7)

In the twentieth century the presence of an omniscient author comes to be read as a metaphor for the divine, and must necessarily be proscribed in a system of values which makes even a bird's-eye-view seem unrealistic (Sarraute, 1956, 125–55). The limitations that any situated perspective inevitably creates are nowadays considered to be an integral part of reality. Or, as Butor writes 'this ignorance is one of the fundamental aspects of human reality', so that the introduction of a narrative point of view must therefore be seen as a 'step forward in realism' (1964, 62).

Robbe-Grillet writes even more vehemently in favour of locating the narrative of a novel in the subjective experience of human reality. He distinguishes modern fiction, and his own in particular, from the divine objectivity of Balzac's *Comédie humaine*: 'In our books', he writes, 'it is *a man* who sees, feels, imagines, a man located in space and time, conditioned by his passions, a man like you and me. And the book tells us only about his limited, uncertain experience.' (1963, 118) Some notion of relativity, then, provides a major motivation for narrative techniques based on a limited point of view, and it is for this reason that they have come to be regarded as a cornerstone in the realistic representation of human experience.

The writings of the new novelists reveal a surprising degree of unanimity concerning the need for a realist motivation for narrative strategies, and, in contrast to their essays on character, for example, those on the question of point of view reveal no trace of unease about the illusory basis of this mimetic effect. This lack of squeamishness is particularly strange in view of the fact that a given motivation can never fully account for all aspects of a given technique. In general, it seems that every gain in realism achieved in one aspect by one technique entails a simultaneous loss in another. So that, for example, the kind of monologue used by Faulkner in *Light in August* or by Sartre in *Les chemins de la liberté* provides an 'enrichment of insight' on the one hand, but, on the other, carries with it the handicap that 'extensive verbalisation of this nature invites a psychological interpretation, and may seem to imply a high degree of rationalising self-consciousness in the character which may, in many cases, conflict with his or her temperament or situation' (Pascal, 1977, 2). This problem (created by the use of soliloquy as a narrative device) can be solved by the introduction of a first-person narrator. But this solution, in its own turn, brings other problems: the 'freedom in regard to the fictional self entails a large limitation in regard to other characters that hampers the impersonal third-person narrator, who is allowed the right of access to all secret places' (Pascal, 1977, 3). Similarly, first-person narrative, which has the advantage of providing a plausible basis for the narration as language, still has the inherent disadvantage of all story-telling, namely the 'distorting power of distance' (Pascal, 1977, 4). But in overcoming this last disadvantage by closing the gap between narration and action in an effort to convey the feeling of lived experience, new drawbacks are introduced: the insistent self-awareness of the narrator and the continual transformation of action into words cannot be sustained for any length of time without appearing to contradict the verisimilitude which the technique was designed to foster. So it appears that there is no narrative strategy capable of granting equally satisfactory answers to the questions 'qui voit?' and 'qui parle?'. To give a realistic answer to the one implies a proportional loss of realism in the answer to the other. The literal-mindedness involved in asking (like Sarraute's suspicious child) 'qui voit?' and 'qui parle?' starts a process that is endless and finally self-destructive because the answers can never be fully adequate.

One way of getting out of the impasse into which the quest for narrational realism inevitably leads us is to abandon it altogether, and to evaluate the relationship between a story and its manner of presentation in quite other terms. In this change of approach the work of the French linguist Emile Benveniste has been repeatedly used as a source of critical tools.[2] Writing specifically about the temporal structures of the French verbal system, Benveniste distinguishes between two sub-systems: the historical and the discursive, the one constituting *histoire* the other *discours* (1966, 237–50). The historical system (exemplified by the preterite) is marked by the fact that it enables events to speak for themselves, as it were, and can proceed without reference to the context in which the narrative is uttered: 'there is not even [...] a narrator any more. Events

[2] The best-known examples are Barthes, 1966 and Genette's essay 'Frontières du récit' (1969, 49–69). See also Culler, 1975, 197–200 and Bellos, 1978.

are presented in the way that they occurred as they appear on the horizon of the story. No one speaks here; events seem to narrate themselves. The fundamental tense is the aorist, which is the tense of events outside the person of a narrator.' (1966, 241) The discursive system is represented by any element in an utterance which cannot be interpreted without reference to the context of that utterance, for example, the present tense and words such as *here*, *now*, etc. In his study of the pronominal system, 'La nature des pronoms' (1966, 251–7), Benveniste discovers the same dual system in operation. There is one system where the pronouns can be fully understood only by reference to the discourse in which they are uttered – notably *I* and *you*: *I* is always and only 'I, the speaker of this utterance'. On the other hand, the third-person pronoun *he* needs no such point of reference and in this sense can be compared to the aorist or preterite in the tense system. *I* and *you* belong with the present tense in the discursive system.

Gérard Genette takes up this distinction in his essay on narrative, 'Les frontières du récit' (1969, 49–69), and argues that the opposition between *récit* and *discours* is fundamental. He claims that the two systems are mutually incompatible and suggests that we therefore regard the history of the novel as a perpetual (and finally impossible) struggle to reconcile them: 'Indeed we know that the novel has never succeeded in resolving the problem posed by this relationship in a convincing and definite way' (67). According to this view, narrative strategies in the novel would interest us by the degree to which they succeed in resolving the inevitable conflicts between the two systems represented by *récit* and *discours*, and we would regard the purpose of story-telling in fiction not in realist terms, but as a kind of amplification of a contradiction inherent in language itself.

Jean Ricardou's similar distinction between *narration* and *fiction* (1967, 161–70) is also designed to make us see the novel as revealing something about the nature of language itself. Only, here *fiction* is used to refer to the illusion of reality created by the text, and *narration* to the language of which the text consists. Again, the two elements are seen as being in conflict, and where the *fiction* has the upper hand the 'naturalist illusion' is created, but where *narration* has the edge, the literal or anti-naturalist aspects of the text are privileged. Or, as Ricardou puts it in his comment on *L'emploi du temps*, 'with the axis of the narration being developed at the expense of that of the fiction, one can see how the novel ceases to be the writing of a story to become the story of a writing' (166). Again, narrative strategies are to be evaluated according to the degree to which they draw attention to the nature of language itself.

The advantage of this relatively formalist kind of approach is that it manages to find significance in narrative strategies while at the same time dispensing with the extremely unwieldy and finally unproductive apparatus involved in realist interpretations of different ways of telling stories. But the disadvantage of these concepts is that they abandon altogether the notion of speakers. It is, of course, true that language exists independently of each of us, but, as speakers of language we are all involved in some relationship with language. Do we speak it? or does it speak us? do we express ourselves through language? or are we invented by language? The remainder of this chapter will be devoted to exploring the hypothesis that it is this problematic, unstable and centrally important relationship between ourselves and language that is highlighted in the nouveau roman through the deployment of different kinds of narrative strategy.

The first person and its narrative dramas: 'Portrait d'un inconnu'

Portrait d'un inconnu is narrated in the first person and, if we are to take our cue from Nathalie Sarraute's remarks in *L'ère du soupçon,* we should see this particular narrative form as having a dual realist function: first, the greater anonymity of the first-person pronoun (as opposed to the third) corresponds to contemporary ideas concerning character, and, secondly, it provides a source for the narrative discourse and 'satisfies the legitimate curiosity of the reader' by creating an 'appearance of lived experience, of authenticity' (1956, 68–9). The restrictions that the realism of this narrative technique imposes are summarised by Norman Friedman in his discussion of the "'I'' as witness':

The natural consequence of this narrative frame is that the witness has no more than ordinary access to the mental states of others; its distinguishing characteristic, then, is that the author has surrendered his omniscience altogether regarding all the other characters involved, and has chosen to allow his witness to tell the reader only what he as observer may legitimately discover. The reader has available to him only the thoughts, feelings, and perceptions of the witness-narrator; he therefore views the story from what may be called the wandering periphery. (1955b, 1174)

It is this expulsion of the reader, and with him the narrator, to the wandering periphery that constitutes the main drawback to the first-person narrative used with a realist purpose, and it is one that is particularly keenly felt in the case of Nathalie Sarraute's fiction.

In all the novels, be they first-person narratives (like *Portrait d'un inconnu* or *Martereau*) or apparently narratorless fictions (like the subsequent ones), we find that the psychological themes demonstrate both that people are mutually opaque and that everyone is prone to tropism, and the 'terrible desire to establish contact' (1956, 33). A first-person narrator is clearly well suited to the representation of the opacity of the other, as it is to the representation of the narrator's experience in trying to break through the mask to establish contact. The difficulty comes in conveying the universality of this psychology. And in this thematic context, the use of the first person may even end by contradicting the anonymity which it was originally supposed to guarantee, by defining the narrator as a certain kind of character in opposition to those we see from without. It is in establishing the universality of the subjective experience associated with a first-person narrative that the greatest *invraisemblances* are likely to occur. For, in order to describe the very experiences which the other is set on concealing, the text must break the laws of *vraisemblance* which follow from the use of a narrator-witness, namely that he has 'no more than ordinary access to the mental states of others'.

It is no surprise, therefore, to find that the narration of *Por-*

trait d'un inconnu does repeatedly transgress the realist limitations of the narrator's position in order to give an account of the inner lives of other characters. Indeed, most of the novel's major scenes are based on such transgressions; for example, when the old man wakes in the night, when he discovers the leak in the bathroom, or when the daughter asks him for money. Some critics have recuperated these transgressions in broad psychological terms: Cranaki and Belaval speak of 'knowledge through feeling' (1965, 93); Gerda Zeltner and Valerie Minogue explain them as a mark of the superiority of creativity and imagination over direct perception (Zeltner, 1962; Minogue, 1973b); and Valerie Minogue specifically relates the compensating powers of creativity to the limited point of view associated with a first-person narration (Minogue, 1976). This kind of metaphorical alibi for what is, strictly speaking, not a justifiable strategy in realist terms need not necessarily seem implausible as long as the stance is coherently and consistently maintained. Coherence and consistency are at least as effective in establishing narrational realism as any particular technique.[3] The reason why the first-person narration of *Portrait d'un inconnu* is ultimately *invraisemblable* is not because it is impossible to accept metaphorical alibis such as 'knowledge through feeling' or what the text itself calls 'this supernatural flair for things', but because the novel seems so insistently to bring together incompatible narrative stances.

This is the case, for example, in the episode where the narrator watches the old man and his friend from a bridge above a railway station. The narrator presents himself as being physically situated in the scene with a limited point of view on it *and nevertheless* as having an intuitive access to the feelings and emotions of the other characters:

[3]This point is made by Friedman in his discussion of the author-narrator so abhorrent to realist sensibilities in the twentieth century: 'he [the author-narrator] need not retire behind his work, so long as his point of view is adequately established and *coherently maintained. It is more a matter of consistency than this or that degree of "impersonality";*' (1955, 1181, my emphasis). This view is also set out by Genette in his discussion of narrative strategies: 'Le critère décisif n'est pas tant de possibilité matérielle ou même de vraisemblance psychologique, que de *cohérence textuelle* et de tonalité narrative' (1972, 222, my emphasis).

The old woman walking along beside him, and to whom he has given his arm, is the wife of his friend . . . – I recognise her, it is her alright, she has aged, she is all wrinkled, her as well, she is wearing a black plush coat which is so worn that it has a reddish sheen as if it had gone rusty, she is carrying a shopping bag, *it must be* a humble bundle of black oilcloth, *I cannot see very well* – the footbridge is high above the platform and *I can't see* because of the smoke and the people moving about on the platform who keep hiding them from me – *I guess rather* just from the air of tenderness and understanding concern with which he takes the bundle from her hands and places it on the ground between them in front of the bench where they sit down next to each other, while they wait for the train.

He likes it, *I know*, the humble oilcloth bundle and the dirty platform filled with the smell of sulphur, the houses, the little gardens: it was to sniff and inhale it with the sickly-sweet, ambiguous delight that one gets from smelling one's own smells that he came here. A bit like I did too. (104–5, my emphases)

The restrictions in vision imposed by the narrator's position on the bridge, the smoke from the engines and the crowds on the platform seem quite redundant, since the knowledge that he is after can be acquired by intuition ('I guess', 'I know'). Either of these stances used separately would be effective in realist terms, but used together they seem mutually invalidating.

The narrational realism of the later scenes, where the narrator's intuitive grasp becomes increasingly assured, is seriously impaired when he interrupts to situate himself in relation to his narrative. For instance, he is not present in the long section dealing with the daughter's attempt to get money for medical treatment from her father (169–209) which takes place behind closed doors in the father's flat, and he specifically states that the only eavesdroppers are the concierge pretending to dust the banisters on the stairs outside and the maid washing up in the kitchen. The narrator's absence from the scene he is describing only becomes an acute problem when he makes it one through references to himself, as in the following remarks:

Only I, if I had been at the next table, only I might perhaps have been able to catch – I have such a perverted mind – in the last tremblings of his laugh as it fades, buried in his lowered cheeks, a sort of vague reflection of the smile he has, secret and directed at himself, a smile just for him, which I know; but no one around him can glimpse the brief flash as it passes and is lost in him, burying itself in a hole like a mouse. (180–2)

This passage not only draws our attention to the narrator's absence from the scene, but compounds the peculiarity by making the very intuition on which the narration of the whole scene depends merely a hypothetical consequence of his hypothetical physical presence, so that the logical basis of the narration at this stage is: *if* I were on the scene, I would *perhaps* be intuitively aware of the old man's mental life which I am now (intuitively, presumably?) describing. The illogicality and redundancy of this intervention is entirely counterproductive in terms of the realist effect that the narrator's self-identification is normally supposed to produce.

The full extent of the narrational *invraisemblance* inherent in the narrator's double narrative alibi (limited point of view and intuition) can be gauged and explored if we examine two versions of the same episode which the novel gives. The episode in question relates a chance encounter between the narrator himself and the old man's daughter. The first version is given as part of the narrative proper, and the second is constituted by a later conversational retelling of the episode when the narrator meets his friend L'Alter. The conversational version, curiously enough, displays none of the *invraisemblances* of the narrated version.

The episode begins with the narrator sitting alone on a bench in a square, and until the point where the daughter walks on to the scene, the use of the first person is entirely appropriate to the material of the narrative, which is chiefly concerned with the narrator's mental state. But on the daughter's arrival some changes have to be made in order to justify the kinds of comment that the text wants to make about her, namely, that behind the façade of a twentieth-century Eugénie Grandet she is as much prone to the murky psychology of the Sarrautean tropism as the narrator himself. In order to make this kind of statement possible, the narrator attributes to himself a special sensitivity which operates in the presence of the old man and his daughter. He uses the word 'premonition' and speaks of 'the vague excitement – a mixture of fear and eager expectations –

which I always feel before I even see them' (30); and elsewhere he speaks of being a 'conducting rod through which all
the currents that charged the atmosphere were passing' (144).
This constitutes an alibi for any otherwise implausible statement that the narrative might wish to make. The conversational
version, however, dispenses with all alibis of this kind. In the
textual narrative, the narrator goes on to state that the daughter
possesses the same special sensitivity which may explain her
surly aggression towards himself:

She had seen me. There was no doubt about it. She has the same
supernatural flair for things. She senses it: she senses me behind
her, and she also senses me behind her looking in a mirror, as I leave
a theatre in the crowd. She had had a premonition that she would see
me, she had noticed me at once sitting on the bench, seen my head
above the boxwood hedge next to the motionless little old people,
or perhaps it was the line of my crossed legs glimpsed between the
bars of the railings. (31)

This passage (which has no parallel in the conversational version) narrates with confidence what the daughter sees and feels.
The self-reference in the narrator's account ('There was no
doubt about it', 'certainly', 'perhaps') does nothing to qualify or
contest the validity of 'she had seen me', 'she senses it', which
directly assert the existence of a secret tropistic life behind the
mask, an existence which the narrator is elsewhere so uncertain
of. In the conversational version, where the narrator and
L'Alter are discussing precisely this uncertainty, the remarks
that the narrator makes about the daughter are clearly based
on inference from observable facts: 'she was afraid, she wasn't
prepared for it, she was literally trembling' (46). Trembling is
a plausible enough sign of fear. In the first, textual, version,
the narrator is making statements which are somewhat incon-
sistent with his stated epistemological position and which are
only superficially justified by the thin alibi of special sensitivity.
The alibi is thin because it is only intermittently invoked and
is not used in the conversational version of the same event.

This inconsistency about the narrator's position persists,
but as long as he remains on the scene that he is describing,
there is no outright scandal about his position in the story and

the information that the narrative provides. On page 34, however, the narrative follows the daughter off the scene, leaving
the narrator behind:

She must be walking very fast now, she has wasted her time clowning
there with me, she must catch up, she hurries, there is something
obstinate and grasping, something blind and implacable in the way
she proceeds in the right direction, cuts across the roads, her back still
hollowed, as if someone was about to kick her from behind, her long
thin legs striding ahead.

She would find it funny, I am sure, if she had time still to think about
me, she would find it funny, now that she feels free, and is not afraid
of me any more, if she knew that I was still there following her and
spying on her ... She walks up the dark, silent staircase, with walls
covered in wallpaper made to look like Cordoba leather. She fumbles
in her handbag for the key, quick, she has no time to lose, it is late, and
then like me a while ago, she probably feels a sort of trembling, a sweet
and painful excitement rising and growing.

This passage is full of inconsistencies about the narrator's position in relation to his narrative. The first sentence 'she *must* be
walking very fast now' implies that the narrator's remarks are
based on hypothesis. The confident tone of 'there is something
obstinate' etc., in contrast, suggests that the narrator really is
following her and spying on her (although this spying could be
read as a metaphor and thus indicate conjecture). When the text
says 'she fumbles in her handbag for the key' is this based on the
narrator's observation or on his supposition? And who says
'quick', an exclamation which one reads as an utterance? Are
we to read 'she has wasted her time clowning there with me;
she must catch up' as a report of the girl's thoughts, and, if so,
how does the narrator know what she is thinking? It could,
of course, be conjecture, but even as conjecture its confident
tone contradicts the Sarrautean norm whereby no character
may be sure of what thoughts and feelings go on behind the
mask of external appearance, a norm which initially gave rise
to a first-person narrative. These almost deliberate inconsistencies concerning the narrator are teasing, especially when
the conversational version poses no such problem:

But afterwards, as soon as she left, I suddenly saw in the expression of her back, something which struck me, something grasping and

heavy. A sort of terrible determination . . . She was going to the old man, I am certain. Crushing everything in her path. A blind, implacable force. A ballista. (46–7)

Here the narrator's remarks are consistent and plausibly based on conjecture derived from observable facts and, presumably, things that he knows about her already. When compared with the conversational account, the textual version appears to abound in unnecessary contortions and incompatibilities.

What follows aggravates the anomaly still further. Whereas the conversational version allows one to postulate an imaginative leap to justify what the narrator asserts, the textual version maintains its concrete inconsistencies. What L'Alter hears is this:

Listen, but joking apart, this time I think I have got it, that I am on the right track. [. . .] I tell you, I think I see them now: all those currents in them, those flutterings and tremblings. (47–8)

The 'I think' acts as sufficient explanation for the statements that it qualifies. The textual version is not so straightforward:

I can come. She is quiet. I can cling on like a stubborn little lapdog that won't let go. I shall only ever be able to tear off a tiny piece of living matter . . .
He is there, in his study, lurking like a huge spider on the watch; heavy, motionless; he looks all turned in on himself, he is waiting. He stands up as soon as he hears her voice coming from the hallway, her too gentle voice, the one she always has when she talks to the maid, the same one as with me a while ago, a tiny, toneless, strangled voice. He walks quickly across the room and hurries to position himself with his back to the door, in front of the mantlepiece where he pretends to be tidying up his papers. Like her, he has these furtive leaps, these last minute preparations, these speedy recoveries: sometimes one can catch him hurriedly readjusting his face behind the door before one opens it. (35–6)

This is, of course, a much more interesting passage than its conversational equivalent, but it proves almost impossible to coax it into any consistency about the narrator's point of view. The first paragraph can be more or less accounted for as the narrator's hypothesis, with the last four sentences ('I can come' etc.) constituting a sort of metaphorical justification for the assertions that the narrator is making. But what follows is almost a double transgression in that the narrator leaves the daughter and describes the father whom even she cannot see and who is explicitly alone. The extent of this transgression is emphasised by the narrator's self-reference ('the same one as with *me* a while ago'). The last half-sentence although not an explicit self-reference ('*one* can catch him') if taken literally, is still a practical impossibility: on the one hand the information about the way the old man behaves when he is alone is given as if it were the result of direct observation, and on the other the inclusion of information about what someone does when they are alone (even down to indicating where the old man is putting on a mask 'he *pretends* to be tidying up his papers') can only really be attributed to some kind of narrative licence which is incompatible with direct observation. It is precisely this mixture of hypothesis and direct observation which creates the disturbance. We have a narrator who appears limited to a point of view where he can only observe the external appearance of others who may use it as a mask to deceive observers and conceal what goes on within, so that the narrator has no power to tell us about anybody except himself. But there are moments when that narrator is able to tell us with confidence what lies behind the mask of others, and to show that behind all the masks, everybody is prone to the same impulses. It is not clear what enables the narrator to break out of his limited point of view.

The uncertainty about the narrator's basis for his narrative continues to be emphasised as the episode draws to a close:

She stands in the doorway . . . And almost at once it begins between them . . . They uncoil like snakes . . . But I feel that I am beginning to lose my grip, they have got the upper hand, they shake me off on the way, I let go . . . She must be asking for something, he refuses, she insists. It almost certainly has something to do with money. [. . .] There must be the noise of blows, shouts . . . And then silence. A few more doors slammed. A smell of valerian in the narrow corridor . . . It's done . . . Here she is coming out again, with her eyes and cheeks still red. She strides off in a hurry, her back humble and furtive as always. Only her neck straining forward is full of an aggressive rigidity, and

her face looks like a clenched fist: 'What a swine he was', she says to
herself.

She is closed now, walled in on all sides, much stronger than a while
ago. She would not see me, she would not even notice me, this time, if
I was huddled up, like I sometimes am, under the opposite porchway,
my eyes fixed on the double glass doors shining at the far end of the
hallway like black water, waiting for them to appear. Or perhaps she
would just throw me a sideways glance in passing, an amused and
knowing look, if she happened to see me, huddled there in the porchway on the watch. (36–7)

The text here is doubly confusing because it multiplies the
number of vantage-points from which the narrator might plausibly be said to be observing or imagining. Either he is completely off the scene (perhaps still on the bench in the square?),
or he is somewhere in the vicinity (outside the study door?
in the street?). And in addition, the text vacillates between
implied observation or eavesdropping, and implied supposition in relation to the same events: 'She stands in the doorway'
reads like direct observation, whereas 'There *must* be the noise
of blows' reads like a supposition from a vantage-point well
outside the real scene. The disturbance created by the text in
its uncertainties about whether the scene is imagined or observed, and in either case from what position, is not justified
by the needs of the story itself. The conversational version has
none of these ambiguities and manages to harmonise without
contradiction the two narrative positions of limited point of
view and intuitive grasp.

In trying to account for the *invraisemblances* of the narrated
version of the encounter, we should first try to establish what
function the conversation with L'Alter has as an episode in its
own right (beyond the fact that it makes us aware of the pecu-
liarities of the narrational basis of the text). In the conversation
episode the narration itself of the events already described is
presented as constituting a certain kind of action and as having
a certain kind of effect on the narrator's interlocutor. As a
result, the interest is not so much on the events as on their narration, the discourse in which they are related.

L'Alter is first introduced as one of the few people with whom
the narrator can share his language and his vision of the world.

There are not many who 'feel it at once, [who] are well acquainted with it: all these expressions which seem obscure and vaguely indecent to other people, are everyday language between me and them, technical terms which the initiated are familiar with' (19). As one of these people, L'Alter makes it possible for the narrator to use his preferred kind of language without fear of rejection, and the narrator proceeds without inhibition to tell L'Alter of his own ideas concerning the inner life of the old man and his daughter:

I tell you, I think I see them now: all those currents in them, those flutterings and tremblings, those teeming, shameful, cringing desires inside them, what we used to call their 'little demons' you only have to plant one word, one good big image into it all, and as soon as it penetrates, it's like a particle of crystal falling into a supersaturated liquid: everything is suddenly transfixed and goes hard. They get covered by a carapace. They become inert and heavy ... I see them – the old man as well, in spite of his disillusioned airs of a man who has 'understood and forgiven everything', which he always puts on, the old man is just like her, they are the same. (48)

By this stage in the novel we have become initiated into the narrator's special metaphorical language which is the means whereby he tries to convey his view of human nature, and we can see the narrator giving full rein to it here. But it is clear that on this occasion L'Alter is made to feel uncomfortable by it: 'I feel that he does not like it' and 'He seems ill at ease, embarrassed' (48). The intimacy between the two friends is soured by the narrator's insistence on using a language which on this occasion L'Alter cannot accept as the discourse of truth and insight. And the narrator's sense that his language and its corresponding vision are not shared leads to the destruction of the truth which he had thought that they embodied:

Look at it now, my beautiful find, my little 'vision', look what it has become, after we have set upon it once again in our unhealthy games like children or cats: it lies between the two of us now, mutilated, inert and grey, a dead mouse. (51)

The presence of quotation marks around the narrator's discourse and the account of his interlocutor's unfavourable response serve to remind us yet again that the narrator is the

source of a special kind of discourse and that the drama of the
novel lies as much in the fate of his discourse as in the events
that it relates.

Seen in these terms, the two versions of the encounter with the
daughter are better regarded as two consecutive episodes in the
narrative of the narrator's discourse, rather than as two parallel narrations of the same narrative events. In this light, then,
the first episode would appear (narratively speaking) as an
account of the hesitant acquisition of the narrator's discourse,
followed in the second episode by an account of its fate when
put to the test. This view that the episodes constitute a sequence
in the narrative of the narrator's language is confirmed by the
two brief intervening episodes. Both have to do with the evaluation of different kinds of language and are fleetingly alluded to
in the conversation with L'Alter. The first recounts a chance
meeting between the narrator and the old man, where the old
man is shown very aggressively using all kinds of clichés in
order to assure himself of the narrator's vulnerability:

With his subtle intuition he vaguely senses something inside me, a tiny,
frightened animal trembling and huddling deep inside me. He
searches around, like one does with the tip of an iron rod to winkle out
a crab in the cavity of a rock, somewhat at random to begin with:
'Well, still got plans this year? trips abroad? Corsica? Italy? eh? eh?
(37–8)

The old man hides his own vulnerability behind a language of
clichés and banalities which is both a weapon against others
and a protection for himself. In the episode following on from
this one there is a generalised account of the way in which an
anonymous group of women (to which the daughter also
belongs) are able to gather all the clichés in the world around
themselves and turn them into 'this cocoon, this impenetrable
covering, [...] this armour in which they would then step out,
under the benevolent gaze of the concierges' (43). This linguistic armour is not only their chief protection for their vulnerable
inner life, but is also the daughter's most effective weapon in
her confrontations with her father.

As far as the apparent story goes, these scenes have no chronological relation with each other or with what comes before and after them (the two versions of the encounter with the daughter). But if we regard the true narrative as consisting of a sequential account of the adventures of the narrator's own discourse, then it becomes possible to see these four sections as a tale which begins with the narrator's hesitant discovery of the validity of his own discourse, is followed by his increasing confidence in the view that the language of others has little truth value and is merely a strategic cover for the inner life which his own discourse actually seeks to represent, and finally concludes with the (temporary) destruction of this fragile discourse. In other words, this is a tale of consolidation followed by defeat.

The *invraisemblances* in the narrative point of view which are so frequent in this novel can be re-evaluated once we accept that its chief concerns are neither with the events which it recounts nor with the mind of their narrator. If we read the novel as the narrative of the fate of a certain kind of language (its own), conventional questions about the realism of its relations either with its supposed speaker or with its supposed referents will come to have only incidental relevance. The textual coherence that Genette says is the fundamental criterion for the acceptability of a narrative strategy is provided by the drama of this discursive adventure. From the beginning to the end of the novel, the narrator appears not so much as someone with a story to tell, but as someone whose language is on trial, and the very first page of the novel shows that language undergoing its first test. The uncoded, metaphorical language of the narrator is set against the familiar, conventional language of an anonymous *they* in a conversation about someone whom we can retrospectively identify as the old man's daughter. The narrator's words are as follows:

I asked them if they didn't feel like me, if they hadn't sometimes felt something peculiar, a vague emanation, something coming out of her and sticking to them. (15)

Their reply to this question is in a quite different discursive register:

'I find her a bit tiresome', they said to me. 'I find her rather a bore.'

And the following page sees the second round in these discursive hostilities, which open with the narrator asking:

'didn't they find, hadn't they sometimes felt something coming out of her, something soft and sticky, which somehow clung and sucked and which you had to remove and pull off your skin like a damp compress with a stale, sickly smell'. (16)

And 'they' quickly translate these unfamiliar metaphors back into a conventional remark:

'Yes, she seems to set great store by being liked.'

The narrator's own commentary on these exchanges makes it quite clear that the utterances of each party are in conflict with each other. He is trying to insert his own language into the linguistic currency in a manner that will cause as little offence as possible: 'I began by being matter of fact and natural, so as not to startle them' (15). While 'they' are trying to silence the threat that they see this kind of talk as posing:

they rebuffed me at once, with a sharp rap. (15)

it was dangerous, too strong, and they loathed that kind of thing. (16)

they said that to calm me down, to put an end to it, they wanted to call me back to order. (16)

By presenting these two different kinds of language in the form of a conflict, the text is able to make us perceive different discursive registers and, more importantly, it is able to show us the discourses as being, to a certain extent, independent of their respective speakers. The narrator has to manoeuvre his language as carefully as possible in his attempt to get it accepted, and 'they' employ their language as a weapon and a device for maintaining order.

In neither case is it suggested that language is in any way expressive of the minds or emotions of its speakers. The narrator does not express himself through his narration; he is simply the agent responsible for it, and it is not so much he as his language which is the hero of the novel's narrative, from this first encounter with the enemy to the final defeat at the hands of Dumontet's talk of house-prices, home-renovation and the

best way to catch pike. Behind the strangely clumsy realism of
the narrative strategy which is supposed to link the story and
its means of presentation in *Portrait d'un inconnu* there is another narrative at work, where the discourse is not an index
of the narrator's psyche nor simply the vehicle for the plot,
but its chief protagonist.

The missing 'I': 'La jalousie'

The ambiguity of the title of *La jalousie* leads directly to questions concerning its narrative organisation. If we take the title
to refer to the emotion of jealousy, then we must almost inevitably assume that there is an *I* behind the narrative discourse
(although the first-person pronoun never once appears in the
narration), and that it is the jealousy experienced by that absent *I* which motivates the novel's narrative organisation and
provides the *telos* for the whole fiction. If, however, we take
the title to refer to a venetian blind (the other meaning of the
word in French), there is no need to find a speaker for this apparently speakerless narration, and we could assume instead that
the major concern of the novel lies with the exact representation
of external reality (including, for example, a blind). In the
first case we attribute the narration to a narrator-protagonist,
and in the second to a camera, following Norman Friedman's
terminology (1955b). In other words, the ambiguity of the
title forces us to make a choice between almost irreconcilable
narrative strategies: either the narration is inhabited, organised
and motivated by an experiencing mind, or else it is simply
the objective imprint left by the external world, a 'camera
with its shutter open, quite passive, recording, not thinking'
(Friedman, 1955b, 1179).

Both the novel itself and Robbe-Grillet's critical and theoretical writing provide justification for both assumptions.[4] In
support of the 'camera' interpretation, there are actual blinds
in the novel, combined with detailed and apparently wholly

---

[4] For a discussion of these contradictory positions in Robbe-Grillet's theoretical
writings see Heath, 1972, 67–131.

objective descriptions of external reality. This kind of exact and objective description also seems to fulfil the demands made by Robbe-Grillet in his essay 'Nature, humanisme, tragédie' (1963, 45–67), which was originally published in 1958, one year after the appearance of *La jalousie*, and which vehemently denounces the false humanising of objects through metaphor and tragedy. Literature should demonstrate that 'Man looks at the world, and the world does not look back at him' (1963, 53). Description should emphasise the exteriority of things and the world, showing that 'things are there and that they are nothing more than things' (65). Read in the light of this kind of programme, *La jalousie* appears to consist of a sustained sequence of descriptions of a variety of objects (shadows falling on a balcony, a banana plantation, a blind over a window, etc.) whose achievement is indeed to demonstrate that the world is there and that it has no meaning.

Nevertheless, the novel also contains sufficient grounds for suspicion concerning an adulterous affair between the two characters Franck and A . . . to make jealousy an equally appropriate theme. In addition, if we are at all sensitive to the demands of *vraisemblance* we are likely to want to identify the undesignated occupant of the third chair on the balcony, of the third setting at table, to find a recipient for the third glass of cognac and mineral water apéritif, to find a speaker for the implied question about the saltiness of the soup (24) or for the opinions about native truck drivers with which Franck so strongly disagrees. And if we postulate a jealous husband (as the apparently empty chairs and place-settings invite us to do) it seems plausible also to construe him as the source of the narration, and to see hesitations or qualifications in the discourse as signs of his presence, as in 'he murmurs a few words: *doubtless* to thank her' (18, my emphasis). The existence of this narrator makes a far more likely and interesting *telos* for this fiction than the one provided by the camera interpretation, and the theoretical writings include essays which lend ample support for such a view. In writing specifically about the nouveau roman Robbe-Grillet states: 'Objects in our novels have no existence outside human perception, real or imaginary'

(1963, 116). (This remark dates from 1961.) This version of the narrative basis of the novel puts a quite different complexion on the many descriptions of the external world, for it makes everything meaningful as a sign of the narrator's emotional state. 'Robbe-Grillet describes jealousy by letting jealousy describe the world', as one critic has put it (Bersani, 1970, 285).

But if commonsense and the demands of *vraisemblance* encourage us to postulate a jealous husband, his presence in the text can never be more than precarious on account of the crucial absence of an *I* in the narrative discourse. Without this *I* there is no guarantee of his existence.[5] Everything points to the presence of the husband, but nothing confirms it. As Morrissette says, *La jalousie* contains more repetitions of scenes and fragments of scenes than almost any other novel in history (1963, 140), but without the confirmation of the first person in the narration we can never be sure whether the repetitions take place in the narrator's mind (and so become a sign of his obsessions), or whether they take place in the external reality which is organised around routine events and interchangeable objects: meals are always preceded by the same apéritif, Franck's remark about the comfort of the chairs on the veranda becomes customary, A . . . 's brushing her hair is presumably a daily ritual, Franck is always having engine-trouble with his cars and lorries, the work on the banana plantation is routine and repetitive, all the insect noises are the same, all engines are the same (as Franck himself remarks), A . . . 's dressing-table where she sits to brush her hair is exactly like all dressing-tables in colonial houses, etc. But to iron out these uncertainties by opting either for the camera or for the husband is to fail to account for the effect of the absent *I* and to eliminate the central drama of the novel.

By asking ourselves whether the narrative strategy of the novel adequately supports the story it has to tell and judging it purely in terms of its mimetic value, we risk placing unfair

---

[5] Some critics have, however, taken the husband's existence for granted and gone on to explain the absence of the *I* in psychological or thematic terms, e.g. Morrissette, 1963, Bernal, 1964 and Leenhardt, 1973.

limitations on the potential interest of the novel. Instead, we could perhaps turn the question round and ask ourselves how far the *story* mimics the drama of the *narration*, a proposal made by Ricardou in his discussion of *Projet pour une révolution à New York*: 'fiction here is not some pre-existing substance which can be poured into a mould. *It derives from the narrative process* and in a way helps to describe it. Most often, *the fiction is a fiction of the narration.* [...] In a sense, the fiction is an immense metaphor of its narration.' (1971, 219–20, my emphases) In the case of *La jalousie* this would mean that we could retain the camera/narrator ambiguity and see how far it is mirrored or paralleled in the story (or fiction, as Ricardou terms it).

The central question raised by the narrational ambiguity concerns interpretation: are the construction of the novel and the descriptions of objects and events to be read as signs of a deforming vision, or as objective representations of a material and non-signifying world? And it is precisely this uncertainty that is reflected in the jealous husband's interpretation of the world in which he lives, and particularly of the behaviour of A ... and Franck. His activity consists entirely in trying to decide whether what he sees is just what it appears to be, or whether it is a sign of his wife's adultery. This uncertainty is never made explicit in these terms, but in postulating the husband, this is the dilemma that follows from his existence.

The ambiguity is already implicit in the description of the layout of the chairs on the balcony a few pages after the beginning of the novel:

It is she who arranged the chairs, this evening, when she had them brought onto the veranda. The one that she reserved for Franck and her own are next to each other, against the wall of the house – with their backs to this wall, of course – underneath the study window. So that she has Franck's chair on her left, and on her right – but further forward – the little table with the bottles on. The two other chairs have been placed on the other side of the table, even further to the right, so as not to block the view between the two first ones and the balustrade of the veranda. Again because of the 'view', these other two chairs have not been turned towards the rest of the group: they have been put at an angle, sideways on to the openwork balustrade and the

upper end of the valley. This arrangement means that the people sitting in them have to turn their heads right round to the left, if they
want to see A . . . – especially in the case of the fourth chair, furthest
away.

The third one, which is a folding chair made of canvas stretched
over a metal frame is set decidedly further back, between the fourth
one and the table. But it is this less comfortable one which has remained empty. (19–20)

We are clearly being invited to seat a hypostasised husband
in the fourth chair and, having installed him, we then become
alerted to the possibility that the chairs have been arranged
neither by accident nor for the view, but in order to bring
Franck and A . . . close together and to keep the husband at a
distance. This suspicion is reinforced by the sentence preceding
the description of the chairs, where A . . . and Franck are so
close together that Franck's words to A . . . are inaudible:

She rests her other hand on the arm of the chair that Franck is sitting
in and leans towards him, so close that their heads touch. He murmurs
a few words: doubtless to thank her. (18)

Some pages later the usual apéritif is being served on the
balcony. A . . . dispenses three glasses, and so the husband is
once again conjured into being. Immediately afterwards A . . .,
who brought the drinks but not the customary ice-cubes, offers
ice to Franck but makes no move to fetch it herself. We can
plausibly infer that the husband gets up to go in search of it,
since we then read a description of the house as one walks from
the balcony to the pantry; for the laws of reading make it likely
that such a description is motivated by the presence of a character on the scene, in this case, the husband.[6] When he finds that
the boy was just bringing the ice and on his mistress's orders,
the question could occur to the jealous husband: did A . . .
deliberately 'forget' the ice so that she and Franck could be
alone together for a moment? And furthermore, (as later scenes

[6] See Hamon, 1972. He points out that description in a text is almost invariably accompanied by some narrative motivation, very often given in the presence of a
character: 'La description, avant même de commencer, doit [. . .] se justifier, et elle
se caractérise alors par tout un *remplissage* vraisemblablisant destiné à servir d'alibi,
[. . .] (pour introduire la description D il faut introduire un personnage X qui devra
regarder le décor D)' (472).

invite one to speculate) was the husband's absence carefully engineered so that A . . . can pass a letter to Franck? Was it all design or accident? Was it a sign of A . . .'s adultery or was it sheer coincidence? These alternatives exist for nearly every incident concerning A . . . and Franck. Does A . . . accompany Franck to town because she has shopping to do, or does she go in order to be alone with him? Did they spend a night in a hotel (together?) because the car really broke down or are they lying? When A . . . leans inside Franck's car on her return is she picking up a parcel or kissing him? Are they innocent or guilty? Is the narrative a record of suspicion or reality? Is it sign or representation?

This problem is thematised not only in the story of Franck and A . . . but also in the repeated accounts of the native's song that is heard during the course of the novel. The song is disturbing because of its incomprehensibility; it is described as a 'native tune, with incomprehensible words' (99). Is the song merely a series of arbitrary noises or does it have a musical principle behind it?

Because of the special character of this type of melody, it is difficult to determine whether the singing has stopped for some chance reason – to do with the manual work which the singer must be carrying out at the same time, for example – or else whether the tune ended naturally at that point. (100)

At moments, the poem is so unlike what is conventionally called a song, a lament, a refrain, that the western listener is entitled to wonder whether it is not something quite different. In spite of obvious repeats the notes do not seem to be linked by any musical law. Altogether, there is no tune, no melody, no rhythm. It was as if the man was just uttering incoherent fragments to go with his work. (194–5)

Defined as a 'poem' by the text, its meaninglessness seems finally to be confirmed by the repetitions and variants on which it is built. It expresses nothing and refers to nothing:

Doubtless it is still the same poem which continues. Although the themes sometimes get blurred; they come back a little later, strengthened and almost identical. Nevertheless, these repetitions, these tiny variants, these breaks, these flashbacks, can give rise to modifications which – though they are barely perceptible – eventually end up a long way from the starting point. (101)

The poetic effect of the repetitions in the song directly contradicts the psychological effect that many critics have attributed
to the repetitions in the novel. If we postulate the jealous husband as the source of the narrative discourse in the novel, then
its repetitions can be seen as an expression or sign of his obses-
sive jealousy. Or, as Morrissette puts it: 'The repetitions are
transformed, amplified or reduced in line with the inner needs
of the narrator' (1963, 140). And the contrast between the
native's song and the novel about jealousy is emphasised
further by the absence of the singer: it is the *disembodied* voice
of the second driver which is heard (99–100). These contradictions in the interpretation of similar structures in the novel
and the song might very well then lead us to wonder whether,
in reading the narrative as the expression of the husband's
jealousy, we are making it impossible to read it as a 'poem',
as literature.

La jalousie also thematises the implications of the alternative
interpretation of the narration, namely that it is the direct and
undistorted record of events and objects in the external world.
Here the episode of the centipede (episodes?) plays an exemplary role. This is one of the most frequently repeated scenes in
the novel and also has the highest number of variants. As such
it has usually been interpreted as an index of the husband's
mounting jealousy. The husband's supposed interest in the
episode is attributed to possible signs of connivance between
A . . . and Franck. However, one of the major elements of the
episode which has nothing to do with Franck and A . . . concerns the mark left by the centipede after Franck has squashed
it against the wall. The mark is described as being both an exact
and an incomplete representation of the insect:

In order to see the details of the mark clearly, in order to make out
where it came from, it is necessary to get very close to the wall and turn
towards the pantry door. The picture of the squashed centipede
appears then not as a complete drawing, but as a composition of
fragments which are accurate enough for there to be no doubt.
Several of the bits of the body or the appendages have left a flawless
imprint of their outline, and are reproduced as faithfully as an anato-
mical plate: one of the antennae, two curved mandibles, the head and
the first segment, half of the second, three large legs. Then comes the

vaguer outline of the rest: bits of leg and the partial shape of a body convulsed in a question mark. (56)

As an image of the nature of representation, the squashing of the centipede on the wall constitutes a near ideal. The representation is not mediated by an artist or by materials alien to its nature (paint, words, etc.). The trace of the animal is as near to being the thing itself as any realist could dream of. Nevertheless, however faithful and direct a representation, it is not complete, but fragmented.

In emphasising the exactness of the representation of the insect, later versions are equally careful to stress its incompletion. The implication behind these passages is, perhaps, that the ideal of a direct representation of the world can never be fully realised, and that even a plain white wall (or a camera?) can never fully and adequately receive the imprint of reality. This is especially true when we consider the status of the novel itself as a record of the real, for in its own descriptive representation of the mark left on the wall, it constantly draws on analogies borrowed from its own medium – writing: the parts of the insect's body are *printed* on the wall (56), the body is twisted into the form of a *question-mark* (56), the mark looks like *brown ink* (129), and the husband (?) tries to erase it first with a *rubber* and then with the razor-blade which A . . . had already used to scratch out a *word* on a piece of paper. These allusions act as a reminder that however near to the ideal the representation of the centipede on the dining-room wall may be, it is one that the novel itself can never even approach, since the insistent self-reference of writing will always interpose itself between the object and its description.

Another variation on this theme of representation can be seen in the window-pane which looks onto the yard at the back of the house. In the pane of glass we have the classic image of the undistorted representation of reality. The transparency of the glass supposedly guarantees the authenticity of what is seen. In Robbe-Grillet's pane of glass, however, there are flaws which make an exact observation of external reality impossible. In so far as this pane of glass has received any critical attention, it is usually in connection with the husband's uncertainty about whether A . . . exchanges a kiss with Franck on her return from town, for it is through this distorting window that the scene is observed. But most of the passages where the window is mentioned also stress the flaws in its transparency. For example, one of the windows has been opened, with the result that the glass, instead of revealing what lies beyond it, reflects another part of the yard: 'one of the windows, without a speck of dust on its panes, has been opened onto the yard which is, in addition, reflected in one half of it' (57). It may be spotlessly clean, but in mirroring the yard this window's relation with reality becomes decidedly oblique.

There are also a number of small flaws in the glass which pervert and distort the picture that appears through it:

> In the left half, the reflected landscape is more vivid although it is also darker. But it is distorted by faults in the glass, so that round spots or crescent shapes of greenery, the colour of the banana trees, wander about in the middle of the yard in front of the sheds.
>
> Although it has been cut into by one of these moving rings of foliage, the large blue saloon nevertheless remains recognisable, as does A . . .'s dress, standing next to the car. (57–8)

The glass, instead of mediating the whole landscape that lies beyond it, distorts it by breaking it into fragments and rearranging them so that bits of banana plantation are brought into the yard, and Franck's car is made to incorporate a ring of leaves. This kind of distortion can be read as a *mise en abyme* of the whole construction of *La jalousie*, and is particularly pertinent in these pages where the text passes to and fro between two apparently unconnected scenes. But apart from this specific self-reference of the *mise en abyme*, the window-pane passages can be read as articulating the theme of representation which derives from the ambiguity of the narrative base.

The impossibility of ever achieving a full and adequate representation of anything is outlined here by the way in which the medium (glass) can be seen to actively intervene in its mediation of reality. Not only does it distort and rearrange reality, but it actually draws or inscribes its own images onto that reality:

> Beyond the coarse and spotlessly clean glass, there is only the pebbly

yard, and then, rising towards the road and the edge of the plateau, the green mass of the banana trees. The flaws in the glass *draw* moving circles in their uniform foliage. (55, my emphasis)

The circular shapes perceived in the banana trees are constructed and projected by the glass, not transmitted by it from without. And later on, these shapes are used to obliterate the reality which lies beyond the window. There is a patch of oil on the ground in the yard which the glass can completely wipe out by interposing itself between the outside world and the spectator within:

It is easy to make this mark disappear by using the flaws in the very coarse glass in the window: it just takes a bit of trial and error to bring the blackened surface into one of the blind spots in the pane.

The mark begins by getting wider, as one of its sides bulges to make a round protuberance which is larger than the original object. But, a few millimetres further on, the bulge is transformed into a series of thin concentric crescent shapes, which are then reduced to mere lines, while the other side of the mark retracts leaving behind a stalk-shaped appendage. This swells in turn for a moment; then everything suddenly disappears.

Beyond the pane, in the angle between the central upright and the cross-piece, there is only the dusty grey-brown gravel which covers the ground in the yard. (126–7)

Again, the novel could be seen to be talking about itself: just as the glass succeeds in wiping out the oil patch by interposing its supposedly transparent self, so one could say that the writing of the novel succeeds in effacing or distorting the things that seem to exist beyond it. Instead of allowing us to perceive an emotional and mental source for the narrative and to get a picture of a banana plantation in the colonies, it casts in doubt the dual concepts of expressivity (behind writing) and representation (of a reality beyond writing). The absence of the *I*, in particular, succeeds in ensuring a void which Robbe-Grillet himself has called an 'organising void',[7] or what Blanchot identifies as the 'absence which allows everything to be said, everything to be seen' (1959, 200).

[7] *Robbe-Grillet*, 1976, II, 195. In this discussion Robbe-Grillet describes his first three novels as variations on the theme of the void: 'Quand je repense aux *Gommes*, au *Voyeur*, à *La jalousie*, ce qui me frappe, c'est une approche croissante de ce qu'est ce vide central de l'oeuvre' (194).

It does indeed seem that if we accept the ambiguity of the narrative organisation of this novel we may encounter a void in realist terms, but we also benefit from seeing whole new areas of the text to come into focus. The profound unrealism of the ambiguity in the novel allows us to hear the articulation of themes through which it meditates on its own existence as a text.

Free indirect speech as language on the loose: 'Vous les entendez?'

Free indirect speech is a narrative style which is generally regarded as being a major feature of modern fiction. Flaubert is conventionally cited as an early master of the style which later came into its own in the novels of Virginia Woolf, William Faulkner and James Joyce. Known by many names (*style indirect libre* in French, *erlebte Rede* in German, with 'free indirect style', 'quasi-direct discourse', 'narrated monologue' and 'free indirect discourse' as English variants),[8] the presence of free indirect speech in a novel is usually only intermittent and, strictly speaking, cannot be classified as a narrative strategy. It does, nevertheless, lend itself to being exploited by the largely modern strategies which Friedman categorises as 'multiple selective omniscience' and 'selective omniscience', and its extensive use in the narrative economy of so much modern fiction justifies its inclusion in a discussion of narrative discourse.

Its values for the fiction of the late nineteenth and early twentieth centuries lay in the increased effacement of the author that it allows, and in the extension of psychological realism that its use can imply. Pascal sees it as one of the many devices developed by novelists to help them in what he regards as their central creative purpose, the presentation of the 'inner life, the mental and emotional activities and responses of their invented characters' (1977, 2). He sees it as having advantages over other devices such as epic monologue, first-person narration (retrospective or present-tense), epistolary forms, and other

[8] For a survey of the history and practical use of this concept see Pascal, 1977. McHale, 1978, has a more extensive and theoretical account of what he calls 'free indirect discourse'.

such realist strategies, in that it does not entail either a restriction in point of view or unwanted psychological side-effects, such as excessive self-consciousness. In this way, free indirect speech apparently lends itself to the requirements of realist motivations for narrative discourse as a representation of the inner life.

Grammatically speaking free indirect speech uses the tense and pronoun of a third-person narrative, but in its use of deictics (*here, now, this,* etc.) it corresponds to the character's (and not the narrator's) situation and point of view. The last sentence of the following lines from Virginia Woolf's *To the Lighthouse* (also quoted and discussed in Banfield, 1973) provide a typical example of free indirect speech, and the presence of both direct speech and straightforward third-person narration in the preceding sentence act as good points of comparison:

'It must have been fifteen – no, twenty years ago – that I last saw her', she was saying, turning back to him again as if she could not lose a moment of talk, for she was absorbed by what they were saying. So he had actually heard from her this evening! (100)

The temporal orientation of the words 'this evening' together with the expressive implications of the exclamation mark act as markers of the character's point of view; on the other hand, the pluperfect 'had heard' belongs to the temporal sequence of the narration proper. Neither author nor character says *I* and so the text is not burdened with the occasionally embarrassing consequences of the first person, and yet, at the same time, the impression of speech conveys a sense of psychological and emotional immediacy. Free indirect speech does seem, then, to doubly fulfil contemporary requirements for narrational realism.

But this duality is also the source of a gross *invraisemblance*. 'We hear in "style indirect libre" a dual voice, which, through vocabulary, sentence structure, and intonation subtly fuses the two voices of the character and the narrator', says Pascal (1977, 26); and the title of his book, *The Dual Voice*, suggests that he sees this duality as the very essence of free indirect speech. It is not simply that sentences and paragraphs can be carved up on the basis of grammatical markers and redistributed between narrator and character, but rather that those markers act as a sign that every element of the narrative discourse has two potential origins. Voloshinov speaks in this context of the 'double intonation' of *each word* (1973, 156), and suggests that this duality ultimately prevents free indirect speech from being read as the record of an actual voice. Although a narrator's evaluation of a character's utterance can be conveyed by voice when the narrator's view is dominant, it is the ambiguity and to-and-fro between narrator and character that constitutes the essence of free indirect speech and makes a vocal rendering of it impossible. It is for this reason that free indirect style occurs chiefly in a 'silent register', namely the discourse of prose fiction. 'Only this "silencing" of prose could have made possible the multileveledness and voice-defying complexity of intonational structures that are so characteristic for modern literature' (Voloshinov, 1973, 156). Many writers on free indirect speech acknowledge its exclusively literary existence (e.g. Bally, 1914 and, by implication, Banfield, 1973), and although the explanations given tend to vary, it seems reasonable to argue that it is precisely the ambiguity or indeterminacy of its vocal origin that marks it as written, literary and finally *invraisemblable*.

These indeterminate origins of free indirect speech could be used as support for Derrida's attack on what he calls the metaphysics of presence. We commonly imagine, he says, that the voice expresses the soul, that meaning is present in the voice, that the 'voice is closest to the signified, whether one defines it strictly as meaning [. . .] or more loosely as thing' (1967, 22). This phonocentrism (as Derrida dubs it) is the root-cause of what he sees as a fundamental misconception about the nature and organisation of language, and of written language in particular. Writing is commonly and wrongly regarded as being secondary to speech, a derivative and debased form of speech, as the 'external representation of language and of this "thought-sound"' (47). Derrida's argument is that language (with writing as a primary and not a derivative linguistic form) is a system based on differences, and this view is designed to replace the false conception of language as having its source in the soul. As a certain kind of writing, free indirect speech certainly seems a pertinent example of the conception that Derrida is trying to put over, for the indeterminacy of its origins makes it impossible to decide whose mind or soul lies behind it, whether narrator or character is present in it. If this style prevents us from tracking down a mind behind it, from finding even an illusory inhabitant for it, then, for all its apparent gains in narrational realism, it must be regarded as being finally non-representational, as a product of literary writing.

Indeed, the representational status of free indirect speech is further vitiated by ambiguities in what it refers to, for it can convey actual words uttered by a character, *or* thoughts which are privately voiced in the mind, *or* thoughts and feelings which are experienced by the character but never articulated in language; but it is never obliged to make clear which of these is the case in any given instance. This word–thought–feeling confusion on which free indirect speech rests has the effect of undermining the distinction between *diegesis* and *mimesis* which is one of the oldest in critical discourse and goes back as far as Plato.[9] *Diegesis* consists in the representation of objects, events, and actions, whereas *mimesis* consists in the representation of actual utterances. *Diegesis* concerns things (*de re*) and *mimesis* concerns speech (*de dicto*), but in free indirect speech this distinction cannot always be made. Consider, for example, the following phrase from Virginia Woolf's *Mrs Dalloway*: 'but here the other clock [...] came shuffling in with its lap full of odds and ends' (141).[10] The ambiguity of the style prevents us from paraphrasing it and making decisions as to whether this is an unarticulated perception, or a verbalised thought, or (although here commonsense and context make it less likely) an actual utterance. We cannot rewrite the sentence in any other terms because we cannot tell whether it should take the form:

[9] These terms have been used and reworked in a variety of ways (e.g. Genette, 1969, 50–6), but it is in Plato's original sense that I shall be using them here, although at the risk of creating a confusion between 'mimesis' in the wider sense of representation, and '*mimesis*' in Plato's restricted sense of 'dramatic representation' or 'dialogue'. See Cornford, 1941, 78–80.

[10] This sentence is also quoted and discussed by Banfield (1973, 33).

She saw the other clock come shuffling in.

or:

She thought, 'Here comes the other clock shuffling in.'

or:

She said, 'Here comes the other clock shuffling in.'

In this way free indirect speech denies us absolute certainty about what is being referred to. Free indirect speech proves, then, to be a doubly disconcerting use of language; it is, as it were, cut adrift from the two points at which we like to imagine language anchored to reality, the speaker and the referent. Seen in this light, it would seem fruitless to pursue a discussion concerning its role in promoting narrational realism.

An examination of Nathalie Sarraute's *Vous les entendez?* should give us a chance to discover some other function for free indirect speech in the narrative discourse of fiction, since, in his study of Sarraute, Newman has claimed that free indirect speech amounts to a fundamental principle of writing in the novels (1976, 99). The discussion of the narrative organisation of *Vous les entendez?* in Chapter 1 above demonstrated that its effect was not primarily realistic, and so it would seem reasonable to assume that if free indirect speech does constitute its basic principle, the discourse of the novel is unlikely to be predominantly a realistic one.

The following passage may serve as a source of examples for further analysis:

1. — Believe it or not, not everyone agrees with you. They don't agree with you at all . . . The other man removes his pipe from his mouth, holds it in his raised hand. . . — Who, for example? — Well, Gautrand. . . Believe it or not, he examined the animal very closely, and he found . . . he thought it was more something from a late epoch, copied from a popular model. Anyway, he wasn't specially excited by it. . . — Well, well . . . the friend replaces the stem of his pipe between his teeth, there is surprise in his still, attentive gaze . . . It must be that excited tone suddenly, that sudden aggression in his voice which he finds a bit strange . . . What do

you care about what Gautrand thinks? He's always so afraid of being
wrong, of not being taken for a connoisseur . . . late epoch or not . . .
Copy or not . . . I think you just have to look . . . He stretches out
his plump hand and places it calmly on the animal's back . . . —
Are you sure about it? You really think so? But Gautrand has
exploded lots of false values . . . his voice trembles . . . He knows
more about it than most people . . . and I must say that sometimes I
wonder too . . .

2.   The friend quickly withdraws his hand, there is fear as well as
surprise in his eyes . . . the dismay of someone who thought he was
with a friend and who all of a sudden sees his expression, his voice,
his tone change, who suddenly feels the sharp chill of handcuffs
on his wrist, hears the click, cannot believe his senses . . . struggles . . .
— But I don't understand . . . A moment ago you yourself . . . you
said to me . . . He hears a slight snigger . . . — But who am I? But
what evidence have I given? Have I ever discovered anything
like Gautrand? Do I have collections? Look . . . when I turn it
round this way now I think it looks a bit funny too . . . facile, no?
ha, ha, a bit vulgar? . . . Don't look at me like that. I am not so
sure of having absolute taste . . . I could be wrong, eh? Why not?
I'm quite ready to admit it. I'm quite ready to submit . . . Don't
look so shocked. I'm modest, quite ready to repudiate my mistakes
in the past. I bow to authority when it's in the right. I wonder how
I could have . . .

3.   I must have been crazy to leave my nearest and dearest, to break
such tender ties and worship this wretched thing, go into ecstasies
over this rubbish . . . But it's over. No more heartbreak. No more
wrenches. I am one of you, you over there. You my nearest and
dearest, you my family . . . They come running up . . . they take me
in their arms . . . Yes, you see, we're with you, we won't leave each
other again, we've made it up . . . No, don't squeeze me like that . . .
No, let go of me, I don't want to, I'm frightened . . . no, leave it,
don't take it away from me, I am fond of the animal after all, you
understand . . . If I give it up . . . Don't touch it, it's sacred. I'm
ready to defend it . . . For it . . .

4.   They gently loosen their fingers, they lift it up and turn it round
under the light . . . a wretched thing . . . their strong, gentle hands
hold him back . . . He stammers . . . A wretched thing . . . Yes, it's
true . . . Did you know? — But of course we knew. It sticks out a
mile, come on. Forget it, leave, look at us. He is surrounded by
their fresh happy faces, their fresh laughter splashes him . . . Aren't
they charming . . . they don't need to study early or late epochs,
one look is enough for them . . .

5.   Their mobile, agile, light minds leap, allow themselves to be
tossed about, swept along by anything that moves, opens out,

breaks up, slips, whirls, disappears, returns ... slow, almost imperceptible apparitions ... sudden appearances, unexpected shocks, repetitions with endless nuances ... reflections ... mottlings ... there is nothing that they find more repellent than standing still, settling down, letting themselves be filled up and dozing off with the blissful smile of a well-fed baby ... everything you want, everything you yearn for, you poor old fool ... But don't think about it any more, give it up, come, throw yourself headlong like us. (82–5)

The first paragraph can be fairly easily divided into different discursive categories, with dialogue (*mimesis*) and narrative (*diegesis*) predominating. The exchange between the father and his old friend concerning Gautrand's opinion seems relatively unproblematic:

FATHER: Believe it or not, not everyone agrees with you.
FRIEND: Who for example?
FATHER: Well, Gautrand.
FRIEND: Well, well ... What do you care about what Gautrand thinks?

The elements of narrative help to identify the speakers in this exchange and provide a 'real' context for the conversation: 'the other man removes his pipe from his mouth' and so on. Here we do not need to ask who is speaking, since the impersonal voice of narrative itself as the record of the real constitutes sufficient justification for the presence of these observations.

There is, however, an ambiguous sentence halfway through the paragraph: 'It must be that excited tone suddenly, that sudden aggression in his voice which he finds a bit strange' ('C'est ce ton excité tout à coup, cette agressivité subite dans la voix qui doivent lui apparaître un peu étranges'). The deictics 'ce' and 'cette' and the supposition implied in the word 'must' ('doivent') indicate that this sentence could be read as an instance of free indirect speech, giving the father's point of view. (As the novel is narrated in the present tense and as there is no pronoun referring to the father here, the primary grammatical markers of free indirect speech are not present in this instance.) On the whole, then, this is a relatively straightforward paragraph which through its clear distinctions between *mimesis* and *diegesis* allows us to reconstruct an apparently stable reality of words and gestures which tallies with the core of *données* which constitutes the realist base of the novel: the two old men sitting after dinner admiring the sculpture while the children go upstairs to bed. The potentially disruptive effect of the free indirect speech on the representation of reality is not developed until later on in the passage.

The second paragraph opens with a seemingly unproblematic piece of *diegesis:* 'The friend quickly withdraws his hand, there is fear as well as surprise in his eyes'. But the rest of the sentence with its sustained metaphor interpreting the look in the friend's eyes does raise problems. The introduction of the metaphor into the narrative discourse makes us ask whose view it conveys: the narrator's? the father's? the friend's? But this novel has no identifiable narrator who might be persuaded to accept responsibility for the metaphorical discourse. And yet it is not explicitly attributed either to the father or to the friend by means of a phrase like 'it appeared to the father to be the confusion of someone who . . . etc.' Although the sentence has none of the strict grammatical features (such as deixis) that would enable us to categorise it as free indirect speech, its ambiguity, like that of most free indirect speech, derives from the fact that it is not embedded, so that, even if we do not classify this as free indirect speech proper, its ambiguities allow us to see it as a cognate form of discourse.

The passage returns briefly to utterance ('But I don't understand . . . A moment ago you yourself . . . you said to me') and narrative ('He hears a slight snigger'). But the long utterance from the father which follows is so theatrical in tone and so deviant from the norms of politeness which the situation would encourage one to regard as appropriate, that its status as *mimesis* can be called into question: 'But who am I? What evidence have I given? Have I ever discovered anything like Gautrand?' etc. This does in fact appear to be an utterance rather than a verbalised thought or an articulation of a certain state of mind, but because its tone is such an unlikely one for the context in which it appears, its validity as a record of an actual utterance is cast into doubt. It is perhaps best classified as *pseudo-mimesis*. As such it cuts across the *mimesis–diegesis* distinction in just the same way as free indirect speech does, and may therefore be regarded as another cognate form of this ambiguous style.

The third paragraph begins with what are probably voiced thoughts on the part of the father: 'I must have been crazy' etc. But since this does not carry any speech marks and is not introduced as either speech or thought, there is a potential (although not very powerful) source of ambiguity here too. The presence of the word *you* in the following lines suggests that we are dealing with a voiced utterance: 'I am one of you, you over there,' etc. But there is no clear demarcation that would allow us to be sure that the previous statements are not also voiced aloud or that these apparently voiced utterances are not also thoughts. But whatever the extent of the ambiguity, the utterance has the same hyperbolic and theatrical tone as the previous one, and since the children (to whom these utterances are addressed) did not appear to be present at the beginning of the scene, this passage qualifies as another instance of *pseudo-mimesis*.

For the same reason 'They come running up' must be regarded as *pseudo-diegesis*. The final part of the sentence 'they take me in their arms' would, in principle, also seem to be *pseudo-diegesis* but its anomalous status is exacerbated by the presence of the first-person pronoun. Any term coined to classify this form is likely to be clumsy (*voiced pseudo-diegesis?*) but it is worth identifying as a further category of discourse which, like free indirect speech, blurs the basic distinction between *diegesis* and *mimesis*.

Paragraph five introduces another problematic form created by the presence of highly figurative language which is superficially an utterance attributable to the father, but this attribution is awkward since to regard him as the source of it would be to ascribe to him an articulateness that is thematically and narratively speaking inappropriate. Like the other forms identified above, these metaphors constitute an unrealistic language similar to free indirect speech in that they combine a character's view of things with an obscured source of articulation.

What, then, should we conclude from this identification of

these various types of discourse? If we inventory them again briefly, we find that they fall roughly into two groups, the conventional and the anomalous:

conventional	anomalous
mimesis	free indirect speech
diegesis	pseudo-mimesis
	pseudo-diegesis
	voiced pseudo-diegesis
	metaphor

All of the discourse-types in the second group can be seen as variants of free indirect speech in so far as they share its problematic relation to reality, although strictly speaking they do not share its grammatical features. In this sense, Newman is right to differentiate between free indirect speech as a syntactic form and as a principle of writing, and the above analysis certainly vindicates his claim that his usually incidental style does indeed amount to a principle of writing in Sarraute's fiction.

This claim is all the more valid when the overall function of these anomalous styles is pinpointed. In the passage in question the elaboration of the different styles and the narrative itself grow out of the opening conversation about Gautrand the art expert which is reported in the conventional alternation of *mimesis* and *diegesis*. What follows in the narrative (the father's betrayal of his friend and their shared culture, and the children's ultimate rejection of his new allegiance to them and their modern culture) might or might not be 'real'. We cannot tell whether it is imagined, and if so by whom, or whether it is simply a hypothesis explored by the text. But whatever its ontological status, its chief function is to alert us to the hidden implications and consequences of the opening conversation. We learn that the father is not simply reporting the verdict of an expert, but that his quoting of this verdict is motivated by a radical shift of allegiance from the world of traditional cultural values to the one represented by his children. The remarks about Gautrand are the means whereby he deserts his friend and tries to buy his way into the children's camp.

The narrative is not constructed in the conventional forms of *diegesis* and *mimesis*, but only in the anomalous styles associated with free indirect speech. The innocent authority of *diegesis* and *mimesis* is at odds with the revelation of the crimes that are committed under their disguise, and has to be deconstructed by the anomalous discourses which lack the authority of either speaker or stable referent. These unauthoritative discourses act as a comment on the conventional discourse of the opening paragraph and show that the reality to which the *diegesis* refers (a reality of gestures where pipes are pulled from mouths, hands extended) has no interest or significance, and that the relation of speakers to their language in *mimesis* is a distant and indirect one, that the actions of *diegesis* mean nothing and that *mimesis* is itself an action.

The anomalous discourses act as a comment on other discourses by making us aware that language is never fully inhabited by its speakers and never fully adequate as a representation of reality. In so doing they prove that their own apparently anomalous status is in fact the norm and that it is only by loosening the illusory ties binding speakers to their language and language to the world that we can find significance or value in it. In the case of Nathalie Sarraute, at least, free indirect speech (as the best-known and perhaps the most exemplary of these anomalous discourses) is one of the most powerful tools with which the texts can explore and construct the dramas that come into being when we open our mouths in the hope of describing the world or expressing ourselves.

First-, second- and third-degree narrative: 'Degrés'

Michel Butor's *Degrés* seems at first sight to be simply the 'description of a class' as Pierre Vernier, narrator of Part I and teacher of the lesson in question, describes his enterprise (16). The opening lines of the novel conform to reasonable expectations about just such a description:

I walk into the classroom, and I step up on to the dais.
    When the bell stops ringing, I take out of the briefcase which I have just put on the desk the alphabetical list of pupils, and this other

sheet of white paper, on which they themselves have marked their places inside this room.

Then I sit down, and when there is silence, I begin to call the register.

This kind of account would not normally be expected to give rise to any special problems in the narration; the narrator simply gives a blow-by-blow account of the events that take place while he is in a certain place for a certain length of time.

But as the paragraphs of this first page unfold, factors are introduced which will ultimately prevent the execution of this description on the simple chronological lines which structure the opening of the novel. These are the introduction of the second person ('I do not recognise them yet, except for the few who were with me last year, *you* in particular, Pierre'), the references to family ties between the pupils (the Pierre whom Vernier addresses is his nephew), and a brief allusion to what is going on next door (Henri Jouret, Pierre Eller's other uncle, is taking a class in French literature). The following section introduces a fourth major disruptive element by alluding to other events and lessons that have taken place in the past. By linking the writing to systems outside the strict chronology of the present lesson these four factors succeed in disrupting the whole project, and the account apparently promised in the opening lines is never realised in the novel. In fact there are very few further allusions to Vernier's actual lesson, and when the bell rings at the end of the lesson (383), the narration is in the hands of another narrator (Henri Jouret) and the reference is quickly submerged and lost among the other narratives which the original description engendered and finally succumbs to.

It becomes increasingly clear during the course of the novel that the documentary basis on which we assume description to rest is unrealisable. Just as maps cannot accurately record the physical world, so there is no purely documentary language into which the hour's lesson on the discovery of America could be translated:

I tried to get you to understand that it is impossible to represent the earth accurately without distorting it, just as it is impossible to transfer reality into speech without using a certain kind of projection, a certain system of references, the form and organisation of which depend on what one is trying to demonstrate, and, as a corollary, what one needs to know. (56)

Intelligibility is incompatible with documentary record, and it is primarily the need to make the record of the hour intelligible which lies behind the introduction of the various 'systems of references' which take over the way in which the writing is organised. The hour itself disappears in the network of systems which structure the way in which we make sense of it, until finally it exists simply as a pivot (Vernier speaks of 'this pivotal lesson', 62) an organising absence. The simple narration-story construction is impossible to maintain, for, to make sense of it, there must also be other stories and other narrations, and Butor's novel consists of a to-and-fro between these multiple constructions.

One of the most important systems which structures the writing of the novel is the narration itself. The introduction of a first-person narrator is, according to Butor, doubly justifiable. First, it acknowledges the fact that, in so far as they are told at all, all narratives are told in the first person: 'Every time there is narrative in the novel, the three persons of the verb are bound to be involved: two real persons: the author telling the story, who is the equivalent of the "I" in ordinary conversation, the reader who is being told the story, the "you", and a fictitious person, the hero, the person who the story is being told about, the "he"' (1964, 61). Secondly, there is a 'step forward in realism, through the introduction of a point of view' (62). The introduction of the first person ought, then, at least in theory, to simplify the narration because it coincides with, and indeed endorses the way in which all stories are told. However, once the narrator has been introduced into the text, other things follow and need to be added to the text: 'As soon as one introduces a narrator, one needs to know how his writing is related to his adventure' (64). In the case of Pierre Vernier the relation between his writing and his adventure (the lesson) comes to require more and more space in the text, to the detriment of the adventure itself.

Originally, the proposed description is intended to provide a solution to a personal problem. As Pierre Eller puts it: 'you began to think about the year that was about to begin, about the life of loneliness and sterility which awaited you. You had two ways of getting out of it: literature or marriage.' (162) Vernier chooses literature in preference to, and ultimately, at the expense of marriage. The consequences of Vernier's writing are frequently brought into focus in the context of his relationship with Micheline Pavin. In the early stages of their friendship, Vernier's literary project brings them closer to each other as they discuss it together and Micheline encourages him. Then Vernier asks her to sanction his enterprise by ordering him to write, which she does. But as time goes on the demands of writing come increasingly into conflict with the demands of friendship. Vernier defers saying *tu* to Micheline until his writing is going smoothly; the time that work on the writing takes up is time taken away from Micheline; and the systems he uses to organise his writing begin to make cumulative demands on his time. For example, the presentation of teachers and pupils in triadic groups based on family relationships (like uncles and nephews) is a system which becomes harder and harder to sustain, requiring more and more effort and research into family background. In addition, the location of Vernier's class on the discovery of America in the context of other classes both past and present on other subjects involves him in a potentially inexhaustible amount of reading. And the consequences of these demands affect not only his relationship with Micheline but also his efficiency as a teacher and, in the end, his health too. Henri Jouret says that it is Vernier's project that is the cause of his death at the end of the novel. Addressing his nephew Pierre Eller, Jouret writes: 'You do not know that the book is for you and that he is dying of it' (384). These narratives of love and death leave us in no doubt as to the way in which the narrator's writing is related to his adventure and suggest even that the writing is achieved at the cost of the adventure which it originally set out to narrate.

The 'natural' presence of the second person, the *you*, in the system of narration interferes in a similar way with the narrative which it supposedly serves and supports. To introduce a second person into a novel is, in the first place, simply to acknowledge that all narratives are addressed to a reader. Furthermore, for Butor, the presence of the second person allows the novel to make explicit its didactic function which he regards as inherent in the genre, and he describes the twentieth-century novel as a 'new kind of poetry which is both epic and didactic' (1960, 11). The ignorance which justifies the telling of most tales invites the use of the second person, a solution which is carried to radical extremes in *La modification*.

The *you* of the first and third parts of *Degrés*, Pierre Eller, is repeatedly defined as ignorant, and this ignorance organises and orientates Vernier's narrative:

I am writing for you (60)

to help you see what you were yourself, and so where you come from, and so which direction you are going in, what the vector of your present is. (118)

The narrative becomes intelligible only when it abandons the unrealisable aims of documentary description to become a form of address. But in orientating his narrative towards Eller, Vernier needs the active co-operation of his nephew. He needs Eller to provide him with information about things that Vernier cannot know, and he increasingly involves his nephew in research on his behalf. Eller is sent to seek out information that will become part of the writing that is to be addressed to him. In due course this apparently simple provision of information comes to affect Eller's life, if only in small details at first. For example, meeting his uncle after morning lessons to tell him what he knows makes him late for lunch and so gets him into trouble with his father. And the more Eller becomes involved in actually seeking out the information that his uncle needs, the more his life is affected by it. He is increasingly suspected by his friends of spying on them and when he is finally directly accused and his allegiance put to the test he symbolically walks out of his uncle's class: the information-gathering that was supposed to make possible his uncle's didactic narrative leads him into a situation where he can no longer accept his uncle's didactic function as a teacher (382). The demands of Vernier's writing which begin with the simple, more or less logical presence of a *you* finally deprive him of the friendship of his nephew and a factual base for his narrative. Again, factors inherent in the narrational dimension of the novel succeed in distorting, if not destroying the reality that it narrates.

The *I–you* axis of the narration in *Degrés* is even more complicated than this account suggests, because in each of the three parts of the novel the *I* refers to a different person, and for different reasons. In Part I *I* refers to Pierre Vernier, and *you* to Pierre Eller. In Part II, *I* refers to Pierre Eller and *you* to Pierre Vernier. In Part III *I* refers to Henri Jouret, *you* to Pierre Eller again, and the dying Vernier is referred to as *he*. Rendered schematically, the pronominal system looks like this:

	Part I	Part II	Part III
Vernier	*I*	*you*	*he*
Eller	*you*	*I*	*you*
Jouret	*he*	*he*	*I*

The alternation of pronominal roles is not entirely symmetrical and it is only Vernier who is allotted all three persons. Eller is twice *you*, once *I* and never *he*. Jouret (whose role is relatively insignificant in the pronominal systems of Parts I and II) is twice *he*, once *I* and never *you*. These pronominal transformations are another of the major organising systems that lie behind the writing of *Degrés*, and the writing is at one stage described as a *conjugation* : Eller speaks of the need for a change of narrator in the 'conjugation of this work' (277). But most importantly, it is made quite clear that in this conjugation, the distribution of pronouns does not always correspond to the real positions of the characters. Eller is not 'really' the narrator of Part II despite the fact that he says *I*, and the introduction of Jouret as the ostensible narrator of Part III only makes more pertinent the question asked by the dying Vernier on which the novel closes: 'Qui parle?'

The conjugation of the text shares with its other organising systems the function of drawing our attention to the fictional basis of the novel. These systems do not only serve to make it intelligible, but also proclaim the novel's fictionality. Very early on in the novel Vernier concedes that hypothesis and imagination must inevitably determine and construct his documentary enterprise. He tells of the moment when he began his task of narration:

I began to write these notes, [...] these notes which at that point I wanted to be a literal description, without any imaginative intervention, a simple record of precise facts, which would not have allowed me to give an adequate representation at all,

for, in order to describe the space in which these facts occur, and without which it is impossible to reveal them, one has to imagine an enormous number of others which are impossible to verify [...]

imagine this class in describing it, just as simply seeing it before I also imagined it, seeing you listening to me, but without realising it. (53–4)

Imagination does not simply supplement the verifiable, but actually lies at the base of description, and even perception itself.

Vernier's narration in Part I shows him more and more willing to acknowledge, accept and exploit the part played by fiction in his so-called description:

not only do I have to imagine for you, but I need to imagine for myself; the words that I have written or utter when I say 'This is all I know', even these words only mean something to me because I know so many other things, because so many other things are present at various degrees of historicity;

this fact which is like a nail holding down my text and stopping it from losing its way, exists ultimately for me, for you, for all of us, only because it appears as a focus in the midst of a whole zone of imagination and probability.

and this imagination is all the stronger and all the truer because I can link this moment in your uncle's life, by means of grammatical or other categories to other moments,

this man to other men, this place to other places, this quotation to the rest of the tragedy, this tragedy to others by Racine, this fragment of culture to others,

and so bring some light in the midst of the tremendous confusion where we struggle, a little light which is cast on this instant, which makes it visible, observable, which is reflected on this instant to illuminate the obscure present a little. (117)

Imagination makes irrelevant the factuality of facts, is the only means whereby links can be made between things and so bring light into the darkness and confusion of experience.

It is for this reason that we can be encouraged to recognise the fictionality of the present tense of the narration and see that the opening words of the novel 'I walk into the classroom' are not the guarantee of documentation but a supreme fiction because the moment when they are written is so far removed from the moment to which they refer, and the novel's painstaking precision about dates paradoxically confirms this. As Vernier (but is it Vernier?) has Eller write:

I say now, but it is not really now, just as it is not really me writing; it is a long time since this hour ended and this present tense that I am using is like the support of a bridge linking up these other presents. (186)

The *I* of the narration is not really itself, and its present tense is illusory; and this double fiction serves to explode the narrational realism of the novel. It is the didactic function again which makes necessary this switch to the fictional first person:

To help you to see what you were yourself, and so where you come from, and so which direction you are going in, what the vector of your present is, I must make a tremendous effort of systematic imagination, reconstruction, hypothesis, I must put myself in your place, I must try and see myself through your eyes, and so I must let you speak, which will upset the balance of this narrative. (118)

It is not just the equilibrium of the narrative that is upset by this fictional *I* but the realism of the novel. Nevertheless, the text seems quite happy to live with this fiction as a fiction and is not concerned about the *invraisemblances* which ensue from it. For example, it is in Part II, ostensibly narrated by Pierre Eller, that the bulk of the account of Pierre Vernier's friendship with Micheline Pavin is given, and the boy is given the task of writing about events which, realistically speaking, he cannot know of. It is the fifteen-year-old Eller who tells us that Vernier and Micheline ate grilled lobster together in Greece at a time when he himself was on holiday with his parents in France. He tells us when Vernier thinks of Micheline and what he thinks of her. All that Micheline and Vernier say together in private is narrated by the boy, and yet it is not this kind of *invraisemblance* which finally puts an end to the designation of Pierre Eller as *I*.

On one level it is the change in the relationship between Eller and Vernier which makes the use of the first person for Eller seem a fraud and a lie. It is real events in the timescale of the narration (dated here 11 October 1955: that is, exactly one year after the 'pivotal lesson') which alter the pronominal form that the narration takes. But on another level, it is the fictionality of Pierre Eller as *you* as well as *I* which justifies the shift to the even more fictional pronominal system which structures the narration of Part III. Significantly, it is Eller's fictional *I* which alerts us to the fictional status of the *you* to whom Vernier addresses his narrative. The person addressed is 'not the Pierre Eller that I was on that day [i.e. 12 October 1954], who certainly could not have expressed himself like that, but the one I shall be perhaps in a few years' time' (150). The *you* around whom the narration is organised is at most a hypothesis, not the real Pierre Eller who sits through his uncle's lesson on the discovery and conquest of America, but the hypothetical person that he *might* become in the future. The imagined *I* of Eller's narrative reminds us that Eller as *you* is at best a speculation based on his uncle's imagination. And indeed, we already know from a parenthetical remark in Part I that in any case Eller is not the ultimate addressee of Vernier's narration, but rather a cipher or pretext for a much larger and less precisely defined audience. Vernier describes his 'notes' as being written 'for you, and, less directly, also for your friends, and through you and them, for everyone who has been a pupil in *seconde*, and even, I think one has to go as far as that, for everyone who comes into contact with people who have been in *seconde*' (99). Eller as *you* is not much more substantial than Eller as *I*.

The conjugational system of Part III finally endorses the potential unrealism of the systems of Parts I and II. Eller suggests towards the end of his narration that the first person should pass to 'Uncle Henri, who from now on is certainly much better qualified than me to be designated by the first person in the conjugation of this work' (277). He goes on: 'If you want me to read you, if you don't want me to be repelled by the opening pages, you will have to put the sentences in another mouth than mine' (and *you* here is Vernier). This strongly implies that Jouret is no more really the *I* of his narration than was Eller himself. But whereas in Part II we could continue to see Vernier as an *I* behind the *you* used to refer to him, there is no such possibility in Part III where Vernier is *he* and dying in hospital. We know that Eller as *you* is a hypothesis, but it now appears that the *I* has become so hypothetical that it is impossible to reconstruct a 'real' narrative source behind this fiction.

In becoming *he* the original narrator has adopted what Benveniste calls the pronoun of non-person and lost his power to transform language into discourse. The narration has ditched all pretence of having an origin to validate it and has become entirely self-sustaining. The narration, in shifting by *degrees* through Butor's conjugational system, raises the question 'qui parle?' and simultaneously rules out the possibility of an answer. The pronominal system, instead of providing a realist support for the narration has finally to be seen as the fictional product of a fiction. Butor claims in his essay on personal pronouns in the novel that they are always a more complex version of their real-life counterparts, and his novel seems to suggest that their complexity is in large part due to their fictionality. We cannot reconstruct real, physical individuals behind them, and they are advertised as both the product and the generator of fiction. In the novel it is not speakers who invent fiction (as first seemed to be the case with Vernier in *Degrés*) but fiction which invents its speakers.

In the various ploys adopted by novels to present their narratives we can see not just a narration which is more or less appropriate to its fiction, but a manner of speaking about speech. In the ultimately uninhabited discourse supporting the story, we can detect the novel itself (not as a source or entity behind its language but as the sum total of it) reminding us that language is indeed separate from us, that at best it can be borrowed, wielded or played with, but can never be fully incorporated into our being. Speakers of the language of fiction are themselves fictions, and the minstrel and mere author that Lubbock talks of are no exception. The arbitrary quality of narration which so dismayed Lubbock is not the effect of the author's absolute authority, but on the contrary, is due to the fact that the novel is, at bottom, speakerless. This speakerless language constitutes the essence of fiction, and the speakers invented by it as a motivation for it only serve (as this chapter has shown) to make even more audible the text's eloquent independence.

4

The novel and the poetics of quotation

Speech about speech

The first three chapters of this book have all demonstrated that the nouveau roman will, in telling stories or in presenting characters, inevitably also draw attention to the means whereby it does so. While on one level plot, character and narration can be seen as an elaborate means of constructing motivation for the arbitrary base of fiction, on another level this motivation also appears to provide fiction with a pretext for a seemingly endless discourse upon itself. In this chapter I shall attempt to sketch out a theory of the novel which will not only account for the nouveau roman's curious self-obsession, but will also show it to be simply a more explicit and exaggerated form of a necessary reflexivity endemic to the genre as a whole.

That the nouveau roman is to a greater or lesser degree concerned with itself as fiction is by now a commonplace of critical writings on it. It is generally assumed that this self-reference is achieved by means of subversion, violation or infraction of some supposed fictional norm. Jean Ricardou, who has set the tone for the bulk of critical writings on the nouveau roman has always emphasised the subversive aspects of the nouveau roman and of the so-called radical texts which he sees as its forerunners (Poe, Flaubert, Roussel, Borges, etc.). According to Ricardou it is subversion and violation that make us see in the nouveau roman not 'l'écriture d'une aventure' but 'l'aventure d'une écriture'. With the adventure of writing thus privileged over the writing of adventures, the traditional mainstream of fiction comes to be regarded as a naïve or disingenuous succumbing to the 'naturalist illusion'.

Because he appears to accept rather than explode the illusion of reality, a novelist like Balzac simply becomes uninteresting for a critic like Ricardou. But a theory which polarises literature into oppositions between naturalist and literal, or *lisible* and *scriptible*, can only succeed in somewhat simplistically inverting the old values: where lifelikeness and accuracy of representation were once admired, the subversive strategies of auto-representation or anti-representation become the new signs of literary achievement. In this new order we are supposed to be looking for indications of writing undermining mimesis, and the authors we should read would be mainly marginal or modernist (Ricardou mentions Sade, Lautréamont, Roussel, Flaubert, Poe, Proust, Joyce, Roussel, Kafka, Borges, Mallarmé, Artaud and Bataille, amongst others, 1971, 31–2). The orthodoxy implied in this new order is as restricting as that which it attributes to the traditional realist fiction which it aims to subvert. In any case these opposites do not appear to be necessarily mutually exclusive. Although in some of Robbe-Grillet's novels it is impossible to (re-)construct a consistent and coherent world to which the writing would refer, it is perfectly possible to do so in the case of Butor's fiction. And the same is of course true for most of the writers on Ricardou's list of subversive texts. The contribution that the nouveau roman could make to the theory of fiction would be greatly enhanced if this theory were applicable to all fiction rather than simply to a radical or marginal tradition. The disadvantage of Ricardou's theoretical stance is that it leaves most of the nineteenth century (normally invoked as the great era of fiction) completely out of account.

Bearing in mind, then, that the theoretical aspects of this discussion aim to be comprehensive and not simply applicable to the nouveau roman, let us recapitulate the first three chapters of this book. In the case of plot, it was found that contrary to many of the assertions of the new novelists themselves, narrative in the nouveau roman has been neither abandoned nor wrecked by subversion. Instead, by means of the various forms adopted by the texts in question, they were able to draw attention to the unnatural aspects of all narrative, to tell stories and at the same time to explore the nature of narrative constructs. The novels make us aware of the constructed nature of narrative 'truths', of the arbitrary nature of the narrative *telos*, of the artificial basis of the apparently real and of narrative's proclivity for garrulous self-obsession. In short, the shape of the narrative lens through which we view so much of our experience is itself brought into focus by these novels.

In the case of character, the novels, in varying ways, could be seen to be exploring and exposing the underlying fictional elements of this central element of fiction. The novels make us see that character is a created synonym for thematic coherence, that the representation of the human mind is a pretext for the novel's own inventiveness, that character permits an exploration of the nature of linguistic communication, and that all that is normally understood by the concept of character is simply a certain way of talking. As far as narration is concerned, the novels reveal that no narrational strategy can ever completely fill the gap that exists between speaker and language and between language and the world, that language is to some extent always and irreducibly other. In every case and in every function, the language of fiction is brought into play as the *object* as well as the *means* of its representation.

It is precisely this presentation of language as an object which Mikhail Bakhtin, the Soviet theorist and critic, has postulated as a defining characteristic of the novel as a genre. His theory holds that the focusing on language as an object is not the result of fictional violations peculiar only to certain kinds of novel, but that it is an inherent feature of *all* novels. The novel, he says, is not composed of a coherent, uniform continuum of language, but is a composite of different kinds of discourses, since a major part of its activity consists in quoting the language of other people – primarily, and most manifestly, of its characters. 'It is the representation of the language of another.' (1968, 127) And in representing the language of others, the novel is inevitably involved in some evaluation of the types of language that it quotes. As Voloshinov puts it, 'Reported speech is speech within speech, utterance within utterance, and at the same time also *speech about speech, utterance about utterance'* (1973, 115).[1]

This being so, one of the functions of the novel as a genre will be to promote the perception of different language styles. The novel can be read as a commentary on the languages which it contains. 'The language of the novel is a system of dialogically mutually-illuminating languages. It cannot be described and analysed as a single and unified language.' (Bakhtin, 1968, 130) Within the novel, different styles of language become conscious of themselves as particular styles, as a result of the presence of the other languages with which they coexist. This makes the novel a place where our discoveries concern not so much ourselves or the world, but rather the nature of the language (or languages) in which the world and our selves appear to us. Bakhtin's conclusion runs as follows: 'All novels are to a greater or lesser extent a dialogised system of images of "languages", styles and consciousnesses that are concrete and inseparable from language. Language in the novel does not only represent, but serves as the object of representation. The discourse of the novel is always self-critical.' (132) To quote language is inevitably also to make us conscious of language.

The novel is radically different from both poetry and drama in consisting to a large degree of quotations, of marked transitions from reporting to reported speech. Quoted speech is not a necessary ingredient of poetry, which, at its most basic level, can be regarded as the kind of uniform discourse which Bakhtin says we would be wrong to look for in the novel. In drama, on the other hand, all the speech is equally quoted, and there is no authorial or narrational discourse to necessitate the introduction of quotation marks for the utterances of characters. The novel is unique in systematically alternating quoted and unquoted discourse. The reason for this lies in the hierarchical structure of narrative (and particularly of written

[1] V. N. Voloshinov was at one time a pupil of Bakhtin and disappeared during the 1930s in Stalin's purges. It has been suggested that Bakhtin was the real author of *Marxism and the Philosophy of Language* but published the book under his pupil's name. See Medvedev/Bakhtin, 1978, ix–xxiii; I am grateful to Ann Shukman for providing me with English translations of Bakhtin's original Russian. References are to the more easily available French translation.

narrative), where there is a scale of authority that goes from the author at the top down to the characters at the bottom, with the intervening levels potentially containing an implied author or a narrator. Written narrative allows for the elaboration of a much more hierarchical system of authority than the relatively simple narrator–character arrangement on which oral narratives are generally based. The eighteenth-century novel, with its prefaces and footnotes attributed to editors and publishers, was also able to create further levels of authority over and above the supposed author himself. The effect of this multilayered structure of narrative is to intensify the sense that the discourses of the novel are quoted. In this system it is not just the reported speech of characters that appears quoted, but also, in so far as the narrator can be distinguished from the author, that of the narrator too (although the degree to which his language appears quoted is less than that of the characters). The embedding of the discourses which comprise narrative in fiction means ultimately that a very small proportion of them (if any) can be granted full authority and not considered under the aspect of quotation, since so many of them are a kind of reported speech: the author writes that the narrator tells that the character says . . . , or even (as in many eighteenth-century novels or in Constant's *Adolphe*): the publisher writes that the author writes that the narrator tells that the character says . . . , which can be reconstructed as: the author writes that the publisher writes that the author writes that the narrator tells that the character says . . . , which creates such a complex tissue of embedding that language is made the object of representation at every level of the text.

Within this system it is, of course, the utterances of the characters which are most easily identified as quotations because there are quite specific conventions used for indicating such utterances. These conventions are, to a certain extent, historically determined and range from the simple *modus* (he said) and its variants (she smiled) to typographical markers (inverted commas of various kinds, dashes, etc.), depending on the specific conventions of each language. Since the beginning of the nineteenth century (at least) it has also been a convention that characters should be more or less distinguished by their individual speech styles. These devices are not mutually exclusive, and most modern texts use a combination (with varying emphases) of all three.[2] In any case, whatever the devices available, fiction always adopts some method for indicating the reported or quoted status of the utterances of its characters, and in doing so is able to hold up their language as an object of scrutiny.

To illustrate the way in which speech within speech of this kind becomes also speech about speech, I shall take the example of a letter that Mr Micawber sends to the narrator in Dickens's *David Copperfield*. Here the character's utterance is identified as such not by a simple *modus*, but by a rather more elaborate means. David Copperfield writes 'I was not prepared [...] to receive the following communication', which has the same function as the *modus* of attributing the ensuing utterance to a character and marking a shift from the narrator's own discourse. As the utterance here is in written form, the typographical markers are even more emphatic than is the case for spoken utterances, with the special spatial definition of the utterance on the page, the repetition of quotation marks for each indented line and the use of capitals for the address and the signature. And finally, the speech style of the character is very strongly individuated.

In quoting the letter, it is also necessary to quote the surrounding narrative discourse in order to make the discursive contrast between the two styles as palpable as possible and to show how they react upon each other to create what Bakhtin calls a 'system of dialogically mutually-illuminating languages' (1968, 130):

In a word, I never saw anybody so thoroughly jovial as Mr Micawber was, down to the very last moment of the evening, when I took a hearty farewell of himself and his amiable wife. Consequently, I was not prepared, at seven o'clock next morning, to receive the following communication, dated half-past nine in the evening; a quarter of an hour after I had left him:

[2] For a discussion of individual speech styles see Voloshinov (1973, 150–3). For a more detailed account of these conventions see le Hir, 1961 and Mylne, 1975. Newman has an interesting chapter on the *modus* in Sarraute's fiction (1976, 21–45).

My Dear Young Friend,

'The die is cast – all is over. Hiding the ravages of care with a sickly mask of mirth, I have not informed you, this evening, that there is no hope of the remittance! Under these circumstances, alike humiliating to endure, humiliating to contemplate, and humiliating to relate, I have discharged the pecuniary liability contracted at this establishment, by giving a note of hand, made payable fourteen days after date, at my residence, Pentonville, London. When it becomes due, it will not be taken up. The result is destruction. The bolt is impending, and the tree must fall.

'Let the wretched man who now addresses you, my dear Copperfield, be a beacon to you through life. He writes with that intention, and in that hope. If he could think himself of so much use, one gleam of day might, by possibility, penetrate into the cheerless dungeon of his remaining existence – though his longevity is, at present (to say the least of it), extremely problematical.

'This is the last communication, my dear Copperfield, you will ever receive

'From
'The
'Beggared Outcast,
'Wilkins Micawber.'

I was so shocked by the contents of this heartrending letter, that I ran off directly towards the little hotel with the intention of taking it on my way to Doctor Strong's, and trying to soothe Mr Micawber with a word of comfort. But, half-way there, I met the London coach with Mr and Mrs Micawber up behind: Mr Micawber, the very picture of tranquil enjoyment, smiling at Mrs Micawber's conversation, eating walnuts out of a paper bag, with a bottle sticking out of his breast pocket. As they did not see me, I thought it best, all things considered, not to see them. So, with a great weight taken off my mind, I turned into a by-street that was the nearest way to school, and felt, upon the whole, relieved that they were gone: though I still liked them very much, nevertheless. (263–4)

The languages of Mr Micawber and David Copperfield are differentiated first and foremost by the fact that they provide quite contradictory information. Where David Copperfield says that he 'never saw anyone so thoroughly jovial' as Mr Micawber, Micawber himself speaks of his 'hiding the ravages of care with a sickly mask of mirth'. Even Mr Micawber's capacity for extremely rapid swings of mood cannot account for this contradiction, so that the only way in which it can be resolved is by regarding Mr Micawber's version of his emotional state as rhetorical exaggeration. It is true that as a character Mr Micawber is prone to exaggerate, and so the letter's linguistic exuberance could be seen as just another instance of his 'Micawberishness'. And yet its linguistic characteristics are so prominently displayed as language, and contrast so strongly with David Copperfield's very sober and factual discourse that we cannot avoid some purely linguistic appreciation of this quoted discourse. Micawber's grotesque deployment of clichés, both legal and metaphorical, represents a use of language which modesty and self-respect prevent most of us from emulating for fear of looking stupid. And yet Micawber seems to get away from it, perhaps precisely because we cannot tell how far he really means what he says. Surely the picture of Micawber smiling and eating walnuts on the London coach is not compatible with the 'cheerless dungeon' which he mentions in his letter? Micawber has an inordinate capacity for talk (indeed for little else) combined with a poor sense of how his talk will match up to any real state of affairs. But if neither David Copperfield's narrative discourse, nor Mr Micawber's hyperbolic self-portraiture is able to tell us anything very reliable about Mr Micawber's real state of mind, and, given the low information-value of both discourses, is not that of Mr Micawber infinitely more enjoyable as language? His utterances retroact upon the narrator's language which, with its concern for date, time and place seem poverty-stricken in comparison with the joyous irresponsibility of that of his impecunious financial mentor. A systematic analysis of the quoted discourses in *David Copperfield* would (as it would for any novel) eventually provide an account of the nature of the novel's self-criticism and of the basis of its own linguistic economy.[3]

The self-reference derived from this speech about speech seems as much part of a conventional realist novel such as *David Copperfield*, with its apparently unproblematic plots and

[3] Genette's studies of the language of Proust's characters, although not resting explicitly on a theory formulated in these terms, nevertheless provide an excellent example of its value and efficacy. See 'Proust et le langage indirect' (1969, 223–94) and 'Récit de paroles' (1972, 189–203).

its highly characterful characters, as it is of the supposedly unconventional or anti-conventional fiction of the nouveau
roman. Indeed, it could be said that the greater a novel's
endeavour to establish its realism, the greater its self-reference
will be. For one of the most effective devices at fiction's disposal
for creating a sense of the real is to deny that it is a novel at all.
This denial amounts to a quotation of the kind of novel or the
specific convention from which the new fiction is trying to
dissociate itself. When Balzac writes at the beginning of *Le Père
Goriot* : 'This drama is neither a fiction, nor a novel. *All is true*',
he is asserting that all pre-existing novels which we had assumed
gave us access to the real, are in fact merely conventional, and
that what we had taken to be the thing itself was simply a way of
talking. By alluding to the novel as a genre Balzac is, in effect,
putting it between quotation marks and, in thus severing it
from its referential function, is presenting it as an object for
inspection.

Apart from this kind of global disclaimer, fiction also relies
heavily on internalised and specific disclaimers which function
as quotations or images of language within the text itself, and
operate in a similar way to the utterances of characters. Indeed
Don Quixote, which is often taken to be the first European novel,
is based entirely on the representation of images of the
language of romance literature which are held up in contrast
to other discourses which are supposedly more adequate
representations of reality. Stendhal's *Le rouge et le noir* is typical
in its use of this kind of disclaiming strategy in order to create
a mimetic effect. Over and over again, the text draws attention
to the differences between conventional fictional accounts of
human emotions and experiences, and its own real, authentic
version of them. The following paragraph is a typical instance:

In Paris Julien's position in relation to Madame de Rênal would
have been quickly clarified; but in Paris, *love is the child of novels*.
The young tutor and his timid mistress would have found the explanation of their position in three or four novels, and even in a few couplets
of the Gymnase. *Novels would have outlined the roles they should play,
shown them the model to imitate* ; and sooner or later, although with no
enjoyment and perhaps with reluctance, vanity would have obliged

Julien to follow it.[. . .] Under our darker skies, a penniless young man who is ambitious only because the delicacy of his emotions requires some of the delights that money brings, comes into daily contact with a woman of thirty who is sincerely virtuous, devotes herself to her children, and *does not look to novels for examples of behaviour*. Everything happens slowly, everything develops gradually in the provinces, *things are more natural*.

(*Romans et nouvelles* I, 252, my emphases)

Stendhal here draws a clear distinction between the falseness (and banality) of conventional novelistic discourse about love, and the truthfulness and naturalness of his own. He seems to be promising that his text will be free of the corrupting influence of fictional convention which his disclaiming strategy makes us see as the object as well as the means of representation.

In the case of *Le rouge et le noir* the identification and rejection of fiction's false models is doubly crucial. Not only does the integrity of the novel's own discourse depend upon it, but so does the integrity of the characters. If Stendhal were to adopt and follow fiction's conventional model of love, the realism of his novel (it is suggested) might be threatened; but if Julien and Madame de Rênal were to do so, their love itself would soon be destroyed. Indeed, much of the action in *Le rouge et le noir* and its themes of hypocrisy and vanity serve to emphasise the importance of recognising convention as something separate and different from the authentic self. One may therefore regard the action of this novel as serving to mirror and reinforce on the level of representation the preoccupations of the novelistic discourse itself. It might even be possible to account for the nineteenth-century realist's novel's preference for certain plot types in terms of the degree to which they encourage the identification of convention. The quest for authenticity or the narrative of lost illusions clearly promote this sort of identification and hence make possible the presentation of certain types of discourse as images of language.

So, it appears that the structure of the novel as a genre, in so far as it is based on a discursive hierarchy of narrator and character, and in its traditional commitment to mimesis, will inevitably quote or frame other discourses, and in doing so, will make us see various means of representation as objects of representation. It can be said, then, that the novel has as primary function the task of making us aware of different types of discourse *as* discourse, and in this way it becomes possible to outline a theory of fiction which includes the nouveau roman and does not give it a purely negative role. The nouveau roman deserves the title *anti-novel* only in so far as all fiction does, and *Le rouge et le noir* is as much an anti-novel as *Projet pour une révolution à New York*.

It is no coincidence, then, that the readings of the various novels discussed in the first three chapters of this book are all based to a greater or lesser degree on the identification of framed or directly quoted elements in the text. The question of the teleological nature of narrative which *Les gommes* seems to be concerned with is made pertinent through its allusions to Sophocles' *Oedipus*, a text which is, as it were, quoted by Robbe-Grillet's novel. The questions relating to narrative in *L'emploi du temps* are brought into focus both by the actual quotation of Burton's utterances on the subject, and by the allusions to detective fiction. The imaging of narrative discourse is achieved also by the way in which it is framed in the Theseus tapestry and in the stained-glass window in the cathedral. The peculiar forms of narrative embedding in *La maison de rendez-vous* are a very obvious form of framing which are extremely effective in bringing narrative into focus as its own object. Similarly, the topic of character is framed (and in a literal sense too) by the portrait of the unknown man in *Portrait d'un inconnu*, as the theme of names is in the characters' utterances in *Les fruits d'or*. The stereotyped nature of character-types is also made evident through their being quoted in the characters' utterances in *Entre la vie et la mort*, and by being framed in the shop-window in *Projet pour une révolution à New York*. The linguistic themes of *La modification* and *Les fruits d'or* are constructed on the base of the utterances of the characters.

One might expect narration to be exempt from being framed since it is hierarchically superior to the characters' discourse. But apart from the fact that the characters' discourse tends to retroact upon that of the narrator (as with the narration in

David Copperfield), the specific forms of narration discussed in Chapter 3 all appeared to foreground language as an object by means of certain framing effects within the novels themselves. The nature of the narrator's language in *Portrait d'un inconnu* is brought into focus as an image of language by showing its fate when it is uttered, placed inside quotation marks in a dialogue with the utterances of other characters. In the case of *La jalousie* the narrational ambiguity is given concrete form through being represented on the level of the narrative itself. The case of free indirect speech inevitably raises the question of quotation since it is a narrative style which, by definition, incorporates other voices. Finally, the narrational discourse of Pierre Eller in *Degrés* is framed by that of his uncle, and Vernier's own narration ends by being framed through the effect of the final question 'Qui parle?', which raises fundamental questions concerning Vernier's authority as a narrator. In every case, there is a framing or imaging effect achieved either as the result of the structural qualities of fiction (the alternation of the discourses of narrator and characters) or as the result of the framing of specific objects or images in the represented world of the novel (such as the painting in *Portrait d'un inconnu*).

The reflexivity of the nouveau roman, its concern with itself as fiction seem, then, to derive from its very structure as fiction. Self-criticism in the novel is immanent both in its representation of characters speaking and, paradoxically perhaps, in its most overtly mimetic strategies. Through its explicit manipulation of these elements, the nouveau roman may emphasise its self-preoccupation more insistently than some of its predecessors, but this concern with itself as fiction is nevertheless based on those aspects of the genre which have always been part of its definition as fiction.

Talk as theme: 'Disent les imbéciles'

As long as a novel consists of marked transitions from narrating to quoted discourse it should lend itself to being read around the theme of language, although the significance of this articulation in relation to linguistic themes is one which we are not obliged to perceive if narrative and character are sufficiently powerful cohesive forces in the text. In reading, the first procedure is usually to evaluate an utterance in terms of its relevance to narrative – for example, as a delegated narration of events. As far as character is concerned, an utterance will usually be seen as reflecting in some way on the personality of its speaker. There are, however, some texts which are more likely to impose a reading in terms of the linguistic themes implied in the utterances because of their relative lack of interest and coherence on the level of character and plot, and the more recent novels of Nathalie Sarraute are an example of this. *Portrait d'un inconnu, Martereau* and *Le planétarium* all have sufficiently individuated characters and sufficient narrative coherence to make it possible to read these novels through the framework of character and plot, although what then emerges from them is neither very interesting nor very cogent.[4] But with *Les fruits d'or* the narrative becomes so fragmented and the characters so anonymous that one is forced to search around for other types of coherence, and many readers have found the theme of language itself particularly appropriate.[5]

Furthermore, in her essays on the novel in *L'ère du soupçon* Nathalie Sarraute herself has laid great stress on the importance of dialogue in the modern novel in general and, by implication, in her own fiction in particular. She quotes the English novelist Henry Green in support of this view: 'Henry Green remarks that the novel's centre of gravity is shifting: the place of dialogue is growing larger every day' (1956, 90). The reasons she gives for this supposed shift are, however, quite specific to her own concerns, namely the representation of the tropistic inner life. The tropisms which compose Sarraute's 'psychology' are, she says, on such a diminutive scale that they cannot manifest themselves as perceptible actions. 'But, failing actions, we have words at our disposal. Words have

---

[4] As Newman (1974) demonstrates in the case of *Le planétarium*.

[5] Mary McCarthy refers to *Entre la vie et la mort* as an 'auditory pantomime' (1970, 172). Newman takes up this cue in his study of Sarraute's fiction, aptly entitled *Une poésie des discours* (1976). See also Celia Britton's study, whose title summarises this approach, *Language as Text and Language as Theme* (1973).

the qualities necessary for capturing, protecting and bringing
out into the open these subterranean movements which are
at once impatient and timid.' (1956, 102) The action of the
novel will therefore not consist in gestures or any other kind of
external enterprise but will be carried out under the cloak of
language:

So, as long as their appearance [of words] remains more or less harmless and ordinary, they can be and in fact often are the insidious and
very effective weapon in countless small crimes that take place every
day, without anyone seeing anything wrong in it, and without the
victim even daring to admit it openly to himself.[. . .] Through the
play of actions and reactions which they give rise to, they constitute
the most invaluable of the novelist's instruments. (1956, 103–4)

For Sarraute, then, the psychological drama of her fiction takes
place in and through the utterances of her characters, and to
this extent the dialogue will have an extremely important
narrative function in the novels.

Sarraute also attributes to it an important narrational function. The use of dialogue can provide a solution for an author
too scrupulous to write 'la marquise sortit à cinq heures', or
too disdainful of the 'analysis' or interpretation that constitutes
the narration of a novel like Proust's *A la recherche du temps perdu*,
both of which problematise the authorial function in one way
or another. The expansion of dialogue in the novel is seen as a
means of achieving an author-free fiction. It creates a sense of
immediacy by removing the alienating intermediary of the
authorial voice, and the reader has the 'illusion of carrying out
the actions again himself with greater awareness, with more
order, clarity, and force than he can in real life, but without their
losing that element of indeterminacy, opacity and mystery
which these actions always have for the person who experiences
them' (1956, 118). This discourse of dialogues is ambiguous,
being both more orderly than actual experience and, at the
same time, less orderly than norms of narrational interpretation usually require. It is also unabashedly unrealistic, as
Sarraute makes clear when she describes Ivy Compton-Burnett's
dialogues as the kind of discourse that she is aiming at: 'These
long, stilted sentences, which are as rigid as they are sinuous,

are *not like any conversation one has ever heard*. And yet, if they seem strange, they never give a false or gratuitous impression' (1956, 121, my emphases). The conventional alternation of narratorial discourse and characters' utterances is to be replaced by the alternation of *conversation* and *sous-conversation* to create a fictional discourse which is both representational of the action and, at the same time boldly ambiguous and unrealistic. As a discursive style with such a bizarre and apparently contradictory purpose, Sarraute's dialogue would, under any circumstances, require some attention and explanation. But in the context of the theory set out in this chapter, an examination of the dialogues ought also to throw some light onto the general values of the linguistic system in which they occur. In other words, an exploration of the novel's quoted discourses should yield a reading of the novel as self-criticism.

The title alone of '*Disent les imbéciles*' doubly invites our attention to talk as a topic: it is itself apparently an utterance and it also refers to speech. Someone is saying something about what fools say. The novel itself proves to have little narrative coherence and a high degree of anonymity on the part of the characters, which taken together require us to construct other potential factors of coherence. The text opens on a group of anonymous children crowding round their grandmother, but the interest of the scene seems to consist primarily in what is said, with a key phrase (the opening words of the novel) providing a focus to which the *conversation* and *sous-conversation* return over and over again: 'She's sweet'. One of the children revolts against this 'charming family tableau' (13–14) set up around a 'delightful grandmother, a real grandmother out of a fairy tale', and which is somehow clinched by the utterance of the words 'she's sweet'. The interest of the text is not so much in the picture itself as in the implications of this utterance, and, subsequently, of others which, in narrative terms, have little or no connection with this opening scene: 'he is jealous', 'he'll have a protruding chin', 'he is gifted but not intelligent', and so on. In their own talk the characters mull over these apparently harmless utterances, exploring their significance, implications and connotations. And the degree of attention

accorded to the key utterances transforms them into objects
through which the novel is able to work out and demonstrate
its own linguistic economy.

Take the example of the utterance 'il est jaloux' ('he is jealous').
In narrative terms this is the response of the group to the grand-
child's revolt against the 'charming tableau'. But the psychological aspects of the statement are not pursued by the text, and
we never discover whether the child is 'really' jealous and if so
why. The object of the novel's attention is not the emotion
jealousy but the utterance which invokes the concept. Its interest in the statement as a means of representation is nil, and
instead, the phrase is brought into play as the *object* of representation by a variety of different devices. First, the text's gloss
on the phrase seems deliberately to destroy its referential value;
it is presented as a distortion or betrayal of reality:

That's what we need, that's what will follow all the meanders in one
go, flow into all the folds, hunt down in every nook and cranny, suck
up, collect in a single block and reveal what was scattered, caresses,
signs of affection, respectful touches, heads buried in laps, sudden
outbursts, furious glances full of hatred, all gathered together in
these few words, standing there and plain as daylight: he is jealous.
(15)

This strongly stresses the distinction that exists between word
and reality by presenting words as objects. For example, we
do not usually think of language as *seen*; and in comparing
the words to a liquid which covers and flows around reality,
the text contradicts our general assumption that language *un-*
covers and reveals reality; and when the phrase is said to suck
up and gather together the reality to which it supposedly refers,
its relation to the real is transformed from the passive one
which we usually imagine it to have, into a peculiarly active one

The undermining of the representational potential of the
phrase is completed in the following paragraphs which consist of a phonetic commentary on the word 'jaloux'. The text
concentrates exclusively on this aspect of the word and it is not
presented as having any relevance to its meaning. The word
'jaloux' is a weapon whose cutting edge is created entirely by
its sounds:

Yet it's a word which isn't much to look at, a word which looks perfectly harmless, the 'ja' which opens so candidly and the 'loux' which
rounds off so softly, 'loux' like 'doux' [soft] . . . 'loux' is even softer . . .
But you mustn't trust it, there's nothing more treacherous than these
sound-effects. Remember that there's 'loux' and 'loup' [wolf]. It's
all there, in what you don't pronounce, in the x and the p. It makes all
the difference. And the soft 'loux' next to the confident opening of the
'ja' creates something which instantly transforms everything . . .
No computer in millions of years could ever produce the thing you
know was produced in you and me the moment the word 'jaloux'
was uttered. (15–16)

This word is dangerous not because of what it means, but because of the treachery of its sound-effects. In this way, then,
the text effectively curtails any interest in the referential or
semantic validity of the phrase by emphasising its existence as
an object by means of the metaphors that designate it, and by
means of the exploration of its signifying component.

The text's exposition of the communicative function of the
phrase also serves to stress the status of the utterance as an
object. In every instance it is presented as being directed against
the interlocutor. It is not a message or a piece of information to
be transmitted from sender to receiver, but primarily a weapon
which makes victims of its receivers (16–17). In their communicative function words do indeed prove to be the 'insidious and
very effective weapon in countless small crimes that take place
every day' as Sarraute has it in her discussion of dialogue (1956,
103), and as such these words provide a very good example of
the difference between the kind of psychology which makes
authors 'drop their eyes and blush' (1956, 83), and the kind
which she describes as tropisms. The word 'jealousy' belongs
to the crude psychology which makes modern writers blush,
whereas the utterance of the word becomes part of the 'play
of actions and reactions' (1956, 104) which (according to
Sarraute) constitutes the psychological factor in contemporary
fiction. It is the use that language is put to by the narrative of
these novels which makes it perceptible as an object. Here it
is not just the quotation of discourses but also narrative itself
which transforms the novels into speech about speech.

Furthermore, it is not only this narrative element which
promotes the perception of language as object, but also the

thematic one. The major themes of Sarraute's fiction (authenticity/inauthenticity, anarchy/order, desire for contact/rejection of contact, etc.) are all articulated around and through the quoted language in the novels. The identification of themes here necessarily entails the identification of different types of language, 'images of language, characteristic, typical, limited images which border at times on the ridiculous' (Bakhtin, 1968, 130). An example of the way in which this dual identification takes place can be seen in the following passage. After the utterance of the phrase 'She's sweet. Isn't she a picture' something in the grandmother seems to resist, and the figure supposedly consolidated by the words threatens instead to disintegrate. Panic ensues:

Stop it ... Help ... Bring the partitions, separate, lock up what's flowing out of her, spreading ... stop it ... You've got all you need to channel it, enclose it, quell it, all your categories, all your psychology ... quick, lets build a dyke, shut it in, direct it, bring the specially made words designed for this purpose ... here they are, let's take them: revolt, repressed needs, keen desires, as keen as before, renunciations, grievances, furies, mutilations, petty acts of cowardice, hypocrisy, intrepidity, wickedness, goodness, naïvety, lucidity, sensuality ... There, the flood is gradually abating, I am calming down ... The crisis is over.
   It's reassuring to use these partitions to put everything back in place, to separate and lock up in compartments, properly labelled drawers ... You just have to open them, it's there, known, classified. (21–2)

The chief thematic coherence of this passage lies in the opposition between chaos and order. In this case chaos is associated with reality and order with language. Words are used to contain the threat posed by the reality which 'flows' from the grandmother. The thematic predicates of order and chaos serve to set word and object against each other yet again.
   There is another thematic strand running through this passage which creates an implied opposition between the individual and the crowd. First of all, it is the chorus of grandchildren who are the speakers (pseudo-speakers) behind the discourse, and secondly, the known and the labelled are powerful connoters of the crowd (in Sarraute it is always the crowd which loves a 'category'). The kind of language invoked by

the chorus to re-establish order is the language of the crowd, and so their utterances are presented as a certain *kind* of language. Finally, the theme of authenticity is also implicit, for the crowd and the category are always associated with the inauthentic in Sarraute, so that recognition of the inauthentic also involves the recognition of inauthentic types of language, those constructed, unserious types of discourse which are contrasted in the Sarrautean world to organic discursive models. So much, then, for the means whereby 'all these languages with their direct means of representation become the object of representation' (Bakhtin, 1968, 130) in the novels of Nathalie Sarraute. It remains now to examine the nature and scope of the self-criticism which lies behind the novel's presentation of these language-objects.

In the episode concerned with the phrase which provides the title of the novel some of the strategies involved in using certain kinds of language are evaluated in such a way as to make possible some understanding of the text's own linguistic economy. The function of the phrase is described in the following terms:

One of our masters, and one of the greatest, discovered it, he picked out one of those flabby, slippery ideas, compressed it as he knows how to, reduced it to a few words, put it between quotation marks, and without more ado, without doing anything more to it, without running the risk of getting his hands dirty, without bothering to waste precious moments, he added the simple warning: 'disent les imbéciles' [fools say]. (55)

The master, evidently sophisticated enough to be aware of the otherness of language as illustrated in the pages discussed above, seems to have decided to adopt an extremely pragmatic if not cynical attitude towards its use. His aim is to protect himself from the language of others by placing it between quotation marks and attributing it to fools. The phrase 'disent les imbéciles' is a device for making explicit the object status of utterances and turning them against their original speakers.

When one of the other characters is invited to try out the same strategy, he finds that there is a great deal at stake in adopting it. He is offered the strategy by the anonymous crowd as a means of escape when he has been trapped by the language of another anonymous group: 'Say the words which will save you' (61), 'Believe us, you haven't any choice, it's a question of self-defence' (62). But this character does not have the cynicism of the master, and his desire for sincerity and truth at first prevent him from uttering something which he regards as both a sacrilege and a lie ('There are no such things as [. . .] fools', 57). When he is finally prevailed upon to utter the phrase, he discovers that the quotation marks do not protect him, and both he as the speaker of the utterance and the crowd as its referent are deadened by it:

Fools. Fools. Fools. It's unbelievable. It's him that just said it. Him. These amazing words came from his own mouth: fools.

Look at those people, I am pointing them out to you, look at them carefully. You see, they are fools. Here they are. That's what they are called. They are there, in front of us, immobilised. They are quite stiff . . . they look lifeless . . . They are carefully wrapped up, bound round with bandages, painted masks have been put on their faces . . . But little by little, on looking at them so closely . . . don't you think one gets a feeling . . . don't you recognise it? It's the same one as a while back . . . One feels strangely numb, stiff . . . It's like the onset of asphyxia in a stale atmosphere, in an airtight room . . . We've been locked up with them . . . with these mummies . . . it's a tomb, a sarcophagus . . . and us. (63–4)

Speaker and referent are buried alive in the language-tomb of this inauthentic utterance, and the scruples of the character are fully justified. And yet to treat language as if it were transparent and its speakers sincere is also to fall victim to it, not only because it involves loss of dignity (69), but also because people like the master can trap you and hoist you with your own petard simply by placing quotation marks around your words.

Sincerity and cynicism are equally fatal, so what status should we grant the discourse of the novel itself? Is it cynical, based entirely on convention and category, and therefore potentially destructive of its speaker, its referent and its receiver? Or is it sincere and therefore open to the risk of mawkishness and a conventionality which it has failed to recognise? Or perhaps there are other alternatives? Perhaps the novel's own communicative function operates in a different way? If we accept the conclusions of the previous chapter that the novel is at bottom speakerless, then we can dispose at once of the concepts of sincerity and cynicism, both of which imply the existence of a speaker with specific aims and intentions motivating his use of language. In this way the novel appears neither as the expression of an author desperately and embarrassingly trying to make contact with his readers, nor as the means whereby he can establish his superiority at their expense. The negative consequences that follow from the construction of an author explain the absence of any strictly authorial discourse in the novels and the reasons for the vehemence of Sarraute's condemnation of it. And much of the action of '*Disent les imbéciles*' is concerned with emphasising the distinction between the ideas and writings of a 'great man' on the one hand, and his personality on the other (e.g. 177–9). In the second place, we should see the language of the novel as being exempt from the instrumentality of reference, as not serving to name the reality with which it is concerned. For it is only the inauthentic discourse of the category which makes the mistake of naming. Time and again the novel demonstrates the destructive consequences of naming.

The hallmark of authenticity for this text seems to consist of a peculiar rearrangement of the conventional model of communication. Instead of a *speaker* sending a *message* about a *referent* to a *receiver* (which promotes the instrumentality so keenly condemned by the novels), authentic discourse is one where it is the referent itself which speaks. In the section following the 'disent les imbéciles' episode, this communicative model is proposed and defined as the reverse of the one implied by the utterance 'disent les imbéciles', by means of a conversation that takes place between two anonymous characters:

Look carefully, you'll see . . .
— Fine. Let's look, it might be amusing . . . Let's see what he's showing us . . . — Oh no, don't say that: not 'he' . . . who is 'he'? . . . it is a space without limits which no 'he' can contain . . . — Oh fine, so 'shows us' or rather 'shows' . . . Not 'us' either, I suppose? . . . — No, there mustn't be any 'us' . . . they are infinite spaces . . . without any outline . . . — Very funny . . . So this false 'he' approaches the false 'us' and shows . . . what? What is it? . . . But come on, it's easy

to see what it is, that's called an 'idea' . . . Where does it come from?
Did you invent it? — Me? But 'me' doesn't exist, I've just told you,
you mustn't think about that . . . There's no me here . . . no you . . . .
On no account must you let yourself get side-tracked by these triviali-
ties . . . like unruly schoolboys trying to catch flies . . . you just have
to concentrate on it . . . — On the idea? — Yes, since you insist on
giving it a name . . . You just have to let it enter, unfold. [. . .] Forget
what it's called, don't try and find out where it comes from, you just
have to let it sink in, let it settle . . . a seed which can grow on any
ground, it's got such vitality, such strength . . . If you let it take root,
it will grow, be covered in buds and leaves, put out branches . . .
Don't you find that the air around us is already more bracing, as if it
had been purified . . . that rubbish, that nauseating, rotting stuff
which you clumsily tried to shut in, isolate and point out with your
'disent les imbéciles', is destroyed now, you see, for good this time,
there's nothing left of it. (71–2)

In this passage naming is specifically condemned ('forget what
it is called'), as is the identification of origins ('don't try and find
out where it comes from'), and although the passage takes the
form of a dialogue, the speaker insists that true communication
can only take place when the *I* and the *you* are eliminated
('there's no one here . . . no you'). The communicative impetus
comes from the referent itself, the so-called 'idea', and is realised through organic growth as opposed to exchange which
was the communicative mode implied in the utterances discussed above.

This is all highly metaphorical, but it demonstrates very
clearly that the novel is deeply preoccupied with creating the
right conditions for its own communication to its readers, and
that in its concern with the language of others, it can in large
part be read as a self-critical preparation for a successful
communication.

The novel and the world as library: 'Degrés'

Despite its ultimately fictional base *Degrés* is characterised by a
very powerful mimetic intention, for it aims to provide both
the 'description of a class' and a record of the writing of that
description. It is also a highly citational text and includes about
135 quotations taken from some thirty-five different authors

(van Rossum-Guyon, 1974, 33). Although *Degrés* is somewhat unusual in having such a large number of direct quotations from specific texts, it is typical of all novels in this combination of representation and quotation.

The mimetic contract is established from the very outset of the novel ('I walk into the classroom, and I step up onto the dais'), however fictional these lines may subsequently be proved to be. The narrator defines himself as having a recognisable social role (schoolteacher) and his activity (teaching history and geography) is not only a recognisable element of our culture and society, but probably also touches on the lived experience of most readers who have themselves taken these subjects in school. Finally, the present tense acts as a connoter of mimesis in so far as it attempts to link the time of the narration to that of the narrative. To this extent the novel is highly *vraisemblable*. As the novel progresses we find that there is also a high degree of verifiable material in the text. Its action is carefully located in real time and space, with the 'pivotal lesson' taking place in Paris, between 3 and 4 pm on Tuesday 12 October 1954. A very large number of the allusions in the novel are to real places: the characters frequent streets, cafés and buildings which actually exist. And, just as we ourselves could take a walk down the Boulevard Saint-Germain or order a drink in the Café de Flore, so we could also read all the books mentioned in the novel, from Saint-Simon's *Mémoires* (which appears in the first page of the novel), to the various textbooks and manuals owned and studied by the characters in the book (as they were by real French schoolchildren in 1954). In its deployment of the *vraisemblable* and the verifiable, *Degrés* offers us unequivocal testimony of the good faith of its representational intentions.[6]

Although only an infinitesimal proportion of the proposed description actually appears in the novel, this is the result not so much of a renunciation of mimesis as of an excessive concern with it. It is true that Vernier is forced to acknowledge

---

[6] For a discussion of the verifiable see Butor's essay 'Le roman comme recherche' (1960, 7–11) and van Rossum-Guyon 1970a, 45–80). This study also contains a discussion of the *vraisemblable* in *La modification* (81–113).

that it is the imaginary which will ultimately organise his project and make it intelligible, but nevertheless the greater part
of his effort is devoted to factual research, using every means at
his disposal to find out about the private lives and backgrounds
of the other characters, and reading for himself all the books
read by both boys and teachers (from the science-fiction *Galaxie*
circulated amongst the boys to the Greek grammar used in his
colleague's class). Indeed, Vernier is destroyed not so much by
the effort of writing as by the potentially inexhaustible amount
of work involved in establishing the representational accuracy
of his description. Vernier may be misguided, but if the loss
of his nephew's friendship and even of his own life are the price
he is prepared to pay for mimesis, can we doubt the honest
intentions behind his (and by extension Butor's?) text?

In the classroom itself, Vernier is primarily concerned with
representation. As a teacher of geography, one of his main
preoccupations is with the 'representation of the earth', with
its measurement in degrees and minutes, and with the visual
record of it constituted by maps. As a teacher of history he is
also concerned with the facts of the past, and in the lesson on
the discovery and conquest of America, it is a picture of a certain era that he wants to draw. The theme of discovery adum-
brated around this topic is closely allied to the question of representation, firstly because what is discovered also has to be
represented; this is the case with Marco Polo's *Description du
monde* which describes his discovery of the East (and is one of
the texts used by Vernier for his lesson on the discovery of
America). Secondly, and more interestingly, discoveries alter
the existing representation of things, and the discovery of
America is shown to have had a profound effect on the way in
which men represented the world to themselves. As one of
Vernier's pupils says in answer to questions on the subject,
'people were made to realise that the world wasn't like they
thought' (34), a theme which is taken up again in the essay
by Montaigne ('Des Coches') which Vernier also uses in his
lesson: 'Our world has just found another (and who can tell
us if it is the last of its brothers. . .)' (261).

The theme of representation and the related topics of

discovery and description are repeated in other contexts right through the novel, and particularly in the quoted texts: Keats's poem on his discovery of Chapman's translation of Homer, Livy's account of Hannibal's crossing of the Alps, the pseudo-discovery of Europe in Montesquieu's *Lettres persanes* and the imagined discovery of new worlds in the science-fiction of *Galaxie*. These themes are in turn related to the themes of voyage and travel which also appear frequently in the quoted texts. Finally, all these themes are related to the theme of education, not only because of the metaphorical definition of education as a voyage of discovery, but also because, as Vernier says, the discovery of new worlds in the Renaissance with its effect on the representation of reality also had extremely far-reaching consequences on education itself: 'it is this alteration of the face of the world which made necessary a reform in education, whose achievement has taken a long time, and which has perhaps only just been begun even today' (34). The important quotation from Rabelais about Gargantua's studies which appears intermittently throughout the novel takes on further significance in the light of this remark, as does the whole of the novel itself, both in its representation of a certain educational system (the French lycée of the 1950s) and in its didactic orientation towards its interlocutor, Pierre Eller (it is designed to enable Eller to *represent* himself to himself).

Thus the question of representation touches on most aspects of the series of linked themes which circulate in this novel. With representation itself represented in the text, made the object as well as the means of its activity, the questions that plague Vernier about the accuracy and precision of his own documentation are made doubly pertinent. The novel's representation of representations bears directly on its own mimetic status. Some glimpse of the consequences of this mimetic duplication can be seen in the treatment of the various representations of Julius Caesar which figure in *Degrés*. He appears most frequently in M. Bailly's English lessons, where the boys are slowly working their way through Shakespeare's play. In M. Martin's art class they are given the task of drawing a sculpture of Julius Caesar's head, which immediately multiplies the number of representations to be represented (the sculpture itself and the individual drawings of each of the boys). The difficulties involved in achieving a likeness of this supposed likeness are explicitly stated in the narration:

Michel Daval took the piece of charcoal, began drawing Caesar's ear, his cheek-bone, the tip of his nose, his headband, quite astonished at the result, at the total absence of similarity between this grimacing face which he was creating, and which was growing more and more horrible and sarcastic, and the plaster face of the emperor which he was looking at, stopped, not knowing what to do next, waiting for the teacher to come and put things right. (30)

There are also two further representations of Caesar in the textbook on English literature used by the class studying Shakespeare's *Julius Caesar* – a print (30) and a copy of a painting (47). The difference between these various representations is again stressed when Vernier writes that as Eller looks at the print 'you were wondering how it could possibly be the same man whose features you had been trying to draw, under the supervision of M. Martin, two storeys above, a short while ago; the two faces *looked so unlike each other*' (30–1, my emphasis). The copy of the painting ('in the manner of Rochegrosse') is virtually indecipherable, and Caesar appears simply as a 'black blob with an arm sticking out of it' (48). Finally, he features briefly in an allusion to Plutarch's version of his life from which Jouret takes a passage to give to his class for translation (268). So, Caesar takes the forms of a character in a play, a sculpture, a number of schoolboy drawings, a print, a painting and a biography, but none of these many representations bears any resemblance to the others. Where, then, is the *real* Julius Caesar? The novel makes us realise that there is no reliable means of access to him, but only different ways of representing him which are taught in the various subjects in the school curriculum – English, art and classics. The uncertain definition of the object of these several representations has the effect of making the representations themselves the object of the novel's concern. In our effort to look *through* them at the man behind them, we are forced also to look *at* them.

Indeed, this stress on the means of representation is one of the main features to emerge from Butor's picture of the education which the boys receive at the lycée. They may be learning about the world, but they are learning about it through books. Perhaps there is, in any case, no other way of learning about it, for, as Butor writes in his essay 'La critique et l'invention': 'It is largely through books [. . .] that we know the universe' (1968, 8). The books which form the basis of the boys' education are already drawn to our attention through the place they occupy in the narrative itself where they are bought, covered, taken to and from school, studied, borrowed and forgotten. The lycée is by implication defined by Raillard who calls it the 'place where one is initiated into the discourses which our civilisation feeds on' (1968, 139), and the novel is as much concerned with the nature and adequacy of these discourses as it is with what they portray. For, as Butor writes elsewhere: 'The library gives us the world, but it gives us a false world' (1968, 8). Nevertheless, representing the world as it really is cannot be achieved simply by walking out of the library. There is no escape from the library because 'We are always writing inside literature' (Butor 1968, 18), and in order to rectify the library's false images we have to rewrite the texts in it, adapt and translate the books which no longer represent our world. It is as a realist effort to rewrite the literature in which *Degrés* belongs that the numerous quotations it contains should be seen.

The distance between the quoted texts and the real world is emphasised in a number of ways. First and foremost there is the fact of their quoted status, which is reinforced by their fragmentary presentation. When they are estranged from us in this way, the possibility of looking through them at what they represent is greatly reduced; instead, they appear in all their opacity as objects. Secondly, the form in which they are presented in the text often involves a kind of double quotation, when the fragments are more or less uncomprehendingly read aloud by the boys who seem far less interested in what the passage is saying than in the marks they are going to score for their performance. Seen through the eyes of the schoolboys, Hannibal's journey across the Alps loses a good deal of its significance in relation to the themes of travel and discovery, and becomes simply an exasperating and time-consuming part of homework. 'What a pain in the neck Livy is!' exclaims Michel Daval as he struggles through the passage he has to prepare for class the next day (204). Thirdly, many of the texts quoted are either in a foreign language or, as in the case of Rabelais and Montaigne, in sixteenth-century French. The gap between Rabelais's language and the contemporary French language is emphasised by Eller's repeated misreading of this foreign French where he unintentionally updates the grammar of Rabelais' text (11). Where the texts are Greek, Latin, Italian or English, this difference is even greater, and every word has to be painstakingly translated in order to acquire any meaning at all; the obstacles created by language itself minimise its signifying or referential function and make it primarily an object in the text's representation.

These boys struggle through an alien world of other discourses, laboriously learning the languages which constitute their culture, languages which the novel deconstructs through its portrayal of this toilsome apprenticeship. We are reminded that the world is not automatically given through language, that the novel's mimetic status cannot be guaranteed simply by its good faith, but can be assured only when it has redistributed the surface of the library in order to cut new windows onto the real world (Butor, 1968, 8). Mimesis is achieved largely through the text's self-critical quotation of outmoded or conventional discourses.

Unlike the explicit or implied quotations in *Le Père Goriot* and *Le rouge et le noir*, the texts used as sources for the quotations in *Degrés* are none of them novels; but in so far as they bear on the question of representation, their presence in Butor's novel creates a high degree of novelistic self-consciousness. In general the quoted texts in a novel need not themselves be novels, but it is extremely likely that they will be, for, as Sollers says: 'the novel is the way this society speaks of itself' (1968, 228); or, in Butor's words: 'we are bathed in a novelistic atmosphere' (1968, 7). If the way in which we speak of reality is already novelistic, it is also the task of the novel to make this fact clear to us by distancing our manner of talking, to make it audible *as* a way of talking.

This definition of the novel as self-criticism based on quotation applies as much to the so-called realist novel of the nineteenth century as it does to the somewhat unrealistic fiction of Robbe-Grillet, for example. If the narrative organisation of *La maison de rendez-vous* does not fully support the illusion of a coherent and separate world, it does nevertheless represent to us most effectively the nature of the discourses which we use to talk about the world, particularly the language derived from popular fiction (trash) which we use to talk of sex, money and foreign countries in our society. When we read in the novel: 'Everybody knows Hong-Kong, its harbour, its junks, its sampans, the office-blocks of Kowloon, and the close-fitting dresses with the slit in the side to the thigh, which the Eurasian girls wear' (13), it is true in the sense that we are all steeped in a discursive atmosphere that represents Hong Kong to us in this way, even if, strictly speaking, we have no direct experience of the place. Hong Kong is part of our modern mythology, whose tyranny the novel can free us from by presenting its myths as objects, as Robbe-Grillet does in this and his other later novels.

The citational function of the novel must be regarded as a central feature of the genre, although the form taken by Butor's writing after *Degrés* obliges us to add a few provisos. *Degrés* is the last of Butor's texts to be specifically designated a novel. His subsequent writings deliberately contest genre-categories: *Mobile* is subtitled 'Étude pour une représentation des États-Unis', *Réseau aérien* 'Texte radiophonique', *6 810 000 litres d'eau par seconde* 'Étude stéréophonique', and *Portrait de l'artiste en jeune singe* 'Capriccio', and so on. They are all to a greater or lesser degree both citational and representational in purpose, and to this extent there is justification for placing them under the categories 'Romanesque II' and 'Romanesque III', with 'Romanesque I' being reserved for the novels proper.[7] Butor himself has suggested that coherent narrative is the essential criterion for fiction (1964, 293), but it is perhaps not so much this strictly narrative component that constitutes an essential

---

[7] See Roudaut, 1966 for a discussion of these divisions which have become standard in Butor criticism.

prerequisite of the novel, as the discursive hierarchy that the *telling* of stories involves. Butor's later writing has no particular narrative purpose and so is not really concerned with the telling of stories. As a consequence the narrational discourse is either suppressed, or loses its hierarchical superiority to become a series of stage-directions or simply the utterance of one speaker amongst others. We may say, then, that in order to be a novel, the citational and mimetic elements of a text need to be presented in a narrational structure.

Mimesis, reflexivity and self-quotation: 'Topologie d'une cité fantôme'

The third and final type of quotation to be discussed in this chapter is one which is frequently regarded as supremely characteristic of the nouveau roman: *mise en abyme*.[8] It was Gide who originally coined this term to describe a certain kind of strategy in art: 'In a work of art I rather like to find transposed onto the scale of the characters, the very subject of that work. Nothing illuminates it better or more surely establishes the proportions of the whole.' (*Journal*, 41). Among the examples he gives of this kind of transposition are the mirrors in the paintings of Memling or Metzys, the play within the play in *Hamlet*, and the story within the story in Poe's *Fall of the House of Usher*, and he ends by saying that he can best convey what he has in mind by means of a 'comparison with the device of heraldry that consists in setting in the escutcheon a smaller one "*en abyme*" [at the heart-point]' (41).[9] In other words, Gide's *mise en abyme* consists in a representation or quotation of the work within the work itself, and as such it is a device well-suited to the reflexivity of the nouveau roman.

This reflexive nature was one of the first features to be noted and commented on in writings on the nouveau roman, and was generally taken to be a sign of its subversive character. For

---

[8] See Ricardou, 1967, 171–90 and 1973, 47–75, and Dällenbach, 1977, especially 151–288.

[9] It appears that Gide's use of heraldic terminology is less than precise. This, however, makes no difference to the nature of the device he is describing, nor has it affected the way in which the term is used in critical and theoretical writings. For a discussion of the passage from Gide's *Journal* see Dällenbach, 1977, 15–31.

example, the *anti-roman* which Sartre identifies in his preface to Sarraute's *Portrait d'un inconnu* is constituted by its reflexivity:

> One of the most remarkable features of our literary era is the appearance, here and there, of tough and totally *negative* works which one might call anti-novels. [...] These strange works are hard to classify but they are not a sign of the weakness of the novel as a genre, they simply show that we are living in an era of reflection and that *the novel is in the process of reflecting on itself.* (7–8, my emphases)

For Sartre the novel's self-preoccupation and self-discovery are the result of negation, and this makes the nouveau roman a case apart in the house of fiction. This view is reiterated in Ricardou's discussion of reflexivity as it is found in *mise en abyme* : it is 'primarily the *structural revolt* of a fragment of narrative against the overall narrative which contains it' (1967, 181, my emphasis). It is this revolt which leads to self-revelation: 'As soon as the narrative contests itself, it immediately presents itself as narrative' (182). But the price of self-awareness is, in Ricardou's view, self-negation; for by summarising the story in which it appears, *mise en abyme* functions as a premature revelation of the truth whose deferment and delay are the primary constituents of narrative itself.[10]

Gide, however, makes no mention of any negative aspect of the device, and he attributes to it an entirely revelatory effect. It illuminates and corroborates without subverting. Where there is *mise en abyme* in a work of art 'nothing illuminates it better or more surely establishes the proportions of the whole'. Certainly in thematic terms *mise en abyme* can be seen to operate in an entirely positive manner, for it acts both as a repetition and a condensation of the text's preoccupations and so promotes their identification. 'All reflection is a device for semantic overload,' writes Dällenbach (1977, 62), not only because it repeats and condenses, but also because, like other semantically privileged *topoi* such as allegory or symbol, it signifies on more than one level. A mechanism like this which serves so effectively as a heuristic tool hardly deserves to be seen as the agent of subversion and destruction.

---

[10] Although Bal (1977) claims that *mise en abyme* (or what she calls the 'diagrammatical icon') is an integral part of all narrative.

It is however, not in relation either to narrative or to theme that *mise en abyme* can most interestingly be explored, but rather in the context of representation, and it is here that the nouveau roman's links with its fictional past can most accurately and fully be explored. *Mise en abyme* depends for its existence on the notion of representation and the possibility of distinguishing between reality and artifice. For an item to qualify as *mise en abyme* in a text, it must first have points of analogy with the text as a whole, and, secondly it must, ontologically speaking, be embedded (*emboîté*) in the spatio-temporal world of the text, existing both as an object within it and as a representation or mirror of it (Dällenbach 1977, 65–74). Items which function as *mise en abyme* are able to represent the text in which they appear only by being themselves represented in that text. Their own representations have a different ontological status from those of the text itself, so that the elements which may potentially be regarded as *mise en abyme* in a novel will be (to take *Topologie d'une cité fantôme* as an example) mirrors, paintings, photographs, theatrical performances, frescos, sculptures, or (to take *L'emploi du temps* as another example) stained-glass windows, cathedrals, tapestries, other novels, and so on. Like the quoted discourses of characters or of other literature, these representations operate not just as a means of representation in a text (representing the story of Cain and Abel or the adventures of Theseus), but as objects of its own representation. And, since it is the text itself which is represented by *mise en abyme*, the self-criticism resulting from this strategy will be very intense indeed. The text's own discourse is presented within a frame as if it were the 'language of another' (Bakhtin, 1968, 127), and so implies that the novel can only hear the nature of its own discourse by means of self-quotation.

This highly reflexive device is, nevertheless, equally concerned with the question of mimesis. It is an object which is represented by the text and one which is itself representational. Indeed, the inclusion of representations within a text acts as a powerful connoter of the real, for by this means a text can suggest that what is not representation is real. In *L'emploi du temps* one of the reasons why we assume that Revel's depiction of his life in Bleston is real, is because the text marks it as onto-logically different from Burton's detective novel or from the images in the stained-glass window. This perception of onto-logical difference between the real and the represented is es-sential to all mimesis:

That which is, the being-present (the matrix form of substance, of reality, of the oppositions between form and matter, essence and existence, objectivity and subjectivity, etc.) can be distinguished from appearance, image, phenomenon, etc., that is to say, from that which in presenting it as being-present, reduplicates it, re-presents it and consequently replaces it and de-presents it. (Derrida, 1972, 217)

Although the novel itself is 'only' an appearance or an image, its representation of the distinction between 'that which is' and its 'image' serves to validate its own representational status. Furthermore, one could even go so far as to suggest that the more a novel mirrors itself in its represented images, the greater this validity will be, since the '"works within the work" reflect the novel in the same way as the novel reflects reality', as Dällenbach writes in his discussion of *L'emploi du temps* (1977, 157). The reflexivity of *mise en abyme* is, therefore, very closely bound up with the representational function which has traditionally been associated with the novel.

Moreover, however great the degree of reflexivity in *mise en abyme*, it must always depend for its very existence on the text's status as mimesis. For, unless the text itself is seen as having a fairly substantial representation function, there will be no basis on which to distinguish between real and represented within it, and consequently no means of identifying the re-presented representations which constitute *mise en abyme*. We cannot designate the tapestry in *L'emploi du temps* as *mise en abyme* if we cannot see it as a certain kind of object within a representa-tional context. Paradoxically, therefore, *mise en abyme* with all its reflexive potential comes into its own chiefly in the predo-minantly representational arts, in particular figurative paint-ing, the theatre and the novel which, significantly, are the genres from which Gide draws his examples in his discussion of the device in the *Journal*. Seen in the context of the mimetic function of the novel, *mise en abyme* would seem not to constitute a subversion or negation of the traditional framework of the genre, but an extension or consequence of it. Gide identifies *mise en abyme* in fiction as historically distant as Goethe's *Wilhelm Meister* (1796 and 1829) and Poe's *Fall of the House of Usher* (1839), and although its use may have proliferated dramatically in the nouveau roman, it certainly cannot be regarded as an exclusive feature of those novels. Indeed, now that we have defined the device in relation to mimesis (as dependent on it and supportive of it) its proliferation can be seen as a mark of the nouveau roman's preoccupation with representation rather than as a sign of a rejection of it.

As this book has shown, representation in the novel is not a straightforward procedure. Every major aspect of fiction – plot, character and narration – is an artificial construct which we use both inside and outside fiction on the assumption that they enable us to speak of the real world, but which a closer examination will always reveal as fictitious. The conventional basis of *vraisemblance* has been amply discussed in recent literary theory, and consciousness of this conventionality has clearly haunted the nouveau roman just as it has always haunted realist fiction. This awareness of the problematic nature of representation is a topic which we may read in all *mise en abyme*, for it represents the novel to itself not only as discourse (in the manner of a quotation) but also as representation. As a representation of representation it inevitably raises questions concerning representation, and in this way it becomes possible to see fiction as a laboratory of mimesis (just as it is also the laboratory of narrative, character and language), where *mise en abyme* acts as the most powerful focus for investigation and experimentation.

I shall take Robbe-Grillet's *Topologie d'une cité fantôme* as the pretext for discussion of *mise en abyme* and the novel as the laboratory of mimesis, not only because the device is used so frequently in the text, but also because, like much of Robbe-Grillet's fiction since *Dans le labyrinthe*, the novel appears not to yield a coherent and self-consistent representation of a world. I hope to demonstrate that, despite the confusions in the novel, questions concerning mimesis are implied on almost every page.[11] Robbe-Grillet's city may be imaginary but it can be evoked or even constructed only by mimetic strategies: 'I grope my way forward and I place my hand on the chill wall where, engraving in the schist with the tip of a broad-bladed knife, I now write the word CONSTRUCTION, a *painting "en trompe l'oeil"*, an *imaginary construction* through which I name the ruins of a future deity' (13, my emphases). Construction will always appear as imitation, even when the imitated object exists in the imagination or in the future. Even writing the word 'construction' cannot be achieved without implying that the text is also copying a writing that takes place elsewhere.

The novel contains numerous representational objects, most of which can be regarded as *mise en abyme* because they represent the world in which they appear. They are ontologically embedded in the spatio-temporal world of the text and contain points of analogy with it. The major reflexive items in the text are the various mirrors, the painting, the etching, photographs and cameras, tarot cards, theatrical productions, frescos, stage sets, coins, portraits, dummies (all of which are visual representations), as well as posters, a flag on a ship, inscriptions carved in stone, a guide book, poetry, and old-fashioned novels with psychological dramas (all of which represent writing in some form or another, decipherable or otherwise). Both the world and the text of the novel are mirrored in these items. Although the world of the novel is not entirely coherent, it contains a number of features by which it can (approximately) be identified: adolescent girls incarcerated in a brothel or prison, the ritual and quasi-religious rape and murder of such a girl (sometimes) in a temple on a hill, a goddess, the birth of her child, a young woman and her twin children.

Our view of this world is jeopardised to a certain extent by

[11] The novel's preoccupation with this orthodox topic is doubly significant and doubly striking if we believe Dällenbach when he argues that the already essentially transgressive device of *mise en abyme* is itself disrupted in some of the more recent novels of the nouveau roman (novels which would presumably include this one): 'L'avènement d'un texte disloqué, hyperréflexif (*Les lieux-dits*), aléatoire (*Projet pour une révolution à New York*) ou multipolaire (*Triptyque*) entraîne la crise de la mise en abyme' (1977, 200).

uncertainties due to possible repetitions, imposters and re-
productions contained within it. The girls are all more or less
interchangeable in appearance and certainly all equally fit
for the ritual rape which a good many of them fall victim to.
The goddess has a false counterpart (4) as do the twins (185),
but there seems to be no real basis for distinguishing between
them, nor any narrative consequences resulting from the existence of these fakes. In one sense these duplications and
duplicities in the world of the novel act as obstacles to an unequivocal representation of it; they make that world harder to
reconstruct. But equally, in another sense, they draw our attention to the whole enterprise of mimesis, for they may be read
as variants or exercises on the theme of the duplication on
which all representation rests.

The ambiguities of sameness and difference involved in
mimetic reproduction are particularly acutely and comically
formulated in the novel with reference to the topic of human
reproduction. The parthenogenetic, homosexual and hermaphrodite factors in the continuation of the species as it is depicted in *Topologie* exclude the element of difference on which
it normally depends:

As is generally known, this David was the masculine double of
Vanadé, the hermaphrodite deity of pleasure. He reigned as master
over this nation of girls, and himself had the body of a woman but
the addition of a male organ, which is clearly visible on the pictures
where the god-goddess is depicted in the sky, flying towards his countless wives, who await the glowing cloud, half open, each lying in
front of the gaping doorway of her bedroom on a solitary bed, which
tradition usually represents in the form of a boat-bed. According to
the legend this partially homosexual fertilisation guaranteed the
reproduction of the species, but only produced yet more females,
whose parthenogenetic lineage was thus continued from generation
to generation. (44–5)

But does it in fact make sense to speak of a 'masculine double',
a question which is raised again in the apparently contradictory
image of the identical twins of different sex (61, 185)? The confusion concerning sameness and difference in the real world
of the novel not only creates difficulties in our attempts to
reconstruct that world, but also affects the way we evaluate

the representations in the novel. When the final sacrificial victim proves to be a dummy, how much difference does this make? How far is a representation the same as or different from what it represents? And what is the novel's own status as the representation of the ruined city?

These questions are implied in the novel's presentation of the many mirrors in it. Of all the images of representation contained in the novel, that of the mirror would appear to involve the least distortion, for here representation does not depend on construction, convention or artistry of any kind. We would expect the mirror to contain the greatest degree of likeness. And indeed, the mirror's image does prove to be the same as what it represents. But at the same time it pays the price of a certain irreducible otherness, as the following passage suggests:

The double

She who looks at herself too long has been split into two by the mirror. Here is the improbable lover, other, inaccessible and the same, born of solitude and dreams and of the wandering hand: twice two hands, twice two eyes, twice two breasts. Did I also dream twice two mouths, of twice twice two lips? (123–4)

The image is both the same and different. The human body consists of a mirror image of itself that does not involve onto-logical difference: left mirrors right (or vice versa) to give two hands, eyes and breasts, etc. But reflected in a mirror it both remains the same and becomes other ('inaccessible'), providing us with an image of mimesis itself: 'both similar and different, different because – in as far as – it is similar, the same as and other than what it doubles' (Derrida, 1972, 217). But then seen as the product of the narrator's dream or of his writing hand ('the wandering hand') a certain sameness is restored, so that the girl and her image become simply a pair, as if there were two girls instead of one and her image ('twice two hands, twice two eyes, twice two breasts'). Sameness is restored but at the cost of the girl and her image both appearing as representa-tions, different. If there are two mouths twice over then perhaps the girl and her image are in their turn the copy of another girl and her image? Mimesis is reinstated at the same moment that it appears to be abolished.

The mirror as representation is problematic not just for ontological reasons, but also for the practical reason that in reflecting it inverts. Unlike a painting, a mirror represents left as right and right as left, and this inaccuracy is explored in the text's treatment of the etchings in which the artist depicts one of the girls in the cell in the prison. Etchings are produced by a double mirroring process: the engraving is a mirror-image of what it represents, and the print taken from it mirrors it in turn to restore the original form of the represented object. So when the artist draws exactly what she sees before her without compensating for the inversion of the printing process, her painstakingly accurate representation will, paradoxically, turn out false:

> So at this moment, the engraver's right hand is tracing the outline of the left hand of the image with a flawless line, *reproducing exactly and clearly* each finger of the model's left hand.
> However, the inversion of the drawing when it has been printed means that the definitive image will be performing with her right hand the gesture that the living model is executing with her left hand, since the artist, who *thinks she is copying out her subject*, has failed to take the precaution of reconstructing its lines back to front. (33–4, my emphases)

Falsification here is the direct consequence of representational accuracy. Difference will follow from sameness and sameness can only be produced by difference. Indeed, difference is a concept ingrained in our concept of representational similarity. However accurately the artist reproduces the reality she sees before her, and however much we may imagine her engraving to be the same as what it represents, we do nevertheless also expect it to be separate and distinct from that reality. It is therefore a shock when the text begins to behave as if they were the same and speaks of the 'sharp tip in the engraver's hand which stabs the image's genitals with one blow, the long sharp scream from the model who quickly moves her right hand to the middle of her pubic hair, thus losing her pose' (37). This is a violation in every sense of the word.

And yet is not every representation a kind of violation? The text describes the action in this cell ('la cellule génératrice') as the 'motionless ceremony of violence and representation'.

Certainly, the images reflected by the mirrors in the novel act as reflexive reminders on the part of the text that the mirror's reflection is always at least a distortion if not a violation of the real. Mirrors disrupt so that left appears as right, or backwards as forwards or outside as inside, as the following examples show. A small boy walks towards a window between a sewing machine and a

wardrobe with a mirror in which an articulated dummy is reflected, a young woman made out of a blond and pink plastic material, standing at the far end of the room in an attitude of ecstasy, looking so welcoming inspite of a certain stiffness, or fixity of gesture, that she seems – she is naked too – to be stretching out her arms towards the boy who seems to be walking towards her; but the little boy is only advancing towards his own image reflected by the greenish depths of the mirror, that is to say in the *opposite direction* – with the tip of one foot still resting uncertainly on the floor which he is reluctant to leave completely for fear of losing his precarious balance – so, on the contrary moving away from the flesh-coloured dummy, who, instead of facing him, is in fact behind him, like him, looking towards the pale light in the window. (174–5, my emphasis)

What the mirror represents as movement towards proves in reality to be movement away in a manner which is both exact and deceptive. The mirror in the narrator's own room operates a similar kind of deception:

A large mirror, which takes up the whole of the visible part of the wall behind the table (still the same one), reflects the bluish image of the house opposite, as if the outside of the room was inside, following a mechanism which is not unlike the fanatical temple whose trace I am reconstructing with difficulty, day after day, through the repetitions, contradictions and gaps. (196)

Here the inverted image of reality (outside as inside) sets off a chain of associated images related to the theme of mimesis. The mirror's image is different from the reality which it reflects, but it is like another reality, the temple, which the narrator's text is also trying to copy (trace). Likeness is not the result of simple reflection, a point implied by the indirect means whereby the narrator achieves his own representation of the temple – 'through the repetitions, contradictions and gaps'. In Robbe-Grillet's novel, the representations afforded by techniques of mirroring tend to yield difference rather than sameness, and similarity is created through difference. Does this suggest that the construction of the 'cité fantôme' is best executed by these inversions and differences, or is the painting 'en trompe l'oeil' to be effected by other means?

If we turn to the topic of theatrical representation in the novel, we find the problematics of representation tackled in a somewhat different manner, throwing a different light on the question of the narrator's representational task. The notion of representation is central to the theatre in general and to the way it is represented in *Topologie d'une cité fantôme* in particular. First, because theatre is frequently used for realist purposes (certainly in this novel it represents most exactly scenes which we have previously encountered as part of the 'real' world of the city). Secondly, the French word for a theatrical performance, 'représentation', directly invites speculation about the representational nature of the theatre. Thirdly, because every performance is a re-presentation of the previous night's performance. And finally, in this novel, the theatre is also given the task of representing other representations: in its depiction of the 'cellule génératrice' (also called the 'salle de *reproduction*') it includes the photographer and her camera, the mirror, the tarot cards, and so on. Theatre as *mise en abyme* has its own objects *en abyme*.

Theatre as mimesis is repeatedly defined as different by the text. The apparatus of the stage is referred to over and over again, so that although the world represented on the stage is in one sense the same as the real world, it is also immediately perceptible as different precisely because it is represented. The curtain and the footlights act as markers of this difference and unambiguously divide the auditorium from the stage. And yet at times, the need for it seems to be questioned by the text. The novel is perfectly capable of apparently forgetting the otherness and inaccessibility that it has established. In a description of a theatrical representation of the scene in the cell, the novel turns its attention to one of the tarot cards, and when it proceeds to describe what is represented on the card it almost imperceptibly crosses the bounds of *vraisemblance*, for something this small and this detailed could never actually be seen by an audience. And, then, in a manner highly characteristic of Robbe-Grillet, the description of the woman and her children on the card becomes narrative, and another boundary is also crossed:

It is the picture of a crude drawing of a tall stone tower, whose foot has caught fire in an enormous blaze as if the stone itself was burning, while at the very top, on the small round terrace, a young woman holding her two children by the hand anxiously scans the sea's horizon, as if she still hoped it would bring some last-minute help. On closer inspection, one soon notices that the little boy and the little girl are alike in every feature, like two twins, as you would have expected, and can in fact almost only be distinguished by their clothes which custom assigns to different sexes.

The children are standing on either side of their mother, listening with studious attention, standing stiffly for fear of missing some detail, as she explains the topography of the landscape spread out at their feet.[. . .]

So that her son can get a glimpse over the stone parapet which is too high for him, of the houses nearest the tower, or at least of their roofs that slope in two directions and are covered with Roman tiles, and, vertically beneath, up against the breathtakingly high wall, the blackish rocks (is it a heap of lava?) on which this watchtower was built whose three hundred and thirty-three steps they have climbed with difficulty – because of their abnormal height and their poor state of repair – to round off their Sunday outing, Mrs Hamilton *lets go of the little girl's hand, grasps the boy with both arms under the armpits and hoists him up above the granite ledge, leaning his tiny body further and further out over the abyss.* (67–9, my emphases)

With these gestures the picture comes alive and ceases to be representation. Indeed even the theatre is quite forgotten as the trio go back down the tower and complete their tour of the city until they get a glimpse of the stage itself through a window in the building which had originally been represented on the stage in the theatre. They see the actresses about to start the performance and they watch the curtains open for the beginning of the play. The difference between real and re-presented is re-established by this reference to the curtain, but the characters originally represented *within* a representation on the stage have managed to escape into a building *outside* the theatre . . .

How is this breakout achieved? In large part, precisely through the mimetic element of *mise en abyme*. The image on the tarot card has so many points of analogy with the real world of the 'cité fantôme' that it is enabled to come to life: the woman and her twins, the fire and the proximity of the sea all have their counterparts in the real world, and it is this mimetic similarity which permits the escape from difference. These characters are restored to the real world from a state which is doubly embedded in it (on the card in the theatre) by means of representational fidelity. Moreover, in their apparently transgressive restoration to the spatio-temporal world of the novel, they are freed from mimesis as well as by it: they cease to be imitations and become real instead.

In one sense this episode is a subversion of the norms of the *vraisemblable*, but in another sense is proof of the power of mimesis. Theatre as *mise en abyme* presents the other side of the mimetic coin to that offered by the mirrors. Where the mirror stresses the difference behind apparent sameness, the theatre explores the effects of similarity that can be found in apparent difference, and the novel's own status as mimesis is implicated in this ambiguity: it both constructs and represents its world. The 'cellule génératrice' is also the 'salle de reproduction'. It designates itself both as writing and as mimesis through the reflexive reflections of *mise en abyme*. As the narrator implies, his city, however ghostly or imaginary, is there even before he begins to construct it:

Before I fall asleep, the city, once again, erects its burnt walls in front of my closed eyes, with its blind windows, its gaping doorways which lead nowhere: grey sky, platitude, absent rooms emptied even of their ghosts. The twilight thickens. I grope my way forward and I place my hand on the chill wall where, engraving in the schist with the tip of a broad-bladed knife, I now write the word CONSTRUC-TION, a painting 'en trompe l'oeil', an imaginary construction through which I name the ruins of a future deity. (13)

The writing that is to call the city into being is inscribed by the narrator on to the walls of the city which already exist, exterior to him and resistant to his writing. Mimesis, however problematic it is made, will always reassert itself. The narrator's writing is rendered mimetic, a painting 'en trompe l'oeil', even at the moment when it designates itself most fully as writing. Indeed, the very abundance of *mise en abyme*, with its dependence on and connotation of representation, both in this novel and in the nouveau roman as a whole firmly inscribes this fiction within representation. And of all the reflexive strategies available to literature, it is significant that the nouveau roman should have adopted and developed the one which inevitably and emphatically also entails mimesis.

Mise en abyme is a device which presents in a condensed form a number of the essential elements of all fiction. In so far as its representation of the world also involves self-representation, it typifies all the novelistic strategies discussed in this book, and it seems to confirm the impression that the novel cannot actually speak of itself except by speaking of other things. Equally, seen as a kind of quotation, *mise en abyme* suggests that the novel can only operate its reflexive discourse by delegating it to another speaker – a mirror, a play or a stained-glass window. There is no language of fiction that can assume full responsibility for representing itself or full transparency for representing the world. Each is attenuated by the other, suspended and questioned in a system whose reflecting and reflexive aims are always elaborated in a system composed of more or less quoted languages.

Conclusion

With the nouveau roman, fiction appears to have lost faith in the representational function that it is conventionally or naïvely supposed to have. It is no longer able to give us a world from which we assume it then discreetly and gracefully withdraws. The objects it depicts seem hardly to merit even the scanty attention that they get (the publication of a novel or a history lesson in school), so that we begin to wonder what its mimetic project consists of. In this, the nouveau roman is like the sculpture in Robbe-Grillet's *L'année dernière à Marienbad* which, as Barthes says, is a most admirable symbol

not just because the statue itself implies a variety of uncertain meanings which are nevertheless named (*it is you, it is me, it is classical gods, Helen, Agamemnon*, etc.), but also because the prince and his wife are pointing with certainty to an uncertain object (situated inside the story? in the garden? in the auditorium?): *this*, they say. But what is *this*? Perhaps the whole of literature is in this fragile anaphora which simultaneously points and is silent. (1963, 15–16)

So it is not just the nouveau roman which points and is silent, but *all* literature too, says Barthes. The objects designated by the nouveau roman may be more hesitantly represented than those of Balzac's French society, but any hesitation, however slight it may appear, will instigate an exploration of the poetics of the text. It soon becomes apparent that any representation is grounded in convention. The discourse of fiction does not have its source in the objects it points to, and it is not the innocent medium which secretaries use to record what history dictates. In the novel, questions of poetics are implied in even the most mimetically oriented enterprise, and it is involved in endless self-exploration as it tries to discover itself and the world. In seeking the one, it must, in some ways, always stumble on the other; for the world itself consists in a dense babble of discourses which the novel, in its attempt to perceive its own conventions, is bound to hear; and in seeking to represent the world, the novel is also bound to discover that the perception of that chattering world depends on the recognition and elaboration of its own discourses.

The nouveau roman is undoubtedly the product of a historically specific crisis in the reading of fiction. But, contrary to many of the claims made for it, its role has not been to hasten the end of the era of fiction, nor yet simply to alter or extend the range of ingredients that make up the traditional version of the genre. The nouveau roman is a solution to the crisis as well as a manifestation of it, for it proposes a redefinition of fiction in exactly those areas where it was regarded as most atrophied or problematic: plot, character, narration and representation. By placing these conventions in the foreground of its preoccupations, the nouveau roman revives the very concepts which at first seemed the most ossified and irrelevant. In apparently writing against plot or representation, the nouveau roman has made them more productive and more interesting.

Moreover, this generic redefinition is not just restricted to its own practice, or even to the fiction which follows it. It is retrospective in that it restores to us a new past. Not only has it rearranged the literary hierarchy to give greater prominence to Diderot's *Jacques le fataliste* or to the works of Raymond Roussel, for example, but it has thrown new light on the literature with which we have always lived. In their misreading of Balzac, for example, the new novelists have allowed us to hear a new voice in their precursor's work. And it is the mark of what Harold Bloom calls a 'strong poet' that his work 'makes it seem to us, not as though the precursor were writing it, but as though the later poet himself had written the precursor's characteristic work' (1973, 16). Balzac, as misread by the nouveau roman, appals us with his monstrous confidence in aiming to depict the whole of French society, and is (to use Bloom's terms again) completed by their antithetical and systematic reluctance to embark on any documentary project. But, retroactively, under the influence of the nouveau roman, we also discover in Balzac, for example, alongside the monstrously confident secretary to the France of the early nineteenth century, a whole world of rhetoric. Balzac's documentary enterprise begins to interact with a linguistic enterprise in a way that is peculiar not just to him (as it is peculiar to any writer), but to every text. The nouveau roman makes us realise that the revelation of a society is inextricably bound up with the revelation of language. Each depends on the other, so that each can also be read as a metaphor for the other; our view of history is then coloured by our view of the language through which it is constructed, and our view of that language is equally determined by the kind of history which it elaborates. It is in large part thanks to the nouveau roman that this richer, more interesting Balzac has become available to us.

Bibliography

The novels of Butor, Robbe-Grillet and Sarraute:

Butor, Michel, *Passage de Milan*. Paris: Minuit, 1954.
    L'emploi du temps. Paris: Minuit, 1956.
    La modification. Paris: Minuit, 1957.
    Degrés. Paris: Gallimard, 1960.
Robbe-Grillet, Alain, *Les gommes*. Paris: Minuit, 1953.
    Le voyeur. Paris: Minuit, 1955.
    La jalousie. Paris: Minuit, 1957.
    Dans le labyrinthe. Paris: Minuit, 1959.
    La maison de rendez-vous. Paris: Minuit, 1965.
    Projet pour une révolution à New York. Paris: Minuit, 1970.
    Topologie d'une cité fantôme. Paris: Minuit, 1976.
    Un régicide. Paris: Minuit, 1978.
    Souvenirs au triangle d'or. Paris: Minuit, 1978.
Sarraute, Nathalie, *Portrait d'un inconnu* (1948). Paris, Gallimard, 1956.
    Martereau. Paris: Gallimard, 1953.
    Le planétarium. Paris: Gallimard, 1959.
    Les fruits d'or. Paris: Gallimard, 1963.
    Entre la vie et la mort. Paris: Gallimard, 1968.
    Vous les entendez? Paris: Gallimard, 1972.
    'Disent les imbéciles' Paris: Gallimard, 1976.

With the exception of Butor's *Passage de Milan*, all these novels are
available in English translations.

Other literary texts:

Austen, Jane, *Sense and Sensibility*. Harmondsworth: Penguin, 1969.
Dickens, Charles, *David Copperfield*. London: Oxford University
    Press, 1948.
Gide, André, *Journal 1889–1939*. Paris: Bibliothèque de la Pléiade,
    1948.

Proust, Marcel, *A la recherche du temps perdu*, 3 vols. Paris: Bibliothèque de la Pléiade, 1954.
Robbe-Grillet, Alain, *Glissements progressifs du plaisir* (Ciné-roman). Paris: Minuit, 1973.
Sarraute, Nathalie, *Tropismes* (1939). Paris: Minuit, 1957.
 Isma, suivi de Le silence et Le mensonge. Paris: Gallimard, 1970.
Sophocles, *Three tragedies: Antigone, Oedipus the King, Electra*, trans. H. D. F. Kitto. London: Oxford University Press, 1962.
Stendhal, *Le rouge et le noir*. In *Romans et nouvelles*, vol. I. Paris: Bibliothèque de la Pléiade, 1959.
Woolf, Virginia, *Mrs Dalloway*. Harmondsworth: Penguin, 1969.
 To the Lighthouse. Harmondsworth: Penguin, 1969.

References and general bibliography:

Alter, Jean, 1966. *La vision du monde d'Alain Robbe-Grillet*. Geneva: Droz.
Astier, Pierre, 1969. *Encyclopédie du nouveau roman: la crise du roman français et le nouveau réalisme*. Paris: Nouvelles éditions Debresse.
Auden, W. H. 1962. *The Dyer's Hand*. New York: Random House.
Bakhtine, Mikhail, 1970. *La poétique de Dostoïevski* (1963), trad. Isabelle Kolitcheff. Paris: Seuil. (*Problems of Dostoevsky's Poetics*, Ann-Arbor, Mich.: Ardis, 1973).
 1968. L'énoncé dans le roman (1965). *Langages* 12, 126–32.
Bal, Mieke, 1977. *Narratologie: les instances du récit*. Paris: Klincksieck.
 1979. *Mensen van papier: over personages in de literatuur* (ed.). Assen: Van Gorcum.
Bally, Charles, 1912. Le style indirect libre en français moderne. *Germanisch-Romanische Monatsschrift* 4, 549–56, 597–606.
 1914. Figures de pensée et formes linguistiques. *Germanisch-Romanische Monatsschrift* 6, 405–22, 456–70.
Banfield, Ann, 1973. Narrative style and the grammar of direct and indirect speech. *Foundations of Language* 10:1, 1–39.
Barrère, Jean-Bertrand, 1964. *La cure d'amaigrissement du roman*. Paris: Albin Michel.
Barthes, Roland, 1963. Préface. In Morrissette 1963, pp. 7–16. Paris: Minuit.
 1966. Introduction à l'analyse structurale des récits. *Communications* 8, 1–27.
 1967. *Writing Degree Zero* (1953), trans. Annette Lavers & Colin Smith. London: Cape.
 1970a. *S/Z*. Paris: Seuil. (*S/Z*, London, Cape, 1974).
 1970b. Science versus literature. In *Structuralism: a reader*, ed. Michael Lane, pp. 410–16. London: Cape.

1971. *Essais critiques* (1964). Paris: Seuil. (*Critical Essays*, Evanston, Ill.: Northwestern University Press, 1972).

1972. *Le degré zéro de l'écriture, suivi de Nouveaux essais critiques*. Paris: Seuil.

1975. *Roland Barthes*. Paris: Seuil. (*Roland Barthes*, London: Macmillan, 1977).

Bellos, David, 1978. Narrative and communication. *Signs of Change* 3, 34–52.

Benveniste, Emile, 1966, *Problèmes de linguistique générale*. Paris: Gallimard. (*Problems in General Linguistics*, Coral Gables, FL.: University of Miami Press, 1970).

1974. *Problèmes de linguistique générale II*. Paris: Gallimard.

Bernal, Olga, 1964. *Alain Robbe-Grillet: le roman de l'absence*. Paris: Gallimard.

Bersani, Leo, 1970. *From Balzac to Beckett*. New York: Oxford University Press.

Blanchot, Maurice, 1959. La clarté romanesque. In *Le livre à venir*, pp. 195–201. Paris: Gallimard.

Bloch-Michel, Jean, 1963. *Le présent de l'indicatif*. Paris: Gallimard.

Bloom, Harold, 1973. *The Anxiety of Influence*. New York: Oxford University Press.

de Boisdeffre, Pierre, 1967. *La cafetière est sur la table: contre le 'nouveau roman'*. Paris: La Table Ronde.

Booth, Wayne, 1961. *The Rhetoric of Fiction*. Chicago: University of Chicago Press.

Britton, Celia, 1973. *Language as Text and Language as Theme: an Analysis of the Novels of Nathalie Sarraute*. Ph.D. thesis, University of Essex.

Bronzwaer, W. J. M., 1970. *Tense in the Novel*. Groningen: Walters-Noordhof.

Butor, Michel, 1960. *Répertoire*. Paris: Minuit.

1964. *Répertoire II*. Paris: Minuit.

1968. *Répertoire III*. Paris: Minuit.

Butor, Michel, 1974. (Colloque de Cerisy). Paris: Union générale d'éditions.

Calin, Françoise, 1976. *La vie retrouvée: étude de l'oeuvre romanesque de Nathalie Sarraute*. Paris: Minard.

Charbonnier, Georges, 1967. *Entretiens avec Michel Butor*. Paris: Gallimard.

Cornford, Francis M., 1941. *The Republic of Plato* (ed.). Oxford: Clarendon Press.

Cranaki, Mimica & Belaval, Yvon, 1965. *Nathalie Sarraute*. Paris: Gallimard.

Culler, Jonathan, 1974. *Flaubert: the Uses of Uncertainty*. London: Elek.

1975. *Structuralist Poetics*. London: Routledge & Kegan Paul.

Dällenbach, Lucien, 1972. *Le livre et ses miroirs dans l'oeuvre romanesque de Michel Butor*. Paris: Minard.

1977. *Le récit spéculaire: essai sur la mise en abyme*. Paris: Seuil.

Deleuze, Gilles, 1976. *Proust et les signes* (4th ed.). Paris: PUF. (*Proust and Signs*, London: Allen Lane 1972).

Derrida, Jacques, 1967. *De la grammatologie*. Paris: Minuit. (*Of Grammatology*, Baltimore, Md.: Johns Hopkins University Press, 1977).

1972. *La dissémination*. Paris: Seuil.

Dillon, George I. & Kirchhoff, Frederick, 1976. On the Form and Function of Free Indirect Style. *PTL* 1, 431–40.

Doležel, Lubomír, 1973. *Narrative Modes in Czech Literature*. Toronto: University of Toronto Press.

Eliez-Rüegg, Elisabeth, 1972. *La conscience d'autrui et la conscience des objets dans l'oeuvre de Nathalie Sarraute*. Bern: Herbert Lang.

Forster, E. M., 1949. *Aspects of the Novel* (1927). London: Arnold.

Foucault, Michel, 1966. *Les mots et les choses*. Paris: Gallimard. (*The Order of Things*, London: Tavistock, 1970).

1971. *L'ordre du discours*. Paris: Gallimard.

Friedman, Norman, 1955a. Forms of the Plot. *Journal of General Education* 8 : 4, 241–53.

1955b. Point of View in Fiction: the Development of a Critical Concept. *PMLA* 70 : 4, 1160–84.

Genette, Gérard, 1966. *Figures*. Paris: Seuil.

1969. *Figures ii*. Paris: Seuil.

1972. *Figures iii*. Paris: Seuil.

1976. *Mimologiques*. Paris: Seuil.

Goldmann, Lucien, 1964. *Pour une sociologie du roman*. Paris: Gallimard. (*Towards a Sociology of the Novel*, London: Tavistock, 1975).

Greimas, A. J., 1966. *Sémantique structurale*. Paris: Larousse.

Greimas, A. J. & Courtès, J., 1976. The Cognitive Dimension of Narrative Discourse. *New Literary History* 7 : 3, 433–47.

Hamon, Philippe, 1972. Qu'est-ce qu'une description? *Poétique* 12, 465–85.

1973. Un discours contraint. *Poétique* 16, 411–45.

Heath, Stephen, 1972. *The Nouveau Roman: a Study in the Practice of Writing*. London: Elek.

Helbo, André, 1975. *Michel Butor: vers une littérature du signe*. Brussels: Éditions Complexe.

James, Henry, 1961. *The Notebooks of Henry James*, ed. F. O. Mathiesson & Kenneth B. Murdock. New York: Oxford University Press.

Janvier, Ludovic, 1964. *Une parole exigeante: le nouveau roman*. Paris: Minuit.

Jean, Raymond, 1965. *La littérature et le réel: de Diderot au 'nouveau roman'*. Paris: Albin Michel.

Jefferson, Ann, 1977. What's In a Name? From Surname to Pronoun in the Novels of Nathalie Sarraute. *PTL* 2, 203–20.

1978. Imagery Versus Description: the Problematics of Representation in the Novels of Nathalie Sarraute. *Modern Language Review* 73 : 3, 513–24.

1979. Realisme en retoriek: fictionaliteit en waarheidsillusie bij het personage. In Bal, 1979, pp. 27–36.

Kayser, Wolfgang, 1970. Qui raconte le roman? *Poétique* 4, 498–510.

Kristeva, Julia, 1970. Une poétique ruinée. Preface to Bakhtine 1970, pp. 5–27.

Leenhardt, Jacques, 1973. *Lecture politique du roman: 'La jalousie' d'Alain Robbe-Grillet.* Paris: Minuit.

le Hir, Yves. 1961. Dialogue et typographie. *Information littéraire* 13 : 5, 215–16.

Leiris, Michel, 1958. Le réalisme mythologique de Michel Butor. *Critique* 129, 99–118.

Lorck, E., 1914. Passé défini, imparfait, passé indéfini. *Germanisch-Romanische Monatsschrift* 6, 43–57, 100–13, 177–91.

Lubbock, Percy, 1965. *The Craft of Fiction* (1921). London: Cape.

Matthews, Franklin J., 1972. Préface. In Alain Robbe-Grillet *La maison de rendez-vous,* pp. 7–43. Paris: Union générale d'éditions.

McCarthy, Mary, 1970. *The Writing on the Wall.* London: Weidenfeld and Nicolson.

McHale, Brian, 1978. Free Indirect Discourse: a Survey of Recent Accounts. *PTL* 3, 249–87.

Medvedev, P. N./Bakhtin, N. M., 1978. *The Formal Method in Literary Scholarship* (1928), trans. Albert J. Wehrle. Baltimore, Md.: Johns Hopkins University Press.

Meyer, Herman, 1968. *The Poetics of Quotation in the European Novel* (1961), trans. Theodore & Yelta Ziolkowski. Princeton: Princeton University Press.

Minogue, Valerie, 1973a. The Imagery of Childhood in Nathalie Sarraute's *Portrait d'un inconnu. French Studies* 27 : 2, 177–86.

1973b. Nathalie Sarraute's *Le planétarium:* the Narrator Narrated. *Forum for Modern Language Studies* 9 : 3, 217–34.

1976. Distortion and Creativity in the Subjective Viewpoint: Robbe-Grillet, Butor and Nathalie Sarraute. *Forum for Modern Language Studies* 12 : 1, 37–49.

Morrissette, Bruce, 1963. *Les romans de Robbe-Grillet.* Paris: Minuit. (*Alain Robbe-Grillet,* New York: Columbia University Press, 1965).

Mylne, Vivienne, 1975. Dialogue as Narrative in Eighteenth-century French Fiction. In *Studies in eighteenth-century French Literature Presented to Robert Niklaus,* ed. J. H. Fox *et al.,* pp. 173–92. Exeter: University of Exeter.

Newman, A. S., 1974. For a New Writing – a New criticism: Nathalie Sarraute, *Le planétarium. Australian Journal of French Studies* 11 : 1, 118–28.

1976. *Une poésie des discours: essai sur les romans de Nathalie Sarraute.*
    Geneva: Droz.

Nouveau roman: hier, aujourd'hui, 1972. (Colloque de Cerisy), 2 vols.
    Paris: Union générale d'éditions.

Pascal, Roy, 1977. *The Dual Voice.* Manchester University Press.

Pingaud, Bernard, 1958. Je, vous, il. *Esprit* 26 : 7–8, 91–9.

    1963. Le personnage dans l'oeuvre de Nathalie Sarraute. *Preuves*
    154, 19–34.

Rahv, Betty T., 1974. *From Sartre to the Nouveau Roman.* Port Washing-
    ton, New York: Kennikat Press.

Raillard, Georges, 1968. *Michel Butor.* Paris: Gallimard.

Ricardou, Jean, 1967. *Problèmes du nouveau roman.* Paris: Seuil.

    1971. *Pour une théorie du nouveau roman.* Paris: Seuil.

    1973. *Le nouveau roman.* Paris: Seuil.

Robbe-Grillet, Alain, 1963. *Pour un nouveau roman.* Paris: Minuit.
    (*Towards a New Novel,* London: John Calder, 1970).

Robbe-Grillet, Alain, 1976. (Colloque de Cerisy), 2 vols. Paris: Union
    générale d'éditions.

van Rossum-Guyon, Françoise, 1970a. *Critique du roman: essai sur
    'La modification' de Michel Butor.* Paris: Gallimard.

    1970b. Point due vue ou perspective narrative. *Poétique* 4, 476–97.

    1974. Adventures de la citation chez Butor. In *Butor* 1974, pp. 17–54.

Roudaut, Jean, 1964. *Michel Butor ou le livre futur.* Paris: Gallimard.

    1966. Parenthèse sur la place occupée par l'étude intitulée *6 810 000
    litres d'eau par seconde* parmi les autres ouvrages de Michel Butor.
    Nouvelle revue française 165, 498–509.

Rousset, Jean, 1973. *Narcisse romancier.* Paris: Corti.

Sarraute, Nathalie, 1947. Paul Valéry et l'enfant de l'éléphant. *Temps
    modernes* 16, 610–37.

    1956. *L'ère du soupçon.* Paris: Gallimard. (*Tropisms and The Age of
    Suspicion,* London: John Calder, 1963).

    1961. Rebels in a World of Platitudes. In *The Writer's Dilemma,* ed.
    The Times, pp. 35–41. London: Oxford University Press.

    1963. Forward. In *Tropisms and the Age of Suspicion,* trans. Maria
    Jolas. London: John Calder.

Sartre, Jean-Paul, 1947. *Situations I.* Paris: Gallimard. (*Literary and
    Philosophical Essays,* London: Hutchinson, 1955).

    1948. *Situations II.* Paris: Gallimard. (*What is Literature?,* London:
    Methuen, 1950).

    1956. Préface. In Sarraute *Portrait d'un inconnu* (1948), pp. 7–14.
    Paris: Gallimard.

Scholes, Robert & Kellogg, Robert, 1966. *The Nature of Narrative.*
    New York: Oxford University Press.

Searle, John, 1969. *Speech Acts.* Cambridge: Cambridge University
    Press.

Sollers, Philippe, 1968. *Logiques*. Paris: Seuil.

Sturrock, John, 1969. *The French New Novel*. London: Oxford University Press.

Tamir, Nomi, 1976. Personal Narrative and its Linguistic Foundation. *PTL* 1, 403–29.

Todorov, Tzvetan, 1965. *Théorie de la littérature: textes des formalistes russes* (ed.). Paris: Seuil.

    1971. *Poétique de la Prose*. Paris: Seuil. (*Poetics of Prose*, Oxford: Blackwell, 1978).

    1973. *Poétique* (rev. ed.). Paris: Seuil.

Voloshinov, V. N., 1973. *Marxism and the Philosophy of Language* (1930), trans. Ladislav Matejka & I. R. Titunik. New York: Seminar Press.

Waelti-Walters, Jennifer, 1977. *Michel Butor*. Victoria, British Columbia: Sono Nis Press.

von Wartburg, Walther & Zumthor, Paul, 1973. *Précis de syntaxe du français contemporain* (3rd ed.). Bern: Éditions Francke.

Wunderli-Müller, C., 1970. *Le thème du masque et les banalités dans l'oeuvre de Nathalie Sarraute*. Zurich: Juris Verlag.

Zeltner, Gerda, 1962. Nathalie Sarraute et l'impossible réalisme. *Mercure de France* 1188, 593–608.

Index

217